Rethinking Capitalist Development

Rethinking Capitalist Development

Primitive Accumulation, Governmentality & Post-colonial Capitalism

Kalyan Sanyal

Routledge
Taylor & Francis Group

LONDON   NEW YORK   NEW DELHI

First published 2007 in India
by Routledge
912 Tolstoy House, 15–17 Tolstoy Marg, Connaught Place,
New Delhi 110 001

Simultaneously published in the UK
by Routledge
2 Park Square, Milton Park, Abingdon, Oxon OX14 4RN

Routledge is an imprint of the Taylor & Francis Group, an informa business

© 2007 Kalyan Sanyal

Paperback edition published 2014

Typeset by
Glyph Graphics Private Limited
23, Khosla Complex, Vasundhara Enclave
Delhi 110 096

British Library Cataloguing-in-Publication Data
A catalogue record of this book is available from the British Library

ISBN 978-0-415-73546-9

For Abantikumar and Deepti,
my parents

Ship of fools
On a cruel sea
Ship of fools
Sail away from me

Robert Hunter
The *Annotated* Grateful Dead Lyrics

Contents

Foreword

I have a lump in my throat as I write this. For almost forty years, Kalyan Sanyal was one of my closest friends and intellectual colleagues. We chatted and argued about almost everything in the world, from politics and cinema to poetry and political economy. Together we followed the fortunes of our favorite football team, diligently participated in weekly Hegel and Marx reading circles, walked in political rallies, and, for a few years, were also colleagues in the Department of Economics at the University of Calcutta. Every moment in Kalyan's company was enlivened by his razor-sharp intellect and irrepressible wit. I have lost count of the number of times that I had the urge to pick up the phone and ask him for his views on some piece of news or article that I had read, in the past few months since his utterly untimely death from cancer. His responses, I knew, would have been both enlightening and funny.

As an economist, Kalyan Sanyal had established a solid reputation as an expert in the theory of international trade, the field in which he published most of his academic papers. But from the 1980s, silently and methodically, he had familiarized himself with a literature that most professional economists know very little about. Solidly grounded in Marx and in the tradition of Marxian economics, he began to take a keen interest in the new critical literature on the political history of colonial and postcolonial India. He frequently argued with me over our writings in *Subaltern Studies*, often complaining that our assertions on the autonomy of subaltern politics or indeed our critique of elite nationalism had no persuasive foundation in political economy. He even presented a paper on this subject at the Subaltern Studies Conference in Calcutta in 1989. I now realize that it was partly his instigation that led me to examine the world of informal economy and political society that exists in the slums and streets of Indian cities. Sanyal himself began to team up with some of his students to study the political economy of informal production and labor. It was in 2005 that he gave me the manuscript of *Rethinking Capitalist Development*. I remember reading it with a sense of amazement, not merely because of the scale and power of his arguments but even more for his confident grasp and highly original observations on a literature in which I had immersed myself for decades. Needless to say, we had many discussions about his book, both before and after it was published. In the years since its publication, the book has been hailed, in India and abroad, as a major contribution to the critical literature on postcolonial development.

I did have the opportunity once to have a formal discussion with Sanyal about the book. This was first published in Bengali in the Calcutta journal *Baromas* (2007) and was later included in his Bengali book *Sat Satero* (2011). This may be an appropriate occasion to present some of the highlights of that conversation to the readers of this English edition.

Sanyal insisted that the principal argument of his book is that postcolonial development can no longer be seen in terms of a transition from pre-capitalism to capitalism, which is how most of us had hitherto seen it. In saying this however, he was not reviving an argument advanced from certain sections of the Left which said that the Indian economy had already been transformed into a capitalist one, perhaps from late colonial times. Rather, Sanyal was making a more fundamental claim: contemporary postcolonial capitalism, according to him, is not revolutionary, it does not transform pre-capitalism in its own image; in contrast, it often preserves and sometimes creates forms of labor and production that do not belong to the domain of capital. It was not simply that this was a new phase of capitalism in the era of globalization. On the contrary, Marx's account of the primitive or primary accumulation of capital had left out something that was only now becoming apparent in the phenomenon of postcolonial development. But what was this remainder that had been ignored.

Both in the *Grundrisse* and *Capital*, Marx had described primitive accumulation as process that separates the primary producer — the peasant or the artisan — from his means of production. The latter is then brought within the circuit of capital, and the former, now without any means of employment of his labor, becomes a wage laborer in capitalist production. After this transformation is complete, capital becomes self-subsistent and there is nothing left outside capital. But what if all of those primary producers who lost their means of production in the process of primitive accumulation could not be absorbed in capitalist production? Here, one is not referring to the reserve army of labor, waiting to be employed by capitalists, but to the surplus pool of labor-power that cannot be brought within the domain of capitalist production at all, and must necessarily exist as a component outside of capital. Sanyal reminded his readers that Marx's *Capital* does not speak of this possibility. What of the millions of dispossessed peasants who migrated to the settler colonies of the Americas, Australia, New Zealand and South Africa? What of the thousands (perhaps millions) of peasants who were mobilized as cannon fodder in the endless European wars of the 19th and 20th centuries? What of the thousands of deaths due to famines and epidemics in Europe in the 19th century? What if all of these millions of dispossessed peasants and artisans had somehow stayed alive as palpable remnants of the pre-capitalist past but outside the domain of capitalist production? On what terms could they have been described as an element of capital's present, and yet as its outside?

This is the question that Sanyal thinks is unavoidable for any credible account of postcolonial capitalism. The options of mass emigration, conscription into the army or deaths in famines or epidemics are not available any more. So what happens to this surplus labor-power that is the result of primitive accumulation but cannot be absorbed within the circuit of capital? The answer cannot be found within the theoretical frame of Marx's *Capital*. It requires, according to Sanyal, the abandonment of the idea of transition as a process of transformation of pre-capitalist forms of production into capitalism. Primitive accumulation, he claims, must be seen as a process that not only brings pre-capitalist producers and their means of production within the circuit of capital, but also *creates* an area outside of capital. But,what does capital do with what is outside? What do those who are left outside do to stay alive? These are the questions posed by postcolonial capitalism.

While Sanyal's identification of the question of a redundant surplus population resulting from primitive accumulation impinges upon the system of capitalist production itself, there is also a historical context that determines the relevance of this question. The relevance is established, Sanyal insists, not from within the economic logic of capital, but by the changing political context. In the 18th or 19th century, capital was not burdened with looking after the redundant population of surplus labor. They could emigrate, voluntarily or under coercion (the difference was often unclear), or die in wars or famines. Indeed, within its strictly economic logic, this surplus population, unlike the reserve army of labor, was outside the domain of capital. Capital literally had no need for it and could not care less about its outcome. Following that economic logic, the same should have been the case for capitalist production in postcolonial countries. But something changed in the meantime, namely, the political context within which postcolonial capitalism must develop. Given the spread of the ideas and practices of anticolonial nationalism, popular sovereignty, rights of citizens and humans, and even democracy, today it is no longer possible for political regimes to avoid the responsibility of at least trying to ensure the survival of its population. Hence, Sanyal suggests, the creation of a subsistence economy outside the domain of capital. This is not the old pre-capitalist economy which has been largely destroyed by primitive accumulation. Rather, it is entirely a new creature, with varied forms that are conveniently put together under the label of informal economy.

In his book, Sanyal has described the political management of the redundant surplus population as the reversal of primitive accumulation. During my conversation with him, I suggested that this was a slightly inaccurate description since primitive accumulation was not really being reversed: the dispossessed peasant was not being given back his land or the erstwhile artisan reinstated in his old trade. What was being attempted through fiscal subsidies, poverty-removal programs or market-based initiatives such as microcredit, was the reversal of the consequences of primitive accumulation. Sanyal agreed that this was a more accurate description of his viewpoints. To achieve this, the state was intervening to transfer a certain part of the profits of the capitalist growth economy to the subsistence economy in order to establish the legitimacy of postcolonial capital.

When I asked if the recent trend of development economics aimed at ameliorating the conditions of a surplus population that could not be employed in a capitalist industry had become possible because of the failure of the socialist experiments, especially in China, Sanyal made an interesting point. Development economics from the 1950s, led by US economists, tried to depoliticize the process of development and bring it under the aegis of technical experts. This was the result of the Cold War apprehension that mass unemployment and poverty in the third world might lead to the rise of the dangerous classes and the success of communist movements. Even though the communist threat may have now receded, the fear of the dangerous classes continues. Instead of the communist bogey, the language is now one of protection of human rights. But development as a depoliticized domain run by experts has been the implicit ideology of development economics as an academic discipline from its birth.

This is also the reason why, Sanyal told me, he did not clearly see the problem posed by the redundant surplus population until he read the writings of sociologists, ethnographers and urban geographers.

The fact that primitive accumulation was dispossessing millions of peasants and artisans but not absorbing them in the capitalist economy could have produced a radical critique of postcolonial development strategies. But this possibility was side stepped by the proliferation of the techniques of governmentality on a grand scale in many third-world countries. Development economists began to see this as a distinct possibility from the 1970s. Economists such as Amartya Sen took the lead in persuading governments and international organizations for a new development practice that was needed to politically manage the victims of capitalist growth. The management of poverty must become an integral part of the management of growth.

The redundant surplus population, unlike the reserve army of labor, is now treated as a permanently excluded population, outside the sphere of capitalist production, for whom a distinct sub-economy had to be created and sustained. Although this is often brought under the umbrella of informal economy, Sanyal preferred to identify a distinct sector that he called the need economy, characterized by the logic of subsistence rather than accumulation. Not every unregistered production or service unit is necessarily a part of what Sanyal describes as the need economy — I have to say that this concept remains inadequately described and analyzed in Sanyal's book. This was the work he had begun in collaboration with his former students, to empirically describe and more adequately theorize this sub-economy produced by postcolonial capitalist development. Unfortunately, death intervened.

Every day that passes since I first read this book, I realize more strongly the profound importance and originality of the theoretical breakthrough achieved by Kalyan Sanyal. I have no doubt that his arguments are of major relevance in understanding not just what is happening in countries such as India, but that all-encompassing feature of the modern world that we call 'capitalism'.

20 July 2013   Partha Chatterjee
Department of Anthropology,
Columbia University, New York, and
Centre for Studies in Social Sciences, Calcutta

Preface and Acknowledgements

Scholars of development studies have in recent years drawn our attention to the fact that a significant part of the population in the post-colonial world remains excluded from the 'modern and dynamic' economy governed by the logic of capital. Described as 'a surplus humanity', these outcasts inhabit an economic space of informal survivalism both outside and alongside the world of capital.[1] Although this observation is being highlighted in the context of the emergence of the neo-liberal global capitalist order in the 1990s, political economists had in the past taken note of the phenomenon of exclusion and marginalization in the post-colonial context. Surprisingly, there has been little effort to theoretically grasp the phenomenon in relation to the political economy of post-colonial capitalist formation.

This book attempts to radically rethink capitalist development in the post-colonial world. It foregrounds exclusion and marginalization as integral to the development of capitalism and explores how the 'surplus humanity' ineluctably shapes post-colonial capital in the era of globalization as a complex regime of power with its unique modalities. Capitalist underdevelopment has traditionally been seen, by liberal and Marxist theories alike, as a case of failure on the part of capital to revolutionize and transform the economy after its own image. Departing from this, this book extricates the post-colonial experience from the historicist narrative of transition and articulates it within a political economic framework that conceptualizes underdevelopment as endogenous to capitalist development in the post-colonial context.

During the gestation and maturation of the book, I have immensely benefited from the comments, encouraging as well as critical, I received from many people. Over all these years, I have had long, informal but intense discussions with Arup Mallik and Ajit Chaudhury, my colleagues in the Economics Department of the University of Calcutta. I am sure they have left an indelible mark on the ideas developed in the book. Despite the very busy schedule of a globe-trotting academician, Partha Chatterjee found time to carefully read the entire manuscript, provide detailed comments and suggestions that led to substantial improvement in the argument and its presentation, and finally prodded me into sending it for publication. Without his support and encouragement, this book could never have been completed. Robin Blackburn who read an earlier version of the manuscript, made inspiring comments and very useful suggestions. So did Richard Wolff, who was eager to see it in published form. I am deeply indebted to them. Discussions and exchanges with the following people on the general theme of the book have been particularly fruitful: Jonathan Diskin, Julie Graham, Bhaskar Mukharjee, David Ruccio, Stephen Resnick and Asok Sen. I thank them all.

Anirban Chatterjee, an old friend, who looks after the editorial page of the largest circulating Bangla daily, *Anandabazar Patrika,* has always been generous in allowing space for my column in which I could reflect on the everyday issues related to the Indian experience of development and globalization. This helped me in discerning some of the subtle aspects of the theme of this book.

The list will hardly be complete, if I do not mention the students on whom I tried the material of this book: Anirban Dasgupta, Snehashis Bhattacharyya, Anirban Mukharjee, Rajesh Bhattacharyya, Ushasi Chakraborty, Rituparna Bhattacharyya and Joy Shankar Banerjee. The critical questions they raised at every stage forced me to rethink some of the arguments and further develop them. Most of them are now in graduate program of North American and European Universities. They have sent me books and published materials related to my work from abroad, which I had not known of. Working with Routledge has been a pleasure. Esha Betteille as the editor took active interest in the manuscript from the very beginning and saw it through the review process. Roopa Raveendran has done an excellent job as the copy editor, ceaselessly pointing out my errors in citing references and preparing the bibliography. The book in its final form owes much to her. I must also thank Sharmila Banerjee for providing crucial help in getting the final manuscript ready for the publisher.

Finally, I must thank Saswati, Arani and Avik, for showing all these years more patience and tolerance than I suspect I deserve.

Kalyan Sanyal
August 2006, Calcutta

Note

1. Davis, Mike, Planet of Slums, *New Left Review*, March–April 2004.

Chapter 1

Introduction: Rethinking Capitalist Development

Capitalism is Dead, Long Live Capitalism

The search for an alternative to capitalism seems to be over. The "actually existing socialisms" do not exist anymore; "capitalist China" has turned out to be a roaring success; the entire third world is being integrated into one global capitalist network: the triumph of capitalism seems unquestionable, self evident and total. The world, we are told, is fast embracing capitalism as the most efficient, therefore desirable way of organizing production and distribution of wealth.

The emergence of the discourse of capitalism as the hegemonic discourse has produced, on the one hand, euphoria among those who had always believed in the superiority of capitalism over other possible economic organizations. On the other hand, it has led to a deep sense of frustration and dismay among those who had proposed and argued for alternative forms of economic life. Curiously, both the proponents and the detractors of the new order seem to share a common belief: both seem to have accepted without questioning that the system that is being ushered in worldwide is *capitalistic*— what has triumphed is *capitalism.*

This universal acceptance of the claim that the emerging global order is capitalism has also determined what kind of critical questions can be posed from a third world perspective: Will the emergent capitalism be able to mobilize the developmental possibilities in the third world, or subvert these possibilities by disrupting the economic order? Will the integration into the global capitalist network bring to the third world new economic opportunities, or make it an easy prey for predatory multinational corporations? All these questions rest on the assumption that the object being confronted, and critically evaluated, is none other than capitalism.

But what if one is skeptical about this very assumption? What if one asks: Does the new order conform to the concept of capitalism that was posited in the long theoretical debates over the last century and a half? Is this the same capitalism that the alternative economic and social arrangements (socialism, communism, Gandhi's self-sufficient village economy) have traditionally been pitted against? Once asked, these questions surely contest and unsettle the confidence that underlies the tendency to represent the current system as capitalistic. Can the dominant representation then be defended in the face of such skepticism?

The dominant discourse describes capitalism in terms of two characteristics. First, it is a system organized by the market principles in which individual agents are allowed to respond freely to opportunities offered by the market. The efficiency of the system derives from the putative ability of the market to allocate scarce resources in the best possible way. This is posed in contrast to the arrangements based on planning and regulations on the part of the state that, it is claimed, causes inefficiency and deadweight loss. The market acts as a screening devise: a sieve that separates inefficient activities from efficient ones and allows the latter to continue while keeping the former from being undertaken.

The institution of the market that characterizes capitalism, it is stressed, is not restricted to national boundaries. Capitalism requires that market forces be allowed to work beyond the frontiers of nations. The emergent capitalistic order is described as one in which goods, services and resources are free to move globally, unfettered and without any hindrance, ensuring efficiency on a global scale. In short, capitalism is a global system based on global free trade.

The other major defining characteristic of capitalism in this representation is the institution of private property: capitalism as a system is said to rest on private property rights over economic resources. Such rights allow individual agents to enjoy the fruits of their efforts when they respond to market opportunities, thus acting as the most forceful incentive for using resources rationally, and also for accumulation, innovation and technological progress. This again is posed in contrast with the state ownership of productive resources, i.e., the public sector, and the latter is denigrated as an inefficient arrangement in which the lack of incentive dampens the urge for innovation and improvement.

These two characteristics, free market and private property, thus constitute capitalism in the dominant discourse, and what is being celebrated is the victory of this capitalism. The victory, it is claimed, has finally resolved the age-old debate over capitalism and its alternatives in favor of the former. But, is the victorious capitalism of today the same capitalism that figured in those debates? What is striking in the current representation is that it equates capitalism with market and private property while capitalism traditionally has been defined as a specific mode of production. Private property and the market are both requirements for capitalism, but they alone do not make a system capitalistic. The market can exist in the presence of a variety of non-capitalist modes of production. Indeed the institution of market has a history that is much longer than the history of capitalism—it has coexisted, albeit in less than perfect form, with pre-capitalist forms of production such as slavery and feudalism. The market is capable of accommodating much more than only the capitalist mode of production. Therefore, equating capitalism with market means keeping out of sight the specificity of capitalism.

Neither does the institution of private property, combined with market, make the system necessarily capitalistic. A producer who owns the means of production and produces for the market is neither a capitalist producer nor a wageworker. One can imagine an economy populated solely by such self-employed direct producers engaged in production for the market. Here we have commodity production with private property, yet it is not capitalist production. For, the latter rests not on the existence of private property per se, but on a specific structure of property, i.e., a specific distribution of ownership. In capitalist production, workers, bereft of means of production, sell their labor power for wages and enter into the labor process. The capitalist who has ownership rights over the means of production controls the labor process, and the extracted surplus in the form of profits is used for accumulation. While capitalist production, defined thus, implies the existence of both private property and market, the converse is not true: the combination of the market and private property does not rule out non-capitalist production.

Why then is capitalism, in its representation, being equated with this combination? Or more precise question, why is the combination of private property and the market being universally accepted as capitalism and the victory of the market over state regulation, and private property over state ownership, celebrated/mourned as the victory of capitalism? Privatization and globalization, it is being claimed, will open up new possibilities of development for the third world. But in what sense is it 'capitalist development'? For, neither the market nor private property necessarily accords any privilege to capitalist production. If they succeed in unleashing a process of change in the third world, why then is *capitalism* being allowed to appropriate the entire developmental effectivity of that process and, by implication, ruling out the possibility of the same process nurturing and fostering non-capitalist production as a vehicle of development.

The tendency to subsume under the term 'capitalist development' all developmental possibilities of a market economy, lodging— actually and potentially—different forms of production, derives from a social representation that sees capitalism as the dominant form of the economy. In this representation, capitalism's dominance overshadows other possible, existing forms of production that are always already present, thus pushing the heterogeneity that inheres in the economy to the background. The view of capitalism as a hegemonic system informs not only the prevalent description of the advanced Western economies but also the description of the economy of the third world. The economic formation in the third world is traditionally seen as marked by the presence of both capitalist and pre-capitalist forms of production, but always implicit in the characterization of this formation is a presumed superiority of capitalist production in terms of its inherent strength and dynamism. In the course of development, the capitalist sector is seen as the motor of the development process, a sector that expands its domain ultimately bringing the entire economic space within its own ambit, leading to the dissolution of all other forms of production.

In *The End of Capitalism (As We Knew It)* (1996), J.K. Gibson–Graham contests this "hegemony of capitalism" in the dominant social representation. The title of the book, announcing the end of a system whose victory is being celebrated worldwide, is certainly puzzling at first sight. But *As We Knew It* clarifies her project: what she proclaims is the end of our traditional perception of capitalism. As a social descriptor, this vision of capitalism as a "hegemonic" system, claims Gibson–Graham, is the prevalent discursive practice that keeps out of sight the non-capitalist sites in an economy, and thereby devalues them and confines them to the margin. (She identifies household and self-employment as two such sites of non-capitalist production that obdurately inhabit the economic landscape of capitalism.) Her project is to "deconstruct" this representation of the economy to clear a space where non-capitalist economic sites can be foregrounded and an economy can be seen as necessarily constituted by heterogeneity and difference. In other words, Gibson–Graham's attack targets the "capitalocentric" description of the economy wherein non-capital is defined entirely in terms of its "weakness and lack" in comparison with capital's "strength and fullness." Valorization of non-capital, by freeing it from the subordination to capital and endowing it with an autonomy, Gibson–Graham argues, supplants the discourse of capitalist hegemony with a plurality and heterogeneity of economic forms, opening up a new terrain of anti-capitalist politics.

Gibson–Graham's attempted subversion of the capitalocentric vision of the economy produces an alternative, radically different narrative of globalization. The dominant script of globalization is predicated on the image of capitalism engulfing the third world and bringing it under the power and control of multinational capital. In this script, "only capitalism has the ability to spread and invade", and "[c]apitalism is represented as inherently spatial and as naturally stronger than the forms of non-capitalist economy (traditional economies, 'Third World' economies, socialist economies, communal experiments) because of its presumed capacity to universalize the market for capitalist commodities". Thus, 'globalization according to this script involves the violation and eventual death of "other" non-capitalist forms of economy' (*ibid.*: 125, emphasis in original).

The alternative script subverts this predatory image of multinational capital to see it first as fragile and vulnerable, rather than as strong and powerful, and then focuses on its necessarily contradictory impact on the third world economies. The subversion allows one to discover that while the process of globalization entails an assault on the non-capitalist economy through commodification and proletarianization, it simultaneously creates conditions within which non-capitalist forms of production can emerge and flourish. For instance, internationalization of the financial market and the "invasion" of international financial capital can be seen as fostering, through easier availability of personal credit to purchase personal computers and other equipment, self-employment based non-capitalist production. The fluidity of financial capital here contributes to a proliferation of small businesses as sites of the non-capitalist economy. Commodification does not necessarily mean capitalist production; commodities can be produced in non-capitalist sites, and the conflation of capital and commodity, encouraged by the capitalocentric vision, keeps the possibility of difference within a commodified, market economy out of sight. And according to Gibson–Graham, once the representation of globalization as a uni-directional and irresistible process of capitalist penetration is dispensed with, we can see that "globalization need not constitute or inscribe 'economic development' as inevitably capitalist development" (*ibid*.: 139, emphasis in original).

There is no denying the novelty and force of Gibson–Graham's confrontation with capitalism's hegemony in the representation of the economy. Yet, at the same time, one is struck by the "simpleness" of the concept of hegemony and dominance that informs her project. For her, dominance necessarily takes the form of a monolith that annihilates, suppresses, and silences the "others". And by shattering the monolith, the "others" can be reinvigorated, rehabilitated and posited in radical opposition to the "hegemon". But, can't we see hegemony in its complex form in which dominance works through resuscitation rather than asphyxiation, exclusion rather than subsumption, valorization rather than demotion of the "others"? In which the "others" are brought to light and allowed a voice, rather than suppressed and silenced? If we can, then, with representation recognizing difference rather than monism, we have to conceptualize dominance as expressing itself through difference. Hasn't Michel Foucault told us that power does not necessarily express itself in terms of suppression, denial or occlusion; that it can also work through a mechanism that is productive, that "traverses and produces things, ... induces pleasure, forms of knowledge, produces discourse"? (1980: 119) Gibson–Graham problematizes the economy by unsettling the "hegemony of capitalism"; but in her analysis, the concept of hegemony itself escapes problematization.

The flip side of the simple vision of hegemony as suppression is that when the monolith is unsettled, the "others" that emerge automatically acquire a radical face. But if we allow hegemony to take a complex form, can we see the oppositional character of those "others" uncritically? Shouldn't we explore the possibility that they exist as an integral part of a complex hegemonic order?

Although I find Gibson–Graham's counter-construction highly interesting, it is these questions that provoke me to attempt a different problematization of the conflation of market and capitalism. Instead of arguing that the presence of multiple forms of production in a market economy challenges capitalism's hegemony, I want to further problematize the very concept of capitalism by asking: *Isn't it possible to see capitalism as necessarily a complex of capitalist and non-capitalist production residing in the commodity space? In other words, can't we see capitalist development as process that necessarily produces, brings into existence, non-capitalist economic processes in its own course?* (Here I make a distinction between capitalist production and capitalism: the former, structurally combined with non-capitalist production, constitutes the latter. This will be elaborated in Chapter 2). Gibson–Graham foregrounds economic heterogeneity and strategically deploys it to question the dominance of capitalism in the representation of the economy. I begin by recognizing that it is economic heterogeneity that constitutes capitalism within which capital, as a specific relation of production, exists, and then ask whether that heterogeneity itself can be seen as an expression of capital's hegemony. Our projects are different in a fundamental sense: Gibson–Graham wants to shrink and emaciate capitalism to rehabilitate economic difference; I, on the other hand, seek to produce a vision of capitalism that is malleable and protean, see economic difference as an integral part of that capitalism and explore how capital successfully lives in that world of difference.

The motivation behind my attempt to explore the implications of seeing hegemony as difference stems from the specificity of my purpose: As I mentioned earlier, the vision of capitalism as a force that destroys the non-capitalist economy informs the story of capitalist development told by the political economists. In the vast literature on the political economy of underdevelopment, continued existence of pre-capitalist modes of production has been seen as a sign of capitalism's failure to transform the entire economy. Capitalism in the third world has been characterized as weak and inadequate, incapable of performing its hegemonic role. This view of economic difference as "lack of hegemony" is nothing but the flip side of the assumption that hegemony necessarily implies economic monism. By reducing the experience to a "case of failure", the political economy of capitalist development implicitly endorses a vision of capitalism that is antithetical to difference. It is from this absence of hegemony that I begin my journey. *While Gibson–Graham confronts capitalism's hegemony to revive economic difference, I problematize the supposedly "non-hegemonic capitalism" of the third world to explore if economic heterogeneity can be interpreted as a complex hegemonic order.* An order in which capital's strength and power lies in its ability, not to annihilate its "others", but to negotiate the world of difference. In the following section I subject the political economic literature on the third world to a critical reading to locate my exact point of departure.

Capitalist (under)development: Tales told by Marxists

From the very beginning, the Marxist approach to the question of capitalist (under)development in the third world has been caught up in a dilemma. In order to have a theoretical understanding of the economic formation in the third world, it has recognized the need to eschew the orthodox vision of capitalist development as part of a unilineal process of history. But at the same time, it has been reluctant to radically break with the historical materialist framework in which the process of history is seen as the change from a backward mode of production to a more advanced one, driven by the conflicts between forces and relations of production.[1] The theorization of the economic formation in the third world has thus remained implicitly anchored in the paradigm of historical materialism. As the paradigm privileges the orthodox vision that capitalism develops along an inexorable, unidirectional trajectory of historical change, this anchoring ultimately frustrated all attempts to conceptualize the third world capitalism as capitalism of a different kind with a dynamics of its own. The literature on the third world that emerged in the 1960s and 1970s is best seen as a series of failed attempts to cope with this dilemma.

The orthodox vision, as enunciated by Marx in the *Communist Manifesto*, saw capitalism as a force that constantly invades the economic space that lies beyond its own ambit, "batters down the Chinese wall" and revolutionizes all pre-existing organizations of production. It was an inevitable process whereby all earlier productive systems and divisions of labor break down to make way for the ultimate universality of the capitalist system of production. This view held that capitalist penetration in the third world would produce the same trajectory of development as has been observed in the western homelands of capital. The 1960s witnessed the emergence of a critical response to this view. It was argued that given the nature of capitalist penetration, the possibility of the third world experiencing a full-scale capitalist transformation after the image of the first world was ruled out. This alternative view, elaborated in the works of Frank (1967, 1969, 1978) and Amin (1976, 1977),[2] among others, later came to be known as the Dependency Theory. It touched off a debate that went on for almost a decade, spawning a sizable literature that constitutes the Marxist analysis of political economy of third world capitalism. Although this literature has been intensively discussed, appreciated, and critiqued in the past in numerous debates on the political economy of development, I think it will be profitable to take another look at it and its critiques, in the light of the dilemma I mentioned above.

Dependency and the World System

The dependency theory can be seen as highlighting the "other side" of imperialism: how imperialism shapes the processes in the "imperialized" economy. The main thrust of the analysis lies in its emphasis on the inequality in the global order and the consequent dependence of backward economies on advanced ones. The argument is that third world countries—which form the periphery—are implicated in a global economic order and their economic processes are determined exclusively by the needs of advanced countries—center. The global order integrates the center and the periphery through a network of markets in such a way that the economic surplus generated in the latter gets siphoned to meet the needs of accumulation in the former. The surplus of the periphery is transferred to the center through direct repatriation of profits on foreign capital as well as through unequal exchange in the domain of trade.[3]

In other words, the dependency theory sees development and underdevelopment as two inseparable parts of a global economy and thus rules out the possibility of the periphery developing on the same path charted by the center. In the words of Frank,

" ... development and underdevelopment are the same in that they are the product of a single, but dialectically contradictory, economic structure and process of capitalism. Thus, they cannot be viewed as the product of supposedly different economic structure or systems. One and the same historical process of the expansion and development of capitalism throughout the world has simultaneously generated ... both economic development and structural underdevelopment" (Frank 1969: 9).

The somewhat rough sketch of the world economy presented by dependency theory is further structured and systematized by Immanuel Wallerstein in *The Modern World System* (1974).[4] Dependency theory has seen development and underdevelopment as the two sides of the same coin, but its object of inquiry is underdevelopment at the periphery. Wallerstein's approach is different yet complementary to the dependency theory. His focus is the same as that of the dependency theorists: he sees the core and the periphery as two integral elements of a structure that he calls the world economy, but he explores the core–periphery relation from a different perspective. While the dependency theorists question how the integrated world economy constricts development prospects at the periphery, Wallerstein is concerned with how the same world system makes sustained accumulation and development possible at the center. He envisages the modern world system as distinct from what he calls the "world empire"—the system that precedes the modern one. The world empire allowed the economic surplus to be wasted in unproductive channels (maintenance of huge bureaucracies), instead of using it in productive investments, thereby making accumulation and development impossible. With its collapse, a modern world system based on unfettered trade emerged and it brought about a global division of labor with regional specialization of economic activities. This transformation of the global system in turn led to changes at the conditions of production and unleashed the dynamic of accumulation at the core.

However, according to Wallerstein, a fundamental inequality inheres in this world system. There are two aspects of this inequality: the economic and the political. The emergence of the modern world system entails an international division of labor that has a built-in hierarchy in which high skill and low skill activities are concentrated at the center and the periphery respectively. Since market rewards are typically proportional to the degree of skill in an activity, the regional distribution of skilled and unskilled activities has a strong tendency to be reinforced and maintained over time. On the other hand, the inequality manifests itself in the existence of strong states at the center and weak ones at the periphery. The strong states at the center can effectively intervene in the world market so that the market outcome favors the center, making a flow of surplus from the periphery to the center possible. These twin aspects of the world system make the process of accumulation sustainable at the center, while pushing the periphery into perpetual underdevelopment.

Viewing the third world as capitalism of a different kind, the dependency and world system theories together initiated the much-needed departure from orthodoxy, but at the same time, it invited strong criticism from within the Marxist camp. While the Marxists welcomed the departure, they objected to the particular characterization of the peripheral economic formation offered by these theorists, especially their understanding of capitalism. Capitalism, for the dependency theorists as well as for Wallerstein, is defined entirely in terms of the sphere of circulation. Any economic organization for them is capitalistic if it is integrated into a system of commodity exchange. They explicitly take note of the fact that at the periphery, along with a capitalist industrial sector, a wide range of traditional, archaic systems of production exists as an integral part of the global market network. However, for them, this co-existence is of no importance since all these forms are subsumed within the exchange relation and can be clubbed together and called capitalist.

Circulation, Production and Class: Brenner

The critics, on the other hand, argue that a proper characterization of the peripheral economic formation requires the notion of capitalism to go beyond the sphere of circulation and into the sphere of production, and define itself as a particular system of production. A forceful critique on this line is found in Brenner (1977). According to Brenner, the theoretical underpinning of the characterization of capitalist underdevelopment in the dependency and world system theories is provided by the model put forward by Adam Smith's *The Wealth of Nations* (1997). In Smith's work, a society's wealth and its development is directly related to the degree of the division of labor, which in turn depends on the extent of the market. The division of labor leads to development and prosperity because specialization in production (agriculture/manufacturing separation) and indi-viduation of productive tasks that follow from it fosters invention and increases productivity. Brenner points out that both Frank and Wallerstein—he takes Frank as the representative of the dependency school—have adopted this Smithian vision and envisaged capitalism as a system produced by trade-based division of labor. But this characterization of capitalism, Brenner argues, fails to explain underdevelopment. If, as Wallerstein and Frank maintain, expansion of global trade and commerce is what makes accumulation and development possible at the center, the question that remains unanswered is why the result of this expansion has been different for the periphery. The explanation of underdevelopment, therefore, has to be sought elsewhere. "The method of Book I of *The Wealth of Nations* cannot be used to explain the poverty of nations." (Brenner: 83)

To tell the twin stories of capitalist development and underdevelopment, Brenner claims, capitalism has to be seen as a system of production and its development traced in the process of transformation of the production economy, more specifically, transformation of the socially productive relations of production. The increase in productivity that results from the Smithian division of labor is limited in the absence of continuous innovation in the means of production. It is this ability to innovate and thereby to increase productivity continuously that makes capitalism a system distinct from other systems of production. And this ability flows from the structure of social-productive relations that characterize capitalism. In other words, it is class relations that holds the key to an understanding of capitalist development.

Development of capitalism, therefore, is to be understood in terms of transformation of class relations. There is a specific structure of class associated with capitalism and it is this specificity that needs to be brought to the fore, and capitalism viewed as a system of production distinct from other pre-capitalist systems. Put differently, an understanding of capitalist development requires that the ahistorical notion of capitalism as trade-based division of labor be eschewed in favor of an analysis of conditions under which the capitalist class relations—which is a historically specific set of relations—emerge and ultimately replace the pre-capitalist class relations.

Brenner's critique thus places production and class relations at the center of the story of capitalist development. What needs to be stressed here, however, is that it is not class relations as such but the importance of class struggle that Brenner is highlighting. Both Wallerstein and Frank in their later works talk about class, but they see the emergence of particular class relations as a result of the expansion of trade and commerce. For them, expansion of trade brings about the class relations that are in conformity with production for profits in the market. Brenner's critique, on the other hand, claims that the sphere of circulation does not determine class relations. On the contrary, class conflicts and their outcomes determine the direction of change in the production economy. Success and failure of capitalist transformation depends on whether the nature of class conflicts in a specific situation is able to create the conditions necessary for such a transformation.

In other words, according to Brenner, it is not the structure of class *per se*, but class struggle that determines the trajectory of capitalist development/underdevelopment.[5] By focusing on class struggle, Brenner poses the question of agency in the process of capitalist transformation. I shall come back to this question when I deal with the literature on the Gramscian passive revolution later in this chapter. But Brenner's critique of the neo-Smithian view of capitalism and his emphasis on the centrality of production in the analysis of capitalist transformation provides the perspective for the Althusser inspired Marxist literature on mode of production to which I turn now. Although the literature on modes of production preceded Brenner's critique of Frank and Wallerstein, I find it convenient to begin with Brenner and then go back to the mode of production debate because against the backdrop of Brenner's critique, it is easier to consolidate the disparate writings into a school of thought and identify the different positions within it.

The literature locates its point of departure in the observation by the dependency theorists that a wide variety of forms of production organizations, subsumed within the network of trade and market relations, coexist in the periphery. And this coexistence is viewed as holding the key to the conceptualization of the peripheral economic formation. Invoking the Marxian notion of mode of production, these writers seek to characterize the peripheral capitalism as an articulation of several such modes.

In what follows, the literature on modes of production is read with a specific purpose in mind. At the beginning of this section, I claimed that there is a dilemma inherent in the Marxist approach to capitalist development in the third world. It seeks to explain capitalist underdevelopment but at the same time is unable to break with the historical materialist framework. The Smithian approach of Frank and Wallerstein, in its own way, is a marked departure from the linear progression of historical materialism, in that it presents the peripheral formation as failure of capitalism to "batter down the Chinese wall". The Marxist literature recognizes the need to see the periphery as capitalism of a different kind, a *sui generis*, but by bringing the production economy at the center of the analysis, it allows the historical materialist framework to creep in and subvert the project. In my reading, I intend to bring to the surface this underlying contradiction in the literature.

Articulation of Modes of Production

Mode of production in Marx is defined as a structured combination of the three elements of social production, i.e. labor, non-labor, and means of labor, combined through two connections (Althusser and Balibar 1970, Part III, Ch I). One is the real appropriation connection, which refers to the techno-economic conditions of production that constitute the labor process and the division of labor, and is called the forces of production. The relations of production provide the other connection—relations that, emanating from the structure of property rights and entitlements, bind the three elements in the sphere of production. Productive forces and production relations together constitute the structured combination called mode of production.

Using this definition, different modes such as primitive communist, feudal, slave, and capitalist are identified, each seen as having a specific, structured combination of the three elements. For instance, the capitalist mode is defined as extraction of surplus value from direct producers, who have no property rights over the means of production but are combined with the latter through wage relation, by non-producers who own the means of production. The historical materialist framework sees history as a series of epochs; each characterized by the dominance of one such mode of production. The historical process is seen as a process whereby a "superior" mode rises to dominance to characterize a particular epoch by super-seding the earlier mode. In other words, a higher moment in history supersedes its lower moments. And this process of transition from one mode to another is understood as a dialectical process consist-ing of thesis, antithesis, and supersession in the form of synthesis.

In the Marxist analysis, the third world is envisaged as an arti-culation of the capitalist and pre-capitalist modes of production, which reproduces itself over time without the former superseding the latter. The term "articulation", however, does not mean mere co-existence or horizontal juxtaposition. It is a structured unity where the articulated modes provide the conditions of existence for one other. Moreover, there is a hierarchy in the sense that one mode can be identified as dominant with the others having a subordinate status. The Marxist analysis seeks to identify the conditions of both the existence and reproduction of the articulation.

It was Laclau (1971) who first posed the question of articulation in the particular context of Latin America. In a critique of Frank, he argued that underneath the ubiquitous market–capitalism de-scribed by the dependency theorists, the Latin American economy is constituted by both capitalist and feudal modes of production. Al-though Laclau does not use the term articulation, he emphasizes that the feudal relations exist not as survivals of the past but as an in-separable part of the capitalist mode to form an "indissoluble unity".

But the question is why do the pre-capitalist modes continue to exist in the presence of the capitalist mode? Why does the latter not expand and lead to the dissolution of the earlier modes as suggested by the historical materialist process? In other words, what are the conditions of existence of this indissoluble unity? The literature on articulation is quite vast with overlapping explanations presented by the writers. I have reduced the literature to three distinctly differ-ent positions.

Dominance of Merchant Capital

The first position can be located in the attempt by Kay (1975) to provide a theoretical answer to this question. Bringing to the fore the distinction between merchant capital and industrial capital in Marx's analysis, Kay offered an explanation for the continued presence of the pre-capitalist modes in terms of the dominance of the former. In Marx, merchant capital is capital in the sphere of circulation, engaged in the act of buying and selling at different prices and thereby making a profit. This profit is nothing but a part of surplus produced at the sphere of production and appropriated by the merchant as profit on alienation. This form of capital stands in sharp contrast to capital that is engaged in production of surplus value at the sphere of production. In pre-capitalist societies where industrial capital is yet to arrive, merchant capital is the sole form of capital, while in a fully developed industrial capitalist; it exists as mere extension of industrial capital.

The particular aspect of merchant capital in a pre-capitalist society that is of interest to Kay is its relationship with the sphere of production. This relation, Kay observes, is an ambivalent one. On one hand, merchant capital is indifferent to which particular mode exists at the sphere of production, but on the other, it has a strong incentive to undermine the pre-capitalist modes and reorganize them on a capitalist line. Confined to the sphere of circulation, merchant capital in such societies has no control over the labor process and the organization of production. The class that is dominant in the sphere of production controls the labor process, extracts and appropriates the surplus labor from direct producers and brings it to the sphere of circulation. The merchants are thus dependent on this class for their own existence. What is important for the merchant is not the mode of production that prevails but the fact that the produced goods take the form of commodity and are exchanged for money. Put differently, the question of mode of production is immaterial for the functioning of the merchant as long as what is produced is brought to the market—the sphere of exchange and money in which he operates. This provides the incentive for the merchant capital to ally with the pre-capitalist dominant classes and maintain the status quo at the sphere of production only to ensure an uninterrupted flow of goods to the market.

But at the same time, the merchant capital's drive for accumulation requires an expansion of commodity production, which ultimately disrupts the pre-capitalist organizations. The mercantile accumulation has a strong tendency to undermine the conditions of existence of the pre-capitalist modes, and with it the control of the dominant pre-capitalist class, resulting in a reorganization of production on capitalist line. This is the other side of the relation between the merchant capital and the sphere of production.

The ambivalence that inheres in this interaction infuses the role of the merchant capital in the transition process with an ambiguity: it is conservative and radical at the same time. Kay's explanation of the economic formation in the third world is predicated on the conservative role. The initial form of imperialist penetration in the third world, Kay argues, was in the form of the merchant capital that sought to preserve the earlier modes of production and confined itself in the sphere of circulation. After the industrial revolution, although it came under the dominance of the industrial capital in the world economy, the merchant capital retained its independence as the sole form of capital in the third world. And its conservative aspect subverted the possibility of a full-scale transformation of the pre-capitalist modes of production.

Kay's imaginative argument is from within a well-defined theoretical framework. However, his analysis begs the very question it is supposed to address. His argument rests on the assumption that merchant capital is dominant in its conservative form. But the question that is important for us is why this dominance continues? Why does merchant capital not show its radical face and transform itself into industrial capital? In other words, why does the process of transformation get blocked? Moreover, the situation of merchant capital sounds far less persuasive when we take note of the fact that the post-colonial economic scenario of the third world is marked by the presence of industrial capital to a considerable degree. The central question regarding third world capitalism is: why does industrial capital continue to articulate itself with the earlier modes? Why does it not expand its domain, "batter down the Chinese wall", and bring the entire economy under its sway? Kay locates his story within the historical materialist process but, without addressing this question, assumes that the transition dynamic is absent, and then explains how the existence of pre-capitalist modes can be consistent with the logic of merchant capital. It is the articulation theorists of the structuralist school who addressed the question of articulation of industrial capital with the earlier modes.

The central concern of the structuralists then is to explain the coexistence of multiple modes of production even after merchant capital has been transformed into industrial capital, and identify the conditions under which the complex is reproduced over time. It is in this structuralist approach that I locate the second position. But before I deal with the structuralist explanation, let me mention that there is a view that holds that the articulation is merely a transitional phenomenon. It argues that although industrial capital in the third world is found to be coexisting with other pre-capitalist modes, its economic logic will ultimately lead to the dissolution of those other modes. The logic of industrial capital leaves no option for it other than to continuously expand its own domain, but in the third world, this process of expansion has been protracted for a variety of historical and socio-political reasons specific to those regions. Thus, according to this view, the third world is in a state of transition, albeit a delayed one, and will eventually experience a full-fledged capitalist transformation, repeating the Western trajectory. The claim, as one can see, is predicated on the assumed inevitability of the historical materialist process. Bill Warren (1973) made a forceful presentation of this view and argued that there is no need to problematize the articulation of modes of production as a separate economic formation and look for its conditions of existence. To be more specific, Warren's main concern is to refute dependency and world system theories of underdevelopment. Frank and Wallerstein identify the post-colonial world order as one in which the economic surplus is extracted from the periphery to fuel accumulation at the center, an order that they hold responsible for being the root cause of underdevelopment. Moving to the opposite pole, Warren asserts that the neo-colonial world economic order inevitably provides the thrust that the periphery needs for a full-scale transformation of its economy. This is because the center is in a superior position in relation to the periphery in terms of forces of production (i.e. technology) and the center–periphery interaction, contrary to what the dependency–theorists claim, will transmit this advanced technology with its revolutionizing impact on the economic structure.[6] Thus, Warren discards the central problematic of the Marxist political economy of underdevelopment by identifying the center's penetration into the periphery as the vehicle of the historical materialist process of change and dismisses the third world economic formation as merely a transitory phenomenon.

Warren's argument thus reasserts the orthodox Marxist claim that imperialism has an inevitably progressive impact on the economic formations of the colonies. Keeping this argument in the background will help us identify different theories of articulation and see how they distance themselves from Warren's claim.

Imperialist Penetration

There is a position, an influential one, that locates the reasons for the emergence of articulation in the third world in the nature of imperialist penetration in the post-colonial economy (Amin 1976, Taylor 1979). Imperialist penetration, according to this argument, is necessarily selective about transforming the pre-existing economic formations and division of labor associated with them. It radically transforms only those sectors that either provide raw material and means of production for the industrial capitalist mode without being a source of effective competition to imports, or produce luxury commodities for the local comprador classes, which are the main allies of the imperialist power. In other sectors, such as the artisan industry, which is a potential competitor of imports, the techniques of production and division of labor are largely left unchanged despite their formal subsumption by capitalism. The result is a scenario marked by extremely uneven development within the domain of capitalist production. The restricted nature of imperialist penetration weakens the general thrust of capitalist expansion, enabling the traditional modes to effectively resist such expansion. They continue to exist in articulated relation with the capitalist mode and in turn reinforce the restricted nature of capitalism, bringing the historical materialist process to a halt.[7]

Although it deals with the articulation of modes of production, his explanation shares the spirit of the world system of Frank and Wallerstein: the articulation and the consequent underdevelopment is the result of the nature of imperialist penetration in the post-colonial world. It takes imperialist penetration as necessarily being selective in its role as a transformer and then explains, almost tautologically, the lack of transformation in terms of that selection. In doing this, a distinction is made within the capitalist sector—between industrial capital under imperialist control (export and luxury producing sectors) and the indigenous artisan sector. While the latter gets transformed, the former remains stagnant and therefore, unable to supersede the pre-capitalist modes. It is, however, not clear how this specific pattern of imperialist penetration remains unchanged over time. For example, why does metropolitan capital, in its drive for accumulation, not reach out for the indigenous capitalist sector? And if this sector is a potential threat to imports from the metropolis, why is protecting the peripheral market for metropolitan exports necessarily more desirable to metropolitan capital rather than penetrating the indigenous sector for investment and accumulation? The static nature of the story does not allow it to address these questions.

But the main weakness of the imperialist penetration argument surfaces if we consider that since the 1950s, a large number of countries in Latin America and the then newly independent former colonies of Asia and Africa, turned to the path of capitalist industrialization on a national level through import substitution and restricted entry of metropolitan capital. The purpose was to enable the national bourgeoisie to break away precisely from the imperialism imposed pattern of industrialization that Taylor describes. Yet, the experience shows that capitalist development on the national level has failed to bring the entire economy under its sway—earlier modes continued to exist, constituting outside of capital. And this strongly suggests, contrary to claim made by the imperialist penetration argument, that the inability of capital "to batter down the Chinese Wall" does not stem from its being imperialist or national; the inability must be rooted in a more fundamental characteristic of the capitalist mode of production itself.

Capital's Need

Following this line of inquiry, others in the Structuralist School have seen articulation as a self-reproducing structure and located the logic of its reproduction in what may be called "capital's need". The works of, among others, Meillassoux (1972, 1981, 1983), Rey (1971, 1973) and Wolpe (1980) define this position. According to this view, the pre-capitalist modes continue to exist because they fulfil crucial needs of capital and ensure its conditions of existence. Capitalist production requires supply of cheap labor power and raw materials, and capital typically is unable to secure the entire requirement. It is the pre-capitalist sectors that ensure the conditions of existence of capital by acting as sources of cheap labor and raw materials.

Both Meillassoux and Wolpe base their analysis on African case studies. What they observe in Africa is that there is a domestic subsistence sector acting as a source of cheap labor power to the capitalist plantation and mining sectors. Since part of his subsistence consumption is provided by the subsistence sector, the worker is in a position to work in the capitalist sector for a wage rate that is less than what it otherwise would have been. The wage he receives in the capitalist sector only supplements the "social wage" he is entitled to in the village economy. While the subsistence needs are met by this entitlement, the supplementary cash wage-income from the capitalist sector is used to meet cash obligations such as payment of taxes and purchase of goods produced in the capitalist sector. Thus, the subsistent village economy bears a part of the cost of reproducing labor power, and that enables the capitalist sector to use labor power without having to pay its full reproduction cost. In other words, the pre-capitalist sector implicitly subsidizes capitalist production.[8]

Pursuing a similar line of argument, Rey extends its scope to consider raw materials, besides labor power, in the economic transactions between the two sectors. These raw materials are used as constant capital, as distinct from variable capital (wage-goods), in the capitalist sector. According to Rey, the pre-capitalist sectors serve as a source of cheap raw materials when the capitalist sector either is unable to produce on its own these materials on the required scale or faces a high cost of production. This, however, is basically an extension of the Cheap–Labor–Power argument in the sense that the ability of the pre-capitalist sectors to produce the raw materials at a lower cost stems from the relatively lower reproduction cost of labor power compared to the capitalist sector. In this case, labor power instead of being supplied directly to the capitalist sector is used in the pre-capitalist sector to produce the raw materials; and these raw materials are then made available to the capitalist sector at a low price. Thus, the point made by these writers is that the pre-capitalist sectors serve "capital's need" as supplier of labor and raw materials. And this is where they locate the logic of the articulation of multiple modes. Their claim is that as the pre-capitalist sectors fulfill these crucial needs of capital and help create the latter's conditions of existence, capital, instead of superseding these earlier modes, tries to preserve, nurture, and sometimes even bolster them. The colonial histories of the third world countries, they point out, provide ample testimony to this claim.

It is to be noted here that Rey, Meillassoux and Wolpe see the relationship between capital and the other modes from the angle of cost of production: the pre-capitalist sector serves to reduce the cost of production for the capitalist sector. But, capital has need of another kind that the pre-capitalist sector can be seen as serving:

need for a commodities market produced by capital. The pre-capitalist sectors can be viewed as a market outlet for capitalist production—a solution to the latter's realization crisis. Rosa Luxemburg's *The Accumulation of Capital* (1951), highlights this role of the pre-capitalist sector. It may seem strange—or even outrageous to Marxists of classical persuasion—that I include Luxemburg in a discussion of the structuralist literature of Althusserian inspiration. I am aware of the oddity of this inclusion, but my primary concern here is not so much to identify different schools as water-tight, non-overlapping compartments but to locate different types of explanations of articulation offered by the entire corpus of relevant writings. Although the kind of questions Luxemburg deals with are different, and she envisages the relationship between capital and the earlier modes in a different light, she does discuss at length the economic transactions between them which resonates with the capital's need argument. For Luxemburg, existence of the pre-capitalist sector—she calls it the natural economy—is indispensable for capitalist accumulation. *The Accumulation of Capital* views the capitalist mode of production as one with an inherent problem of realization. The entire capitalist production can be absorbed within the capitalist sector only when it is a case of simple reproduction. In case of expanded reproduction, i.e., when a part of the surplus value is transformed into additional capital to enlarge the production base, the situation she argues, is different. The two classes that constitute capitalist production, workers and capitalists, together are incapable of absorbing the entire production and a part of the surplus value remains unrealized. Therefore, for a society consisting solely of capitalists and workers, the realization of surplus value for the purpose of accumulation is an impossible task.

Solution to this realization problem calls for a third source of demand and it is here that Luxemburg brings in the natural economy. For her, the pre-capitalist sector constitutes the outside of capitalist production, providing a market for the latter's surplus. Capitalist production supplies goods over and above its own requirements, which are to be bought by non-capitalist sectors and countries.

And without this outside, it is impossible for the capitalist mode of production to reproduce itself on an expanded scale. In other words, capitalist accumulation is possible only in the presence of a pre-capitalist sector so that the capitalist sector can sell its surplus product to the latter, therefore, the capitalist mode of production must exist in articulation with the earlier modes.

This is clearly a different kind of "capital's need" argument, different from what Rey et al. suggest. While for the structuralists, the pre-capitalist sectors cater to the needs of capital by the way of supplying cheap labor power and raw material, thereby increasing the rate of profit, Luxemburg sees "the outside" as a market outlet which enables the capitalist sector to realize its surplus, i.e. to transform surplus value into profit. In both cases, the logic of articulation can be said to rest on capital's need but the nature of the needs are different: in one, they arise from the supply side and in the other, from the demand side. Before I fashion a critique of the capital's need argument, let me mention that later writers on the realization crisis have successfully refuted Luxemburg's claim. It is now well known, after Michal Kalecki has clearly and convincingly shown; that the pre-capitalist sector cannot provide a market outlet for the capitalist sector if trade between the two sectors is balanced (Kalecki 1971).[9]

The capital's need explanation, it needs to be pointed out at the outset, is a functional explanation. A functional explanation is one in which reference to the effects of a phenomenon contributes to explaining it. In this case, the existence of pre-capitalist modes is explained by the effect it has on capitalist production in terms of lower cost of labor power and raw material. Why does the articulation exist? Because it benefits the economic interest capital. But it is one thing to show that capital benefits from the articulation and quite another to claim that the articulation exists in order to produce precisely those effects. It may very well be the case that the articulation exists for an entirely different set of reasons, and it happens to have effects favorable to the economic interest of capital.[10]

The question of functionalism kept aside, the argument's weakness becomes apparent once we consider the dynamics of the articulation. What the structuralist does present is a static picture of the articulation in which the pre-capitalist modes are seen to be serving the economic needs of capital. But how is the dynamics of the articulation to be characterized? Is it only a synchronic relation? Can it reproduce itself over time? Once we address these questions, the weakness of the structuralist explanation becomes apparent. The capitalist mode of production, defined as extraction of surplus value from wage-labor for accumulation, is essentially a system of expanded reproduction. The surplus value is transformed into new capital resulting in a continuously expanding production base. If the pre-capitalist sectors exist as a source of cheap raw material and labor power, it must then be increasingly difficult for them to cater to the needs of an expanding capitalist production system. In a dynamic context, the capitalist sector, therefore, cannot afford to depend on a stagnant pre-capitalist sector for fulfilling its (economic) conditions of existence; it must fulfill those conditions within itself. Whether it is cheap raw material, as in Rey, or cheap wage goods, as in Meillessoux and Wolpe, the process of accumulation of capital requires that they be eventually produced within the capitalist sector as a part of the process of expanded reproduction. And it is only then that capital becomes self-subsistent in the sense that it is in a position to ensure its own (economic) conditions of existence.

Thus, in a particular stage of capital's emergence as a mode of production, the pre-capitalist sectors may serve capital's need, and capital may have an incentive to preserve the earlier modes, but the dynamic of accumulation weighs heavily against it and necessitates the ultimate dissolution of those other modes. The articulation that rests on capital's need is therefore contingent and transitory—it cannot be reproduced in the face of expanded reproduction of capital. In other words, there cannot be a dynamic theory of articulation based on capital's need.

The structuralists also recognize that the articulation based on capital's need is transitory. Rey, in his otherwise detailed explanation of the articulation, admits that the articulation is synchronic and is merely a stage in the diachronic account of transition to full-fledged capitalism. He identifies three stages in this transition process. In the first stage, the capitalist sector is dependent on the pre-capitalist sectors for labor and raw material. In the second, capital becomes dominant and is in a position to control and modify the pre-capitalist sectors to suit its own requirements. The final stage is when the capitalist sector transforms the pre-capitalist sectors and brings it within the ambit of its expanded reproduction. Thus for Rey, the economic formation in the third world in the ultimate analysis is only a stage in a delayed transition to full-fledged capitalism.

I would argue that the structuralists do not have a choice in this regard. The economic logic of capital has implicit in it the inevitability of a full-scale transition. Marx's conceptualization of the capitalist mode of production in *Capital* pre-supposes its universality in the sense that capital is seen as having already transformed its outside and brought it within its own economic space. It can ensure its own economic conditions of existence and therefore is self-subsistent. It is capital in *being*, and its pre-history, its *becoming*, remains suspended in its *being*. The structuralists take this Marxian concept and then try to explain its articulation with earlier modes, which, they fail to see, is an exploration into its prehistory—a theoretical journey backward. Articulation thus viewed therefore must be transitory and, once the dynamics of the articulation is considered, the reverse journey to self-subsistent capital is inevitable. I shall elaborate on this in Chapter 2.

The logic of articulation of capital and its outside, pre-capital, therefore cannot be found in the capitalist economic alone; we must look for it elsewhere, in the realm of the other instances: the *political* and the ideological/cultural. To be more precise, the logic has to be sought in the interrelationship of the three instances. The centrality of the "economy" in the Frankian and post-Frankian literature on capitalist underdevelopment must be rejected in favor of an analytical framework that recognizes the specificity of the non-economic instances and foregrounds the question of agency: who are the agents of change? And what are the conditions under which they can act? For, after all, modes of production do not change on their own; they are changed through a politico-social process involving agents of change. A. Foster–Carter puts it, "...modes of production are not the subject of history, so neither they should be subject of sentences" (1978: 55).

As I mentioned earlier, it is Brenner who brings up the question of agency in capitalist transformation, and by shifting the focus on class struggle he foregrounds the question of power, suggesting that the story of capitalist transformation needs to be told in relation to the problematic of power. More important, Brenner's analysis militates against a mechanical view of class struggle. It suggests that although classes originate in the base, i.e., the economic, their conflicts and struggles in the realm of the political do not follow any given trajectory determined by forces that inhere in the economic. On the contrary, the configuration of classes and the dynamics of class struggle can play an important role in determining the dynamics of the economic itself. Brenner illustrates this point with a comparison of the experiences of economic transformation in

England, Eastern Europe and France in the phase of late feudalism: a phase plagued by a rent crisis and widespread decline in population due to the Black Death. He shows that the outcomes of the crisis were different in the three cases, depending on the relative strength of the two contending classes, i.e. landlords and peasants. A relatively stronger landlord class in Eastern Europe was able to cope with the crisis by creating the "second serfdom" which ruled out the possibility of the emergence of a superior mode of production. By contrast, class struggle in England led to the collapse of serfdom, but as landlords were able to retain the ownership of land, they were in a position and also had the incentive to bring about transformation into the capitalist mode of production. In France, serfdom collapsed but peasants acquired land rights and remained independent with active support of the state that saw the peasantry as a source of tax revenue. Unlike in England, the French peasants were less interested in capitalist transformation and remained independent peasant cultivators. Thus, Brenner argues that there is a political variable that explains why as an outcome of the same crisis, capitalist transformation occurred in England but not in Eastern Europe or France.

The implication of Brenner's argument is that the story of capitalist transformation must begin by recognizing that the superstructure has an important role to play in determining the outcome of the process of transformation, making its success and failure contingent on the specific configuration of forces in the sphere of politics and ideology. In other words, it calls for an approach that takes into account the complexities of the question of power, agency and subjectivity that the orthodox base–superstructure hierarchy does not permit[11].

There has been an attempt in this direction by Indian political economists who seek to characterize the post-colonial capitalism in India in terms of class, power, and the state. The need to problematize the state in relation to capitalist (under) development in post-colonial India triggered off in the eighties a debate that resulted in a body of writings (Chatterjee 1988, 1993; Chaudhury 1988, 1992, 1994; Sanyal 1988, 1992; Sen 1988)[12] outlining what Terence Byres has labeled the *neo-Gramscian approach* (Byres 1994: 40). This approach draws on Antonio Gramsci's discussion of hegemony and passive revolution in *The Prison Notebooks* (1975) and deploys these concepts to sketch out the contours of a story involving capital, pre-capital, class, power, and the state.

Class, Power and Hegemony:
The Neo-Gramscian Perspective

The central question for Gramsci is how the bourgeoisie seizes and retains power. In order to address this question, Gramsci abandons the base–superstructure division and with it the orthodox claim that the superstructure (political and ideological) flows from, i.e. is predetermined by the base (economic). The base, he argues, cannot be logically prior to the superstructure since the economy cannot be defined without using superstructural categories (such as property rights). Instead he uses the state–civil society division in which the former is the public sphere and the latter is the sphere of the private. The dominant class rules, Gramsci insists, not on the basis of coercion alone; it also persuades the subordinate classes to give active consent to its rule. The dominated classes accept the ideas propagated by the ruling class, making the latter the intellectual and moral leader of society. To be more precise, the ruling class projects its own sectional interest as the universal interest which the other classes identify with and the universal is reified in the body of the state. In capitalism, the bourgeoisie succeeds in separating civil society from the state with the latter portrayed as an abstract and neutral institution above the sectional interests and conflicts of civil society, and this is in sharp contrast with the directly political nature of civil society in pre-capitalist societies. At the same time, it propagates and diffuses its own world-view through the institutions of civil society (e.g., education, media, family, religious organizations) so that it is established as the world-view of the entire society. The bourgeois ideology thus permeates the practices and beliefs of the general masses, producing a system of general faith–belief in the social order. In terms of the historical materialist framework, hegemony numbs the antithesis and allows the ruling class to "rule by thesis".

This ideological appropriation of the dominated classes by the ruling class is what Gramsci calls hegemony. It is the "entire complex of political and theoretical activity by which the ruling classes not only justify and maintain their domination but also succeed in obtaining the active consent of the governed" (Gramsci 1975: 182). The ruling class in this case becomes the hegemonic class "capable of absorbing the entire society, assimilating it to its own cultural and economic level." (p. 260).

In capitalism the state grants right to every citizen, thereby recognizing them as equal, and individuals in civil society see themselves as "particulars" flowing from the "universal", i.e., right. With its conflicts and contradictions rendered invisible, civil society appears as a harmonious whole consisting of autonomous individuals endowed with rights, and thus the bourgeoisie secures legitimation of its class rule. In the writings of young Marx, one finds penetrating insight into this state–civil society relationship in capitalism. Allow me to quote at length:

> The state abolishes...distinctions of birth, rank, education and occupation, when it declares that birth, social rank, education, occupation are non-political distinctions when it proclaims, without regard to these distinctions, that every member of the nation is an equal participant in national sovereignty, and when it treats all elements of the real life of the nation from the standpoint of the state. Nevertheless the state allows private property, education and occupation to act in their way, i.e. as private property, as education, as occupation, and to exert the influence of their special nature. Far from abolishing these real distinctions, the state only exists on the presupposition of their existence; it feels itself to be a political state and asserts its universality only in opposition to these elements of its being. (1975: 153)

And he goes on to demonstrate the falsity of the bourgeois state's claim to universality:

> Where the political state has attained its true development, man— not only in thought, in consciousness, but in reality, in life—leads a twofold life in the political community in which he considers himself a communal being, and life in civil society in which he acts as a private individual, regards other men as means, degrades himself into means, and becomes the plaything of alien powers. The relation of the political state to civil society is just as spiritual as the relation of heaven to earth....In his most immediate reality, in civil society, man is a secular being. Here, where he regards himself as a real individual, and is so regarded by others, he is a fictitious phenomenon. *In the state ... where man is regarded as a species-being, he is the imaginary member of an illusory sovereignty.... endowed with an unreal universality.* (emphasis mine) (1975: 154)

Here Marx's purpose is to demonstrate that the bourgeois state's claim to universality is a false claim. The concept of hegemony can be seen as addressing the same question from the other end: While contradictions in civil society are discovered and foregrounded by Marx and posited against the universality of the political society, the theory of hegemony starts from these contradictions and then seeks to understand the mechanism and the process by which the universal is produced and reified in the body of the state, and how the contradictions apparently dissolve in favor of a harmonious civil society.

Hegemony, however, is not false-consciousness. Dominated classes accept the universal projected by the ruling class not because they are fooled or misled; they do so because they interpret the universal in their own way and find in it elements with which they can identify consciously. Formal equality granted by the state in capitalism is untrue in so far as the class hierarchy that inheres in the capitalist mode of production is concerned. But, at the same time, the claim that citizens are equal is not entirely false if judged in relation to the explicitly political nature of civil society in pre-capitalism with its sanctioned hierarchy and social stratifications. The consent given by the subaltern to the hegemonic order reflects a particular moment of his consciousness, a moment that can be superseded and it is only at a higher moment of consciousness that the subaltern can see the inequality and hierarchy hidden by the projected universal. Put differently, the ideological unity of the ruler and the ruled in capitalism has a basis rooted in society. And it is in this sense that the dominated classes give *active consent* to the moral and intellectual leadership of the hegemonic class. This unity "is attained through the myriad ways in which the institutions in civil society operate to shape, directly or indirectly, the cognitive and affective structures whereby men perceive and evaluate problematic social reality" (Femia 1980: 24). Thus "what a dominant, hegemonic ideology can do is to provide a more coherent and systematic world view which not only influences the mass of population but serves as a principle of organization of social institutions. Ideology in his [Gramsci's] view does not simply reflect or mirror economic class interest ... it organizes action through the way it is embodied in social relations, institutions and practices, and informs all individual and collective activities." (Sasson 1983: 201–203)

The universal projected by the ruling class, however, is not always a simple one. It may take a complex form, and this complexity is what Gramsci is mainly concerned with. If the dominant and the dominated classes occupy the same cultural space, persuasion by the former produces collaboration as its mirror image in the consciousness of the latter. But if they inhabit diverse cultural spaces, then persuasion by the elite fails to produce the mirror image in the subaltern consciousness. The elite in this case must appropriate the elements of collaboration in subaltern consciousness—elements that are rooted in an autonomous cultural space—and hegemony takes a complex form. In terms of the historical materialist framework, *the thesis here for its own development incorporates a part of the antithesis to produce a surrogate synthesis that blocks the true synthesis.* If the classical case is the one in which the dominant class can project its own ideas and is able to elicit collaboration, i.e., rule by thesis, complex hegemony is the non-classical case in which the thesis is unable to rule on its own.[13]

In case of full-fledged capitalism, the classical case would be the one in which capital (the thesis) can project the idea of "freedom" (of property and contract) as the universal, and labor (the antithesis) collaborates. In other words, legitimization of the capitalist mode of production, in this case, is accomplished through the political ideology of freedom represented by the liberal state. But as the working class emerges as the antithesis of capital, the idea of freedom can no longer serve as the universal idea. The hegemony process would then require that capital appropriate the demands of the working class to construct a new universal that will ideologically unite the two classes. In the case of Western capitalism, the idea of 'welfare' (right to subsistence, health, and education) can be seen as the new universal idea and the welfare state, the reification of this complex form of bourgeoisie hegemony. The thesis (capital) in this case appropriates a part of the antithesis (the working class) and the surrogate synthesis on the level of the welfare state blocks the true synthesis (socialism), thereby bringing the historical materialist process to a halt. Gramsci is primarily concerned with the variety of forms this non-classical, complex case can possibly take on: for him they are Bonapartism/Caesarism, Fascism, and Americanism and Fordism.

Gramsci deals primarily with the non-classical cases in advance capitalism, but he also displaces the question of hegemony on another terrain, the terrain of capital–pre-capital relation. And it is here that the neo-Gramscians find the crucial concept they can muster to characterize the post-colonial capitalist development: the concept of "passive revolution." Gramsci makes the distinction between the classical and non-classical cases also in the context of a transitional society in which the bourgeoisie is struggling to seize power. Here the classical case is the one in which the bourgeoisie, after having established its sway over civil society, launches a frontal attack on the state and the old dominant classes on the basis of its own agenda. But when the bourgeoisie is relatively weak in civil society, it resorts to a passive revolution in which it allies with the old dominant classes to get into macro power on the level of the state, and then engages in molecular transformation of civil society. The bourgeoisie, in this case, has to seek legitimization on the basis of a mixed agenda consisting of, along with its own goals, goals of other groups as well. In other words, the thesis (capital), for its own development, incorporates a part of the antithesis (pre-capital), producing a surrogate synthesis that blocks the true synthesis, (full-fledged capitalism).

[The term pre-capital needs clarification. Neo-Gramscians use it in a theoretical as well as chronological sense. It is a term defined in relation to the concept of capital and located, as the prefix suggests, in a chronology: pre-capital is the property and production relations that precede capital.[14] As pre-capitalist forms of production are varied and many, the exact theoretical content put into this generic term needs to be spelled out. In the Marxist discussion on historical materialism, the prehistory of capitalism is periodized in terms of several different economic and social formations. Each of these epochs is characterized in terms of a specific mode of surplus extraction and a particular structure of property relations. Although forms of property differ across epochs, they share one common feature: the non-separation of labor and means of labor. In the neo-Gramscian perspective, the different pre-capitalist forms are collapsed into a general notion of pre-capital as the unity of labor and means of labor. The unity may derive from collective property or it may take the form of direct ownership of the producer].[15]

The neo-Gramscians have deployed the concept of surrogate synthesis to the Indian context and have seen the Indian post-colonial experience as a case of passive revolution by the Indian bourgeoisie. But before I detail out their argument, it is necessary to situate their position in the specific context of the Indian tradition of Marxist political economy because their story has been presented as a theoretical challenge to the Marxist orthodoxy that had prevailed among the Indian left in the 1960s and 1970s: academic intellectuals and activists alike. The traditional Marxist discourse on the Indian economy and the state was firmly and unabashedly rooted in the orthodox deterministic version of historical materialism. It sought to explain capitalist development, or the lack of it, in India solely in terms of the economic and argued that a particular constellation of economic factors—pre-capitalist institutions and relations, in most cases legacies of the colonial past—were acting as constraints on the inexorable historical materialist process laid down in the *Communist Manifesto* and espoused by the Second International. It produced a body of writings that came to be represented under the rubric of the "mode of production debate" and formed a school of thought that ruled the roost among the Indian left till the end of the 1970s.[16] The neo-Gramscian intervention was an emphatic departure from this economistic vision of capitalist underdevelopment.

The Neo-Gramscian Departure

Seeing capitalist development in these terms, the neo-Gramscians argue, only shows capital's failure to overcome the dominance of pre-capitalist relations. For them, a more useful approach is to inquire how capital copes with and negotiates the pre-capitalist institutions in order to carry out the process of accumulation. As Chaudhury puts it, "the task of the social scientist is to examine how capital reacts to these problems: how capital surmounts, neutralizes and appropriates what stands in capital's way." (1992: 57) In other words, while the traditional Marxist analysis finds postcolonial capital constrained and insufficient, for the neo-Gramscians, it is malleable and protean; what the former identifies as weakness, for the latter, betrays its strength. Passive revolution offers the theoretical framework within which these strategic maneuvers of capital vis-à-vis the pre-capitalist forces can be captured, and it is these maneuvers that constitute the situation of post-colonial capitalism. And this is a story of success, not failure, in which capital succeeds in creating the conditions for accumulation despite the presence of pre-capital.

Let us consider the broad outline of the narrative of the Indian post-colonial capital in terms of the theoretical framework of passive revolution.[17] The neo-Gramscian approach characterized the nationalist movement against the colonial power as a case of passive revolution in which the Indian bourgeoisie entered into a series of alliances with other pre-capitalist dominant classes, and under the leadership of this alliances mass support from the subordinate classes was mobilized. Such alliances were necessary because the bourgeoisie did not represent the national–popular and therefore was unable to launch an attack on its own against the colonial rule to found a modern nation state that would ensure the conditions for expanded reproduction of capital. In the post-colonial situation, the nation is reified in the body of the state, and the bourgeoisie is able to establish its dominance only by coming to terms with the other constituents of the nation to construct a hegemonic order that is necessarily complex. Therefore, instead of undertaking a full-scale assault on the pre-capitalist dominant classes, it seeks "to limit their former power, neutralize them where necessary, attack them only selectively, and in general bring them round to a position of subsidiary allies within a reformed state structure."(Chatterjee 1993: 212) The hegemony in this case does not reflect capital's dominance in "civil society"; it is a complex hegemony that includes both civil society and the pre-capitalist community with the nation as the surrogate synthesis reified in the body of the state.

How does this complex hegemony help create the conditions for capital's expanded reproduction? In the post-colonial Indian economy, the domain of capital consists of a dynamic "modern" sector based on accumulation and innovation. But legitimization of this modern sector requires the state to recognize the other constituent elements of the nation, set for them a goal that is distinct from accumulation, and then mobilize and deploy resources to realize that goal. This role of the state, according to our neo-Gramscian, is a legacy of the anti-colonial movement. The critique of colonial rule, he argues, rested on the claim that colonialism was a fetter on the development of the Indian economy, and only an independent modern state could create the conditions for national economic development. Thus, the post-colonial nation state, from the very beginning, is pre-committed to development. In the case of post-colonial India, adoption of a democratic system based on universal adult suffrage further reinforces this developmental role of the state by forcing it to seek legitimization of the modern sector by addressing the developmental needs of the vast pre-capitalist sector that constitutes the "outside" of capital. In other words, legitimization requires that the state undertake developmental programs for the pre-capitalist sectors alongside the accumulation-based modern sector.[18] It is this process of legitimization and the resultant capital–pre-capital dualism that distances post-colonial capitalism from the classical case of capitalist development.

In the classical case, associated with capitalist development, is a process that Marx refers to as primitive accumulation through which the conditions of expanded capitalist production are created. It is a process whereby direct subsistence producers in the pre-capitalist economy are separated from the means of production and turned into wage laborers who have nothing to sell other than their labor power. On the other hand, the means of production thus freed are converted into capital and then combined with free laborer through wage contracts in the labor market for capitalist production. This process of creation of free wage-labor necessarily involves a variety of coercive measures that are used to destroy all pre-capitalist sub-sistence production and the direct producers' entitlements to sub-sistence in the pre-capitalist social arrangements. The pauperization of subsistence producers as a result of large-scale dispossession and destruction of livelihood, and their ultimate transformation into workers in capitalist production, is a very painful process, as evi-denced in the history of capitalist transformation in the Western Europe.

In post-colonial India, according to the neo-Gramscian argument, representative democracy severely limits the use of the kind of co-ercive power that has been used in the Western European case, thus ruling out the possibility of destruction of the pre-capitalist sub-sistence production through the process of primitive accumulation. On the contrary, "...the ideological construct of the 'passive revo-lution of capital' consciously sought to incorporate within the frame-work of its rule... the entire structures of pre-capitalist community taken in their existent forms." And "in the economic field, the form preferred was that of 'community development' in which the benefits of plan projects, meant for the countryside, was supposed to be shared collectively by the whole community."(Chatterjee 1993: 213). The result is the continued presence of pre-capital along with a growing modern (capitalist) sector.

Although it deals with the Indian case, one can delineate the contours of a general theoretical framework for conceptualizing post-colonial capital in the neo-Gramscian literature. It is built on the following claims:

(1) The post-colonial bourgeoisie has to form alliances with dominant pre-capitalist groups to enter into state power.
(2) The state, representing the national popular, has to legitimize capitalist accumulation on the level of the people–nation.
(3) The need for legitimization rules out the process of primitive accumulation.
(4) The state therefore has to protect, preserve, and promote the pre-capitalist modes of production. The strength of the post-colonial capital thus lies in its ability to use the ideological construct of passive revolution to carry on expanded reproduction in the modern sector and, at the same time ensure reproduction of the pre-capitalist, traditional sectors of the economy.

The post-colonial capital, imaginative deployment of Gramsci in the post-colonial context, distances itself from the traditional Marxist perspective in two important ways. First, unlike the structuralists, it does not seek to explain articulation of modes of production in terms of the capitalist *economic*, i.e. capital's economic needs; articulation, for the neo-Gramscians, arises out of the need to ensure the political and ideological conditions of existence of the post-colonial capital. The modern sector must allow the traditional sector to exist in order to secure the legitimacy of its own existence. Second, and this is more important, nor do the neo-Gramscians see articulation as resulting from the nature of imperialist penetration—a factor that figures so prominently in the Frankian as well as in the post-Frankian theories. The process of legitimization that the neo-Gramscians refer to is a process internal to the nation: it involves capital, pre-capital, and the nation state. I pointed out while critiquing Taylor that an explanation of articulation solely in terms of imperialist penetration is inadequate for addressing the post-colonial experience of those economies in which an inward-looking, closed-door strategy of national economic development based on import substitution has failed to produce a full-fledged capitalist transformation. India is a paradigmatic case of such a failure, and by their attempt to theorize the Indian experience, the neo-Gramscians succeed in foregrounding the contradictory and ambivalent nature of the "post-colonial nation" and situate the question of capitalist transformation in relation to those contradictions and ambivalence.

While the neo-Gramscian approach is certainly a departure from the economistic framework of both orthodox Marxists and the structuralists, it is nonetheless marked with the same contradiction that, as I claimed earlier, the post-Frankian theories of articulation try to cope with. The contradiction between the need to characterize capitalism in the periphery as a *sui generis* with dynamics of its own, and the implicit refusal to break away from the stagist paradigm of historical materialism that reduces the peripheral capitalism to a mere case of failure. For the neo-Gramscians, the post-colonial case is one of successful passive revolution by the bourgeoisie, producing capitalism of a different kind. However, full-scale capitalist transformation, i.e. the classical case, as a possibility, remains embedded in the framework as a reference point, in terms of which the case of passive revolution is seen as a deviant one. The analysis thus remains implicitly anchored in the trajectory of capitalist development implied by the framework of historical materialism. Let me elaborate. The neo-Gramscian claim is that:

.....[P]assive revolution is in fact the general framework of capitalist transition in societies where bourgeoisie hegemony has not been accomplished in the classical way....the dialectic here cannot be blocked in any fundamental sense. Rather, the new forms of dominance of capital become understandable, *not as the immanent supersession of earlier contradictions, but as a part of a constructed hegemony*, effective because of the successful exercise of both coercive and persuasive power, but incomplete and fragmented at the same time because the hegemonic claims are fundamentally contested within the constructed whole. (Chatterjee 1993: 212, my emphasis)

Now consider the explanation of the continued presence of precapital our neo-Gramscian offers. According to him, destruction of the pre-capitalist sectors through the process of primitive accumulation involves extensive use of coercive power, which, in the Indian case, the political framework of representative democracy does not permit. And therefore the state has to preserve and develop the traditional sectors. The question is: if it were possible to use the kind of coercive power the process of primitive accumulation calls for, would there have been a full-scale transition to capitalism? Implicit in this argument is an affirmative answer to this question. It implicitly assumes that the success of primitive accumulation— i.e. separation of subsistence producers from their means of production and transformation of those dispossessed producers into wage-laborers in the capitalist sector, depends only on the presence of an appropriate structure and modality of power.

Viewed thus, the democratic framework poses an obstacle in the way of an otherwise realizable full-scale capitalist transformation. The argument implies that if the process of representative democracy could be withheld, coercive power exercised, and if the society were ready to endure the pain and rigor of primitive accumulation, then it would have been possible, at least in principle, to subsume the entire economy within the expanded reproduction of capital. In other words, primitive accumulation is an unavoidable stage in the trajectory of full-scale capitalist development, and what the story of passive revolution tells us is that the need for legitimization in a framework of representative democracy does not allow the society to pass through this crucial stage. It is somewhat analogous to the claim made by the development economist that the inability to undertake a critical minimum amount of investment perpetually holds back a poor country in a low-level trap of poverty. (One may also point out that in the majority of post-colonial nations, representative democracy is absent, but the ability of the state to exercise its coercive power in favor of the process of primitive accumulation has not resulted in a full-scale capitalist transformation.)

The neo-Gramscian position thus remains implicitly but firmly anchored in the historical materialist paradigm, more precisely, in the Hegelian idea of supersession that informs it. In Hegel, the universal unfolds and develops itself in the course of history, higher moments of history superseding its lower moments, until history reaches its terminus: *idea*. Historical materialism retains this Hegelian idea of supersession and sees historical moments as *thesis* and *antithesis*, and their supersession at the higher moment called *synthesis*. In terms of this Hegelian triad (thesis–antithesis–synthesis), historical materialism narrates the movement of the essence of time toward a goal (communism) with feudalism, capitalism and socialism as its successive moments. In the context of capitalist transformation, feudalism (the thesis) and embryonic capitalism (the antithesis) are seen as two moments of history, and full-fledged capitalism as the synthesis that supersedes both feudalism and capitalism in its nascent form.

Beyond Gramsci: Breaking with Historicism

By assuming that a full-scale capitalist transformation is in principle possible, the neo-Gramscian position implicitly subscribes to the idea of supersession, thereby reducing the case of passive revolution to one of 'blocked dialectic', in which the linear progression of history comes to a halt. The position, however, insists that in passive revolution, "the dialectic ... cannot be assumed to be blocked in any fundamental sense, [r]ather, the new forms of dominance of capital become understandable, not as the immanent supersession of earlier contradictions, but as parts of a constructed hegemony"(Chatterjee 1993: 212). In other words, the "blocked dialectic" here is replaced by the idea of a new form of hegemony that redefines itself in terms of a different dialectic. It further claims that passive revolution should be seen as the general framework, rather than a deviant case, of capitalist transition in the third world (Sen 1988). But if "capitalist transition" is the ultimate destination of the journey, then passive revolution is only a roundabout way of arriving at that destination. For societies that have not experienced the classical case of bourgeois revolution, it is the "general framework" only in the sense that these societies must all take this indirect route to realize the project of transition to capitalism. It certainly complicates the linearity of the trajectory, but the historical materialist framework and the idea of supersession remains intact in the background.

Is it possible to grasp the contradictions and the dynamic of this "constructed hegemony" as long as it implicitly remains anchored in the idea of supersession? Isn't then passive revolution, in the ultimate analysis, only a complex moment of the inexorable process of transition from one mode of production to another? How can we then understand its "different dialectic", unless we abandon the idea supersession and extricate the post-colonial story entirely from the historical materialist framework? I would argue that for an understanding of post-colonial capital, we must break with the historicism that marks the Gramscian concept of passive revolution. Only then are we in a position to see the post-colonial capitalist

development not as the immanent supersession of the earlier contradictions but as a constructed hegemony with a dialectic of its own.
This, for sure, is a theoretical task. *It calls for a characterization of
capitalist development that theoretically rules out the possibility
of capital superseding pre-capital. And this is what marks my point
of departure from the neo-Gramscian literature.* In what follows
I shall conceptualize capitalist development as a process that in its
own course produces pre-capital. While on the one hand, the process
of primitive accumulation, I will argue, leads to the destruction of
the pre-capitalist sectors, on the other, it simultaneously produces a
space that necessitates the recreation of those sectors. In short, pre-
capital's conditions of existence flow from the internal logic of the
expanded reproduction of capital. (This characterization of capitalist development is elaborated in Chapter 2). Seen thus, pre-capital
constitutes an internal 'other' of capital and the possibility of capital
superseding pre-capital becomes a theoretical impossibility. And no
synthesis is possible in the form of a full-fledged capitalism and the
classical case of capitalist transformation by 'battering down the
Chinese wall' turns out to be unrealizable even in principle.

This characterization of capitalist development has three important theoretical implications for the political economy of post-
colonial capitalism. First, it effaces the marks of historicism off the
"surrogate synthesis" of capital and pre-capital. In the Gramscian
notion of passive revolution, pre-capital is exogenous to capital, a
remnant of the past that refuses to go away, and capital must learn
to live with it. But if pre-capital is seen as arising out of, i.e., endogenous to, the capitalist development process itself, then both
capital and pre-capital are freed from the historical/chronological
ordering, and the prefix *pre* gives way to *non*. The "other" of capital
is now *non-capital* which articulates itself with capital, and the institution of market constitutes the space in which the articulation
resides. In other words, commodity relations integrate capital and
non-capital to form the post-colonial *economic*. Conversely, by going
beneath the market, we find the complex of capital and non-capital
perpetually locked in a relation of contradiction and mutuality.

Second, the idea that capital produces non-capital allows us to
capture the dynamics of the post-colonial capitalism. In the structuralist explanation, I pointed out earlier, the relation between capital

and pre-capital is only synchronic and the articulation is not dynamically sustainable. On the other hand, the neo-Gramscians consider accumulation in the modern sector and development of the traditional sector as two parallel processes without explicitly referring to the dynamics of their relationship. Our conceptualization of the post-colonial *economic* allows for a diachronic account of the capital–non-capital complex in terms of the two-sided process of destruction and creation of non-capital.

Most important, conceptualized as a complex of capital and non-capital, the narrative of post-colonial capitalism ceases to be a narrative of transition. Both Marxists and liberals have problematized the economic formation of the third world within a framework of transition: from tradition to modernity, from unreason to reason, from pre-capitalism to capitalism. The modernization theories belonging to the liberal tradition have seen development in third world countries as a set of fundamental structural changes whereby traditional economic, social, and cultural institutions are replaced by a set of modern institutions. The traditional institutions act as a fetter on economic development, and these structural changes—transition from tradition to modernity—create the conditions within which sustained economic growth is possible. To the Marxists, as we have already seen, development has always meant transition from the (stagnant) pre-capitalist mode of production to a (dynamic) capitalist mode of production. For them, the central question has been why this transition remains incomplete in the third world. Thus the two theoretical traditions, despite their different world-views and methodologies, share a notion of transition, a break with a "before" and an "after", in which one "order of things" gives way to another. But the characterization of the post-colonial economic as a complex of capital and non-capital, with the latter emerging in a space produced by of the internal logic of the former, totally dispenses with the notion of transition. If there is a possible transition in this scenario, it is from pre-capitalism to the capital–non-capital complex. *The conceptualization of post-colonial capital in terms of this complex amounts to saying that transition in the historicist sense has already occurred and what we have is capitalism with an inherent heterogeneity.* Capitalist development in this scenario means not a structural shift from non-capital to capital, but the development of the entire capital–non-capital complex.

The political economy of post-colonial capitalism in terms of the dual process of destruction and recreation of non-capital, for sure, is to be understood in relation to the question of power and hegemony. In what follows, I will draw upon Michel Foucault's theory of discursive formation to reformulate the Gramscian notion of hegemony and then deploy it to arrive at a story of capitalist development in the post-colonial world. The discourse theory offers a particularly attractive framework that allows us to re-conceptualize the problematic of hegemony and thereby to have a better grasp of the complexities of the nature and modalities of the post-colonial regime of power. An equally important aspect of my reformulation of the Gramscian problematic is that it situates the post-colonial form of hegemony in the global context. The hegemony process in Gramsci is a process defined entirely on the national level—it is a process that relates class, institutions in (national) civil society and the nation state. But as my purpose is to arrive at an understanding of post-colonial capitalism in today's globalized world, I must go beyond Gramsci and understand the process of legitimation as a global, rather than a national, process rooted in a global discourse of "development". The following chapter lays the necessary theoretical groundwork.

Notes

1. Historical materialism is the Marxist theory of history that understands history as a sequence of epochs each dominated by a specific mode of production. The process of history is envisaged as a process of transition from a relatively backward mode of production to a more advanced one. A mode of production is a structured articulation of a certain level of forces of production (i.e., the level of technology, resources, and skill) and relations of production (i.e., relation between social classes, stemming from their positions within the structure of production and property relations). In the historical materialist framework, forces of production is assumed to develop in a unilinear fashion over time. It is further assumed that corresponding to each level of the development of forces of production, there is only one set of relations of production that are compatible. Thus, as productive forces develop, after a point the existing production relations become incompatible and ultimately become a fetter on their further development. The historical materialist process is a process whereby the old set of production relations dissolves to make way for a new set of relations of production consistent with the higher level of productive forces. In other words, the contradiction between the forces and relations of production is the driving force behind

the transition from one mode of production to the next in the pre-ordained sequence that represents history. In short, historical materialism posits history as a unidirectional trajectory in which contradictions within a specific mode of production at a particular stage of history are resolved in the process of transition from that mode of production to a relatively more advanced one—for example, from feudalism to capitalism—until the process of history ends in communism where all contradictions cease.

2. For other important contributions to the dependency theory, see Cordoso (1973, 1979), Sunkel (1972) and Dos Santos (1970). For an illuminating survey of the literature, see Chilcote (1983).

3. Emmanuel (1971) and Samir Amin (1974)) made attempts to theorize the concept of unequal exchange in terms of the wage differential between the center and the periphery. The crux of their argument is that the wage rate is typically lower in the periphery. In the presence of international mobility of capital profit rates are equalized, and the difference in the wage rates then causes a transfer of value from the low-wage periphery to the high-wage center through the system of prices on the basis of which trade takes place.

4. See also Wallerstein (1979).

5. Brenner, although he highlights the role of class struggle and politics and asserts that capitalist development is not an inevitability and it depends on the specificity of class struggle and its dynamic, however retains the assumption that forces of production develop independently of the relations of production. Laclau-Mouffe (1985), referring to Braverman's work (Braverman 1975), challenged this view and assert that the development of productive forces itself is conditioned by class struggle.

6. Warren's position, though fiercely contested by the Marxist theorists of underdevelopment, is consistent with the early writings of Marx and Engels on colonialism in which imperialism is seen as a progressive force. See Marx and Engels (1974), and for a critique of Warren's position, Ahmed (1983, 2001).

7. This position is contrary to the belief that imperialism has a progressive impact on the economic, cultural and social structure of the colonies that are thought to be backward, stagnant and resistant to any change.

8. It may be interesting to note here that this cost-of-labor-power argument resurfaced in the eighties in an entirely different context. Feminist political economists claimed that in the contemporary advance capitalist economies, the household sector exists as a non-capitalist site where labor-power for the capitalist sector is reproduced. Work done by the housewife within the worker's household (cooking, washing, and child caring) is crucial for the reproduction of labor-power of the worker. As labor expended in these activities remains unpaid, the capitalist employer in effect pays less than the true cost of reproduction of labor-power he uses in the factory (Folbre 1982). In one of the latter works, the household sector has been seen as a site of a 'feudal' class process (Wolff, Resnick and Fraad 2000).

9. The outside can serve as a market for the capitalist sector and mitigate its realization problem only if the latter runs a trade surplus. In other words,

unlike what Luxemburg thought, it is not enough that the capitalist sector exports its excess production to the pre-capitalist sector, solution to the realization crisis requires that there be an excess of exports over imports.

10. For an illuminating discussion of functional explanation and Marxism, see Cohen (1978, ch. x).

11. Brenner however posits the development of forces of production as a linear process not mediated by class struggle and politics. Whether the development of productive forces will lead to a transformation of the relations of production is for Brenner a political question whose answer has to be sought in the specific class configurations and the relative strength of different classes. But class struggle has no role to play in determining the trajectory of the development of technology. For a critique of this, see Laclau and Mouffe (1985).

12. A workshop was held in the Center for Studies in Social Sciences, Calcutta, on 'Antonio Gramsci and South Asia' in July 1987. Papers presented in that workshop were later published in the *Economic and Political Weekly* in January 1988.

13. Considering two spaces, each with its own essence, simple hegemony means that one space recognizes the essence of the other space as its own, forgetting its own true essence. In complex hegemony, the two spaces produce a third surrogate space with a surrogate essence. See Chatterjee (1986), Chaudhury (1986).

14. Here the concept of capital serves as the starting point and then as its negation pre-capital is defined as "what capital is not" but out of which capital's conditions of existence emerge.

15. Within pre-capital the individual exists not as a mere laborer but as a member of the community. The purpose of his labor is not the creation of value but maintenance of himself, his family and the communal body as a whole.

16. For a detailed discussion on the mode of production debate, see Patnaik (1990).

17. The story in its fully-blown form is available in Chatterjee (1993).

18. For an elaboration on this point, see Sanyal (1988).

Chapter 2

Ship of Fools

It was while reading Michel Foucault's *Madness and Civilization* that I first caught a glimpse of what struck me as a metaphor for post-colonial capitalism. One surely would find the association strange, for Foucault's story is about 16th century Europe, a story far removed from today's post-colonial context. Yet, his compelling analysis of the change in the order of things that marked the 16th century European society—a society experiencing the emergence of the rule of reason and capitalism—made visible a specific technology of power that, for me, bore an uncanny resemblance to our lived post-colonial experience at the dawn of the 21st century.

Foucault's story is about how the rule of reason dealt with unreason in 16th century Europe. He begins with the observation that at the end of the Middle Ages, lepers, who had always been excluded from society and confined to the margin of the community, had disappeared. The land at the gates of the cities where lepers had been confined remained as uninhabited wasteland for two centuries until its new inhabitants appeared, the new incarnation of the lepers: they were the poor, vagabonds, criminals, and especially the 'deranged minds' on whom the society would again apply the formulas of exclusion. In delineating the contours of the technology of power to which the Age of Reason subjected the insane who was seen as the personification of unreason, Foucault describes a strange but widely practiced custom of that period in which the insane was handed over by the city authorities to the merchants and pilgrims to be taken on a ship to a voyage on the sea, never to return to the city again:

> Something new appears in the imaginary landscape of the Renaissance; soon it will occupy a privileged place there; the Ship of Fools, a strange 'drunken boat' that glides along the calm rivers of the Rhineland and the Flemish canals. (1988: 7)

Foucault further complicates this phenomenon of exclusion by claiming that exclusion was loaded with an ambivalence: lepers were kept outside the city limits but at the same time were seen as a reminder of God's wrath and punishment; and exclusion was seen as salvation, as spiritual reintegration. "Abandonment is his salvation; his exclusion offers him another form of communion."(*ibid.*: p. 7) Similarly, the insane was banished from the city on an endless voyage, but water was viewed as the great purifier and the journey as one in search of sanity. The insane thus occupied a liminal position on the edge of society, a position not entirely outside the society but not inside either. And for Foucault, it was this act of spatial exclusion on the one side and cultural/spiritual integration on the other that reflected the ambivalence in the way the Age of Reason dealt with its outcasts.

Foucault devotes the entire book to probe the techniques and modalities of this new form of power that sought to organize the social space by exclusion and confinement of the marginals. But it is in his description of "Ship of Fools" that I find a striking metaphor for post-colonial capitalism. The ship carrying its insane cargo, drifting from port to port, with the gates of the cities closed and the insane not allowed to disembark, brings to my mind a similar landscape, the post-colonial one, in which a large part of the population, dispossessed and marginalized, wander around in a wasteland created by "capitalist development".

The "Ship of Fools" marked the landscape of the 16th century, but consider the description of the late 20th century Brazilian economy presented by Ignacy Sachs (1991), a development economist, in an article in a volume dealing with the question of poverty in the contemporary third world economies:

"... Brazil was transformed into a BELINDA ... a Belgium in the middle of an India, with parts of the Nordeste comparable to Bangladesh. Industrialization had the opposite effect to that anticipated by Arthur Lewis. Instead of gradually exhausting the reserve of unskilled labour by drawing it into the modern organized sector, it deepened the process of *exclusion and social segregation*, creating a huge surplus of underemployed labour in the cities, including ... casual agricultural workers *expelled* from the rural areas by the mechanization of the large estates." (99, emphasis mine)

This description makes visible a space at the fringe of the urban center inhabiting those who are "expelled" from the agricultural sector and at the same time *excluded and segregated* from the glittering modern, urban economy. Condemned to a no man's land, they are the outcastes and rejects of the contemporary third world economies.

Sachs goes on to elaborate the process of exclusion. He argues that Brazil with a land–man ratio ten times as high as in Asia could accommodate 66.6 million people in agriculture, which is more than the economically active population of the country by means of settlements on public land and more importantly redistribution of unproductive latifundia to landless people. "The land reform announced in 1985 was supposed to benefit 9.4 million peasant families by 1989 using 71 million hectares of public land and up to 400 million hectares of unproductive private land expropriated with monetary compensation. But the landlords threatened to use weapons. The reform was subsequently watered down."(1991: 103) Driven out from their traditional occupation in agriculture and denied entry into the modern, urban world, these people remind one of the passengers in Foucault's "Ship of Fools"—prisoners of a voyage without destination.

It is not Brazil alone. In describing the African economies, Serge Latouche (1993) brings to focus what he calls the castaways of development. At Ouagadougou, the capital of Burkina Faso, Latouche writes, "the center of the capital, with its infrastructure, machinery, administrative buildings, economic and financial installations, vibrates the rhythm of the 'transnational technopolis', but "once you move beyond the checkpoints marking the town boundaries, you see an *immediate and radical* change. You are truly *on another planet*. This strange planet is a planet of people excluded by development—the unwanted and have-nots."(pp. 33–34, author's emphasis) This picture of Burkina Faso, Latouche claims, is more or less representative of the rest of Africa where a glittering, modern enclave is surrounded by the huge army of what he calls the 'outcasts from the consumer society's banquet' (*ibid.*: 35).

Foregrounding of the phenomenon of exclusion and marginalization in the portrayal of the third world economies, for me, is a representational strategy that is very different from the way the economic formation of the third world is represented in the dominant mainstream discourse of development. The mainstream discourse views underdevelopment as an initial condition waiting to be transformed in the process of modernization and development.

It understands the persistence of underdevelopment as the reflection of insufficiency of development, the inability of the modern sector to expand sufficiently and transmit its dynamic to the underdeveloped periphery; in other words, underdevelopment is the residual of the initial condition that the process of development fails to transform. In contrast to this, I see the representation of underdevelopment in terms of castaways of development—i.e. underdevelopment resulting from the development process itself—signaling a new theoretical space in which a radically new conceptualization of the post-colonial formation is possible. A conceptualization that brings to the fore the phenomenon of exclusion and confinement as an essential condition of capital's existence, and also makes visible the specific technology of power that helps create that condition. This, however, requires that we theoretically posit the idea of a wasteland inhabited by the excluded and incorporate that into the narrative of capitalist development. In the following two sections, I attempt to rethink the Marxian concept of primitive accumulation of capital by explicitly considering exclusion and marginalization of surplus labor power as an inescapable moment of capital's arising, and then conceptualize the post-colonial economic formation as a structural unity of capital and a sub-economy of the marginalized. In other words, my purpose is to inscribe the wasteland of the excluded into the narrative of capital's coming into being.

Primitive Accumulation: the Immanent History of Capital

The idea of primitive accumulation refers to the origin of the capitalist mode of production. Capitalist production requires (a) money in the hands of the capitalist, (b) means of production to be used as constant and variable capital, and (c) free wage-labor. These are the three elements that constitute the structure of capitalist production in which surplus value is extracted from wage-labor to create new capital. The conditions for capitalist accumulation are reproduced within the capitalist mode of production itself, but the question that remains is: Where does capitalist accumulation originate? Through what process do these constituent elements, i.e., money, means of production, and free wage-labor together become available to the capitalist marking the beginning of capitalist accumulation? It is in response to this question that Marx presents the concept of primitive or original accumulation as the process through which the initial conditions of the capitalist mode are created.[1] Yet, at the same time, he asserts that the primitive accumulation is not a moment of the existence of full-fledged capital. I quote from *Grundrisse*:

> "The condition that the capitalist, in order to posit himself as capital, must bring values into circulation which he created with his own labor—or by some other means, excepting only already available previous, wage-labor—belongs among the antediluvian conditions of capital, belongs to its *historic presupposition*, which, precisely as such historic presupposition, are past and gone, and hence belongs to the *history of its formation*, but in no way to its contemporary history, i.e., not to the real system of the mode of production ruled by it." (1973: 459, emphasis in original)

What is being argued here is that once capital has attained its full form, i.e., once it is possible to create capital's conditions of existence within capitalist production, its historic presuppositions cease to be a moment of its reality:

> The conditions and presuppositions of the *becoming*, of the arising, of capital presuppose precisely that it is not yet in *being* but merely in *becoming*; they therefore disappear as real capital arises, capital which itself, on the basis of its own reality, posits the conditions for its realization. (*ibid.*: 459)

It is this reality of capital, its state of *being* that Marx deals with in the three volumes of *Capital*, with the story of its arising, its *becoming*, kept in the realm of prehistory. The "capital in arising", dependent on the "pre-capitalist outside" for its conditions of existence, is not capital as posited by the concept of the capitalist mode of production.

Thus, in Marx's theorization, self-subsistent capital has an *immanent history* of its coming into being, a history of how the preconditions of capitalist accumulation are created but that history is derived from the structural logic of capital in its state of *being*. In other words, it is only after the conditions of existence of capital are fully realized that we can make this theoretical journey into its past and trace the process of its formation. It is a past that flows from the reality of the present and the process of primitive accumulation thus seen—unlike the open ended, chronological history of transition from pre-capitalist to capitalist mode of production—is predestined to end up in self-subsistent capital, capital that has already *become*. When Marx offers a detailed discussion of primitive accumulation in England in the last section of *Capital*, volume I, his purpose is to unfold this immanent history of the already established, self-subsistent English capital, and to demonstrate how the structural changes in the English pre-capitalist system brought about by specific modalities of coercive power, combined with exploitation of her colonies, resulted in the creation of capital's initial conditions.

Marxist development theorists, it seems to me, have missed this ex-post nature of the concept of primitive accumulation: that it is the immanent history of self-subsistent capitalist mode of production which can be grasped only after capital has fully *become*, as distinct from the actual process of transition. Articulation–of–modes–of–production school discussed in the preceding chapter is a telling example of this misperception. These theorists have interpreted the economic formation in the third world as a structurally articulated complex of capitalist and pre-capitalist modes in which the latter serve as the source of cheap raw material and labor power for capitalist production. The *raison d'etre* of pre-capital in their view is that it fulfills capital's economic need. What they fail to see is that if capitalist production, to ensure its self-reproduction, has to depend on its outside, then, as Marx emphatically puts it in *Grundrisse*, it is not self-subsistent capital but only *capital in arising*. Capitalist production is self-subsistent only when its entire requirement of wage goods and capital goods is produced within the domain of capital, as is the case in Marx's description of the capitalist mode of production in *Capital*. In other words, self-subsistence means that department I and II (i.e., the investment good sector and the wage good sector, respectively) mutually support each other in the process of expanded reproduction and do not engage in any transactions with the outside for the renewal of the conditions of their reproduction. Thus, the capitalist mode of production described in *Capital* cannot be seen as articulated with pre-capitalist modes in terms of "capital's need" except as a moment of the immanent history and therefore the capital's need-based articulation theoretically

cannot serve as an explanation of the failure of capitalist transformation in the third world.

In the preceding chapter, I offered a detailed critique of the
neo-Gramscian rendition of passive revolution in the context of
post-colonial India. Let me go back to it for a moment. The neo-
Gramscian's story is about capital's coexistence with pre-capital
and the conditions under which the coexistence is reproduced. The
crux of the argument is that representative democracy in India does
not permit the pains and rigors associated with the destruction of
pre-capitalist organizations of production through primitive accumulation, and this calls for, on the part of capital, the strategy of
passive revolution. The ideological construct of passive revolution
seeks to legitimize the existence of capital (i.e., the modern sector)
by ensuring the conditions of reproduction of both capital and pre-
capital (i.e., the traditional community). I argue that this situation
is rooted in an understanding of primitive accumulation that does
not see it as the immanent history of capital. For, the question of
legitimation of capital can arise only after self-subsistent capital
has come into being, and it is not at all clear how one can talk about
capital's need for legitimation after ruling out the possibility of capital's emergence at the very outset. Is what the neo-Gramscian
calls capital economically self-subsistent? Is it capable of reproducing
its economic conditions of existence entirely on its own? If so, how
could its initial conditions of existence emerge in the absence of
primitive accumulation? On the other hand, if it is not self-subsistent,
then it must be capital in arising which calls for an entirely different
conceptualization of the capital–precapital complex. In other words,
if, as the neo-Gramscian claims, it is the need for legitimation of the
modern sector that calls for the strategy of passive revolution on
the part of the bourgeoisie, therefore for preservation of pre-capital/
community, it is not clear how the modern sector itself came
into being without the necessary dissolution of the pre-capitalist
system of production? In short, the capitalist *economic* remains in-
sufficiently theorized in the neo-Gramscian story. The under-
theorization of the *economic* stems from, as I have already said and
let me iterate, the fact that in this analysis primitive accumulation
is not perceived as the ex-post, immanent prehistory of the *being* of
capital. And therefore the crucial point that remains out of sight is
that if the unity of direct producers and their means of production
(i.e., the pre-capitalist community) has to exist outside the domain

of capital, then the coexistence of self-subsistent capital and pre-capitalist production must be theoretically posited. What we need to do is to theoretically intervene in the concept of becoming/arising of capital and problematize the notion of self-subsistent capital to further complicate the concept of primitive accumulation as its immanent history.

Primitive Accumulation of Capital and Capitalist Accumulation: A Distinction that has Escaped Marxists

Besides failing to grasp primitive accumulation as the immanent history of self-subsistent capital, the Marxist political economy of development has also failed to recognize an important difference between the concept of primitive accumulation of capital and accumulation within the capitalist system of production. I shall explore in detail the profound implications of this failure for the theory of transition and development in Chapter 3. However, it must be noted how on a conceptual plane these two moments of accumulation differ in a fundamental sense. Within the capitalist system of production, surplus is produced in the form of surplus value which is the difference between total labor expended and the labor necessary for the reproduction of labor power (and of course the reproduction of the constant capital that is used up in the production process). It is an "economic surplus" in the sense of being a part of production that is over and above the subsistence level of consumption. Capitalist accumulation is the transformation of this surplus into new capital.

Primitive accumulation on the other hand does not refer to an economic surplus in the same sense. It is the process of transformation of money into real capital, i.e., constant and variable capital. Money accumulates in the hands of potential capitalists through trade, and after the direct producers are dispossessed of their means of labor on which they had ownership right in the pre-capitalist system, this money is used to buy those means of labor and transform them into capital. It is in the market that the means of labor are purchased with money. It is capitalization of the already existing means of labor rather than creation of new capital. When the enclosure movement in England led to the eviction of the peasantry from land, the means of labor (food and raw material) that they earlier had command over now became marketable surplus for the capitalist landlords. This marketable surplus found its way into capitalist production as capital through market exchange. Only when it was combined with commodified labor power within the capitalist system of production, an economic surplus in the form of surplus value started being produced.

Thus, primitive accumulation of capital is not a transfer of economic surplus from the pre-capitalist, agricultural sector to the capitalist industrial sector. The means of labor, once they are freed from pre-capitalist production, flow to the capitalist sector in the form of marketable surplus. Seen from an accounting perspective, it occurs under balanced trade between the two sectors.

The Marxist development theorists have seen primitive accumulation as a transfer of surplus, and therefore the process of primitive accumulation working through balanced trade in the inter-sectoral market has remained out of their sight. And this has led to the failure on their part to recognize how the process of capitalist development is depoliticized in the mainstream discourse of development. But more on this in Chapter 3.

Not Even the Chains of Wage-Slavery: Surplus Labor Power and the Arising of Post-Colonial Capital

In Marx, when the process of arising of capital is finally over—when capital has *become* and its *becoming* remains suspended in its being as prehistory—capital is not only self-subsistent but is also the universal mode of production. Universality of capital implies that nothing exists beyond its domain, no outside for it to cope with or relate to, that through the process of primitive accumulation, the pre-capitalist system of production has totally dissolved to create the initial conditions of capital. In other words, the process of capital's becoming means the dissolution of the earlier modes of production and structures of property relations, but universality of the capitalist mode of production implies that the process of demolition of the old order to create the conditions of capital has left no wreckage.

In characterizing post-colonial capital in terms of the concept of primitive accumulation, it is precisely at this point that I locate my point of departure. I would imagine a scenario in which direct producers are estranged from their means of production, the latter are then transformed into constant and variable capital, but not all those who are dispossessed find a place within the system of capitalist production. Bereft of any direct access to means of labor, the dispossessed are left only with labor power, but their exclusion from the space of capitalist production does not allow them to turn their labor power into a commodity. They are condemned to the world of the excluded, the redundant, the dispensable, having nothing to lose, not even the chains of wage-slavery. Primitive accumulation of capital thus produces a vast wasteland inhabited by people whose lives as producers have been subverted and destroyed by the thrust of the process of expansion of capital, but for whom the doors of the world of capital remain forever closed. It is this wasteland, constituted by the shadowy figures of the rejected, the marginal, the leftovers of capital's arising, the wreckage and debris, that remains as an outside of "self-subsistent" capital.

In analyzing the capitalist mode of production, Marx, one may point out, does recognize the phenomenon of surplus labor power, and there have been attempts to address the question of surplus labor in the third world in terms of Marx's analysis (Veltmeyer 1983), but the wasteland inhabited by the excluded that I describe, I must stress, is fundamentally different from what Marx calls the relative surplus population or the reserve army of the proletariat in *Capital*. In volume I, Marx writes, "[e]very laborer belongs to it during the time when he is only partially employed or wholly unemployed" (p. 600) and

> "[t]he fact that the means of production, and the productiveness of labor, increase more rapidly than the productive population, expresses itself, therefore, capitalistically in the inverse form that the laboring population always increases more rapidly than the conditions under which capital can employ this increase for its own self-expansion." (p. 604)[2]

The reserve army of the proletariat for Marx is the product of the internal logic of self-subsistent capital, the nature and dynamics of its accumulation and the contradiction inherent in the process of its self-expansion. Capitalist accumulation does not imply merely a quantitative expansion of capital but also a qualitative change in its composition. Capital constantly seeks to increase the rate of exploitation by increasing the productiveness of labor, and in order to make labor more productive, it changes the composition of new investments in favor of the constant part of the capital as opposed to the variable part, leading to a higher organic composition of the newly created capital. At the same time, composition of the existing capital also changes in the same direction due to the tendency towards centralization. Thus with accumulation, the variable part of the capital grows at a much lower rate than the overall rate of accumulation, and since it is the variable part of the capital that serves as the basis of employment of labor, the rate of growth of employment falls short of the rate of accumulation. And "it is capitalist accumulation itself that constantly produces and produces in direct ratio of its own energy and extent, a relatively redundant population of laborers, i.e., a population of greater extent than suffices for the average needs of the self expansion of capital, and therefore a surplus population" (p. 590).

The reserve army therefore arises out of the very nature of capitalist accumulation, and the surplus population that constitutes the reserve army resides within rather than outside the domain of the capitalist mode of production. Unemployment and pauperism is the mirror image of employment, and the reserve army is an extension of the active labor force—an appendage that is brought into being and reproduced by the capitalist mode of production itself. And it belongs to the *being* of self-subsistent capital. That the surplus population is a moment of the capitalist mode itself becomes apparent once we consider the following assertion in *Grundrisse*:

"[S]ince the necessary development of the productive forces as posited by capital consists in increasing the relation of surplus labour to necessary labour, or in decreasing the portion of necessary labor required for a given amount of surplus labour, then, if a definite amount of labour capacity is given, the relation of necessary labour needed by capital must continuously decline, i.e., part of these labour capacities must become superfluous, since a portion of them suffices to perform the quantity of surplus labour for which the whole amount was required previously. The positing of a specific portion of labour capacities as superfluous ... is therefore *a* necessary consequence of the growth of surplus labour relative to necessary." (p. 609, emphasis mine)

Surplus labor can be produced only on the basis of necessary labor, i.e., labor required for its own reproduction, and the drive on the part of capital to increase the rate of exploitation serves to reduce the requirement of necessary labor and therefore produces redundancy of labor power. Moreover, Marx is quite explicit on the reserve army being an extension of the active labor force, a reservoir of labor power, maintained by the society on behalf of capital, to be drawn upon by the latter when needed. "[S]ociety", he writes, "... undertakes for Mr Capitalist the business of keeping his virtual instrument of labour, its wear and tear, intact as reserve for later use."(p. 610)

Surplus labor power thus exists within the space defined by capitalist production, and exists as an integral part of the *being* of capital. In contrast, surplus labor power in our conceptualization of post-colonial capital is not the product of capital that is self-subsistent, it is created by the process of primitive accumulation; those who constitute the surplus population are not the casualties of capitalist accumulation but of the arising of capital. And therefore they as a category belong to capital's *becoming*. Marx's reserve army as a category supplements the working class, in that it is maintained for later use by capital; the inhabitants of the wasteland resist being captured in terms of any such characterization as their exclusion from the domain of capital is permanent. Marx's reserve army is located in a space on the fringe of the universalized capitalist mode of production. The wasteland in our situation is a space outside capital that challenges the latter's universality.[3]

At the beginning of this chapter, I referred to observations made by Ignacy Sachs and Serge Latouche on marginalization and exclusion in the context of the economies of Brazil and Burkina Faso respectively. They are not the only ones. The observation that capitalist development has produced a wasteland inhabited by the dispossessed is widely shared by recent critiques of the post war development paradigm. In an attempt to highlight the subversive impact of (capitalist) development, Ivan Illich (1997) draws our attention to the redundant part of the population in the third world whose traditional entitlements within a subsistence, moral economy have been destroyed by the irresistible thrust of development, but who are at the same time denied access to the formal cash economy. Allow me this rather longish quote:

"People who have lost their subsistence outside the cash economy ... lack the power to behave according to economic rationality;

they cannot, for example, afford to trade food for shelter or for clothing or tools. *They are neither members of the economy, nor are they capable of living, feeling and acting as they did before they lost the support of a moral economy of subsistence.* The new category of economic cripples, thus defined, may in fact survive, but they do not fully partake of the characteristic of homo economicus. They exist—all over the world—but they are marginal, not just to the national economy but to modern humanity itself, since the latter, from the time of Mandeville, has been defined in terms of the ability to make choices under the assumptions of scarcity. Unlike their ancestors, they do have urgent economic needs, and unlike legitimate participants in the modern economy—no matter how poor—any choice between alternative satisfactions, which is implied in the concept of economic need, is ruled out for them." (1997: 127)

Here Illich makes visible the indeterminate space between the traditional subsistence economy and the modern commodity economy, a space constituted by people who are dispossessed to an extent where even the value of the only endowment they are left with—their labor power—is unrealizable within the commodity economy. This space is kept invisible in the mainstream discussions on development by the strategic use of the term "unemployment", a term that is theoretically internal to the modern, formal economy, signaling merely an anomaly that can be solved in terms of the internal logic of the commodity economy itself.

But it is important to note that while the phenomenon of exclusion and marginalization has not escaped the attention of radical development theorists, there has hardly been any attempt to grasp it as a theoretical category and to explore its implications for an understanding of post-colonial capitalist development. What is its relationship with the emergence, consolidation, and reproduction of the capitalist mode of production? How does it ineluctably shape not only the post-colonial *economic* but the political and ideological instances as well? These questions have never been addressed within the core of the discourse of the political economy of development. In short, the role of the "excluded" as a fundamental constituent of the post-colonial formation remains to be worked out on the theoretical plane. For radical theorists such as Latouche and Illich—Rahnema (1997), Vandana Shiva (1989) and Esteva (1997), to name a few others—see the army of the dispossessed as the victim of "development" which they understand as the process of integration of the natural economies into the network of market exchange, modern technology, and their attendant institutions. The relevance, weight, and force of what they say are undeniable, but at the same time their critiques betray an uncompromising reluctance to understand development and transition/modernization in the light of the arising and self-realization of capital as a specific mode of production. On the other hand, in conceptualizing the relationship between marginality and capitalist transformation, radical theorists who intellectually root their critical stance in the traditional Marxian political economy have not been able to carve out any new theoretical space either. Some of them have taken cognizance of the fact that redundancy and marginality indelibly marks the third world landscape, but they are eager to interpret the surplus population as a phenomenon testifying to the Marxian notion of the reserve army. Consider, for example, the following remarks by Henry Veltmeyer (1983):

Accounting for more than a third of the economically active population in major urban centers and in some countries up to one half of the urban workforce, this surplus population has been studied for sometime as a marginal phenomenon and thus fated to disappear with the advance of large-scale industrial capitalism. *As a major component of the industrial reserve army in its various forms, it is a structured and growing part of the urban economy in peripheral formations.* (pp. 212–213, my emphasis)

A better explanation of these developments can be found in the *general law of capital accumulation, according to which an expanding mass of functioning capital brings about a corresponding increase in surplus population* at lower wage rates. (pp. 213, my emphasis)

I argue that the *class structure of peripheral formations* revolve around the production of a relative surplus population and that certain characteristic features ... of this structure serve to expand capital under conditions of *superexploitation.* (pp. 204–205, my emphasis)

The space of the excluded is thus reduced to the reserve army and thereby allowed to be subsumed within the "general law of capital accumulation", a law that governs the reproduction of the Hegelian *being* of self-subsistent capital. And by doing this, the dispossessed is posited as a victim of capital's super-exploitation, a source of super-surplus value, and in effect integrated into the network of capitalist class relations.

The theoretical stance I adopt is radically different from this received wisdom of the traditional Marxist political economy. My position derives from the claim that the phenomenon of exclusion as a theoretical category belongs not to the realm of self-subsistent capital but to capital's arising, its *becoming*, a process conceptualized in a space that captures the relation between capital and pre-capital. The wasteland of the dispossessed is the result of the process of primitive accumulation and the dispossessed as a theoretical category is excluded from the very space in which class-based exploitation is defined.

The central point is that Marx's rendition of primitive accumulation as the immanent history of capital does not recognize the existence of this wasteland. After capital comes into its own, it is the universal mode of production, self-constituting and self-reproducing, without, as I said earlier, any outside to cope with or relate to. The silence about the wreckage and debris left by primitive accumulation, the obliteration of the space of the dispossessed from the story of the capitalist mode of production, is a discursive violence. My purpose in this book is to inscribe the wasteland and its shadowy inhabitants into the heart of the *becoming* of capital to unsettle the smooth, linear trajectory of its immanent history. The repressed has returned, with a vengeance.

To inscribe the space constituted by the redundant, uncommodified, surplus labor power into the immanent history of capital's arising is to complicate the concept of self-subsistent, real capital. As stated earlier, in Marx, capital is self-subsistent only when the requirements of expanded capitalist reproduction are met within the capitalist system of production:

"While the process in which money or value for itself originally becomes capital presupposes on the part of the capitalist an accumulation. Which he has undertaken as a *not-capitalist*, i.e., while the presuppositions under which money becomes capital appears as given, external *presuppositions* for the arising of capital—[nevertheless] as soon as capital has become capital as such, it creates its own presuppositions, i.e., the possession of the real conditions of the creation of new values *without exchange*— by means of its own production process." (1973: 459–460, emphasis in original)

Clearly, capital is self-subsistent only when it possesses the conditions of creation of new values *without exchange*, i.e. for expanded reproduction of capital, there is no need to engage in exchange with a non-capitalist outside. What is to be noted is that here Marx defines self-subsistence entirely in terms of the economic requirements, i.e. the requirement of labor power and capital—both constant and variable. The implicit assumption is that when capital's economic conditions of existence are created and can be reproduced, the political and ideological conditions of existence are automatically ensured. But once we take into account the wasteland and its inhabitants as an outside of capital, the latter ceases to be self-subsistent even though it is capable of creating and reproducing its economic conditions of existence on its own. For its political and ideological conditions of existence, capital is not self-constituting and to secure the legitimation of its existence, it has to address the outside in politico-ideological terms. In other words, capital's political and ideological conditions of existence require that the dispossessed producers inhabiting the outside be reunited with means of labor so that they can subsist by engaging in economic activities outside the domain of capital. What follows is a process whereby the means of labor are made to flow from the domain of capital to its outside where producers are reunited with the means of production to engage in *non-capitalist production*. More specifically, a part of the surplus produced in the capitalist sector is not transformed into new capital but transferred to the surplus population to constitute the conditions of existence of non-capitalist production. While primitive accumulation seeks to transform the means of labor into capital and subsume them within the domain of capitalist relations, this process of transfer is a reverse flow that extricates them from the space of capital and reunites them with labor. *I characterize this decapitalization of means of labor as a reversal of primitive accumulation. The result is a need-based economy in which the dispossessed are rehabilitated in non-capitalist production activities; and the rehabilitation, I further argue, is made possible by interventions brought about by the discourse of development.*

I anticipate a question at this point. Why must capital's existence be legitimized in the first place? What if the dispossessed are allowed to perish? In other words, why is their rehabilitation in a need economy essential as a politico-ideological condition for capital's reproduction? This question will be dealt with in detail in Chapter 4. Nevertheless, here is a brief response to it. The need for legitimation, I would argue, does not flow from any inherent characteristic of capital: there is nothing in the internal logic of capital that requires that its castaways be allowed to subsist. In fact, the history of capital's arising in the Western Europe is marked with numerous instances in which the dispossessed in huge number simply perished in famines and epidemics, and there was no obligation on the part of capital to ensure their survival. However, the context today has changed radically and the conditions of capital's reproduction have become far more complex. The discourses of democracy and human rights have emerged and consolidated themselves to form an inescapable and integral part of the political and social order. As relatively autonomous discourses, they have constituted an environment within which capital has to reproduce itself. A crucial condition of that reproduction is that the victims of primitive accumulation be addressed in terms of what Michel Foucault has called "governmentality"—interventions on the part of the developmental state (and non-state organizations) to promote the well-being of the population—and what I identify as a reversal of primitive accumulation refers to this realm of welfarist governmentality: the creation of the need economy is an imperative of governance.

Beyond "Being" and "Becoming"

The need for legitimation thus necessitates a reversal of primitive accumulation through developmental intervention but creation of a need economy is not the end of the story. The expansionary thrust of capital continues to subvert the need-based economy separating the direct producers from their means of labor and excluding them from the production economy. This predatory face of capital, its tendency to invade whatever lies beyond its domain, is what *The Communist Manifesto* so penetratingly described as the "battering down of the Chinese Wall". But at the same time, the process of rehabilitation, of reuniting labor and means of labor, continues to be operative. It is this simultaneous process of primitive accumulation and its reversal, the process of destruction and recreation of the non-capitalist outside, of dissolution and conservation of the need-based economy that characterizes the arising of capital in the post-colonial context. The need-based economy as a site for non-capitalist activities gets effaced here only to reappear there in the next moment in a double-faced process of obliteration and reconstitution. The exclusion of the dispossessed and their simultaneous rehabilitation in a sub-economy of need-based production made possible through the agencies produced by the development discourse bears an uncanny resemblance to Foucault's description of the spatial separation and cultural/spiritual reintegration of the insane outcasts.

Thus, unlike the way it has been dealt with in the Marxist literature on capitalist development, primitive accumulation does not refer to a one time change, it is not a process that works itself out once capital's initial conditions are created. It is not what Balibar has termed the "prehistory of capital", an originary moment of capital that dissolves once capital has arisen.[4] It is a continuous and ongoing process that capital is perpetually engaged in; primitive accumulation is an inescapable moment of capital.

Seen thus, the post-colonial capital never *becomes* in the Hegelian sense. On the one hand, it engages in primitive accumulation, invades what lies beyond, usurps the economic space and becomes self-subsistent in so far as its expanded reproduction is concerned. But on the other, its political and ideological conditions of existence, the need for legitimation, demand that it leave a part of the economic space to a non-capitalist need economy—a reversal of primitive accumulation. Like the proverbial Sisyphus, capital is engaged in a task that is never accomplished: its arising is never complete; its universality never fully established; its *being* is forever postponed. In other words, inscription of the wasteland, in what Marx calls the immanent history of capital, condemns the post-colonial capital to a perpetual state of becoming.

The theoretical implication of conceptualizing post-colonial capital in these terms is that the post-colonial context resists being captured in terms of the Hegelian categories of *being* and *becoming*. We have to abandon this framework and see post-colonial capitalism as necessarily a complex of capital and a non-capitalist need economy. This, at the same time, extricates the story of post-colonial capital entirely from the historical materialist paradigm and the Hegelian idea of supersession that informs it. For, if capital necessarily exists as a complex of capital and a non-capitalist outside, then the historical materialist trajectory of stages in which capital supersedes pre-capitalist modes becomes totally irrelevant ruling out full-fledged transformation even as a possibility. And this marks our departure from the Gramscian narrative of passive revolution that presents the post-colonial scenario as a case of blocked transition while full transition remains the reference point in relation to which the post-colonial case is seen as a deviant one.

My characterization of capital in the post-colonial context distances itself from the traditional Marxian understanding of capital's "coming into being" by asserting that when a wasteland, as a site for a need economy, exists as an outside of capital, the universality of the capitalist mode of production becomes a false claim. Capital can then posit itself as the universal only by denying the existence of the outside: an act of discursive violence. But even if we take the Marxian model on its own terms—assume that the process of capital's arising finally culminates into self-subsistent, universal capital, with no outside constituted by the dispossessed—even then we find capital's posited universality problematic once we explicitly consider the question of the reproduction of labor power. For Marx, once capital has arisen, it no longer needs to engage in exchange with any non-capitalist outside for neither labor power nor the means of labor. But the claim that capital is entirely on its own falls through as soon as we bring to the fore the fact that labor power is not reproduced at the site of capitalist production; household as a non-capitalist site exists where the reproduction of labor power takes place. In the Marxian value calculus, the subsistence basket that the worker receives from the capitalist is treated as the value of labor power, i.e., its cost of reproduction. Labor power, however, is reproduced in the household and the process of reproduction involves not only the subsistence basket received as wages but also the labor performed by the members of the household. These include the labor required to transform commodities in the wage-basket into articles of consumption and also affective, emotional labor that goes into rearing the child—the prospective source of labor power. Thus, the household as a site of non-capitalist production is crucial for the expanded reproduction of capital, and capital continues to engage in exchange with a non-capitalist outside. But the Marxian value calculations completely suppress these indispensable production activities undertaken in the household and capital's claim to self-subsistence and universality is predicated on the act of obliteration of the household from the discourse on capital.[5]

The Marxian discourse thus posits capital's universality by adopting a particular representational strategy that denies the existence of the household as an outside of capital. However, when we in the post-colonial context foreground the space of the dispossessed as an outside, it is worth noting that these two outsides are different in a fundamental sense. The relationship between capital and the household is one of extraction/appropriation, in which capital extracts the labor performed in the household in the form of reproduced labor power. The post-colonial wasteland in contrast is the space of the excluded, a space constituted by people who do not perform, in fact are not given the option to perform any labor for capital. They are eager to enter into a relationship of exploitation with capital because it is only by acting as a source of surplus value for capital that they can perform the necessary labor for their own reproduction. But they remain mere spectators of the thrilling Marxian drama of surplus value and exploitation that is enacted within the capitalist factory. The Marxian discourse is totally silent about these inhabitants of the wasteland, the army of redundant labor power rendered superfluous and kept away from the factory gate, and about their desire to be producers of surplus value, to be the victims of capitalist exploitation. It is this silence that probably provokes McCloskey to comment:

> ... the critiques of capitalism sneer indignantly at the jobs available.... Free to take jobs with Nike. After all, a wretchedly paying job making athletic shoes for the American market is hardly unalienated work, the leaning intellectuals say. But ask the woman ... if she had rather take the shoe company not make the offer. Ask her if Nike doesn't pay more than taking in washing. Look at the length of queue that forms when Nike opens a new plant in Indonesia. And ask her if she would rather not have any market opportunities at all...." (2000: 4)

In sum, the post-colonial wasteland is the space of the rejected, the marginal, and unlike the household, it has no role to play in the

creation of the *economic conditions* of capital's expanded reproduction. The relationship here is not one of extraction/appropriation,
rather it is one defined in terms of exclusion and rejection; in other
words, in terms of refusal on the part of capital to engage in an
extractive/appropriative relationship.[6] But like the household, this
space of the excluded challenges capital's political and cultural/ideo-
logical universality, unsettling the state of its *being*.

Beyond the Narrative of Transition: The Post-Colonial *Economic*

The post-colonial *economic*, in our conceptualization, is constituted
by a dual process: on the one hand, the ongoing process of primitive
accumulation of capital estranges direct producers from their means
of labor, creating a wasteland constituted by the expropriated and
dispossessed, and in a parallel process of reversal of primitive accumulation a need economy is created for their rehabilitation. The
dynamics of the post-colonial economic formation is to be understood in terms of this simultaneous process of destruction and
creation, dissolution and conservation, obliteration and reinscription
of the need economy. Dispossession and rehabilitation are the two
contradictory forces that together define the economic landscape
of post-colonial capitalism.

But what makes this process of rehabilitation possible? Who
institutes the need economy? How are its conditions of existence
created and reproduced? What are the agencies that converge to
ensure the conditions for its reproduction? I see the process of recreation and renewal of need economy as being rooted in a global
discourse of development and the agencies produced by that discourse. In the following chapters of the book, I shall argue that the
discourse of development must be understood as distinct from the
narrative of transition from pre-capitalist to capitalist mode of production that lies at the heart of the Marxist theory of underdevelopment. By focusing on such aspects of post-colonial reality—poverty,
need, entitlement and standard of living, development—as a
discourse with international organizations as its vehicles brings into
play both state and non-state agencies and practices that intervene
and act upon the economic space with the aim of ensuring the reproduction of the need economy. Central to the discourse of development is the observation that acute poverty marks post-colonial

societies, where poverty is defined in terms of denial of access to necessities such as food, shelter, health, education, etc. Development is posited as a systematic and sustained process of elimination of poverty by enabling the poor to get access to those necessities. The goal of development is to engage the dispossessed and excluded in production activities by uniting them with the means of labor, that is, by allowing them to have access to productive resources. And it is here that a reversal of primitive accumulation occurs whereby resources are made to flow from the domain of capital to the wasteland to institute a need economy. Uncannily, it reminds one of the passengers of Foucault's "ship of fools" who were excluded from the society but at same time reunited with it culturally/spiritually through the idea of salvation. Similarly, the dispossessed in the post-colonial economy is denied entry into the space of capital but is simultaneously reintegrated into the economy in the space of development. Like water in the case of Foucault's fools, development is the purifier that salvages the poor and the wretched. The need economy is the post-colonial space of confinement.

What is important is that production activities in the need economy are predominantly non-capitalist, such as self-employment based production, household production with family labor or different forms of collective/communal organizations of production. These non-capitalist forms of production are seen by the development discourse as the appropriate and effective ways of constituting the need economy. In the subsequent chapters of this book, I will probe the discourse of development to give a detailed account of how the process of development creates, nurtures, and fosters non-capitalist production in the need economy. At this point, it suffices to say that development does not see the solution to the problem of poverty necessarily in terms of an overall capitalist transformation; its emphasis rather is on re-energization of traditional non-capitalist institutions and forms of production to be used as effective instruments for achieving the goal set in terms of consumption or standard of living of the marginalized and the dispossessed.

The space of non-capital is however constantly under the threat of subversion by an encroaching capitalist space. Its conditions of existence are undermined by the predatory expansion of capital, but at the same time are recreated and renewed by developmental interventions. It is this process of subversion and recreation what constitutes the dynamics of the post-colonial *economic*.

Thus, post-colonial capital can never be self-subsistent, it has to articulate itself with non-capital and exist within the capital–non-capital complex—which I call post-colonial capitalism. This conceptualization of post-colonial capitalism distances itself from the theories of articulation dealt with in the preceding chapter in a number of important ways. First, this is not a capital's–need-based explanation of non-capital. In the structuralist theory of Rey and Wolpe discussed in the preceding chapter, the explanation of articulation was sought in the observation that pre-capitalist modes cater to capital's need for raw materials and labor power. In contrast, non-capital in my construct is a site where the dispossessed are rehabilitated. The need economy may be implicated in economic transactions with the capitalist sector, but its reason for being does not emanate from those economic flows. It needs to be emphasized that non-capital here does not flow directly from the logic of capitalist accumulation. What primitive accumulation produces is a wasteland, a space of the dispossessed, where non-capitalist modes can emerge but their emergence is an autonomous process driven by an entirely different logic, a logic that has to be sought in the discourse of development and its relationship to the regime of capital in the post-colonial context.

Second, the existence of non-capital in this conceptualization does not result from any weakening of the transformative capacity of capital, as in the imperialist penetration-based argument. In that explanation, as we have seen in the preceding chapter, imperialist penetration weakens the expansionary thrust of post-colonial capital thereby allowing the continued existence of the earlier modes of production. In our case, non-capital is not the result of any weakness on the part of capital to carry out its transformative project; on the contrary, it is the force and vigor of capital's primitive accumulation, its ability to usurp the economic space that lies beyond that produces dispossession and marginalization, and therefore, a space for non-capital. In other words, non-capital is the sign not of capital's failure but of its success in carrying out primitive accumulation.

And finally, the post-colonial *economic* I have described is free from historicism that marks the other theories of articulation. One recurrent concern of mine from the beginning has been to break with the historicism underlying the Marxist understanding of the third world and to relocate post-colonial capital on a non-historicist terrain.

And here lies the most important implication of my conceptualization of the post-colonial *economic*: it completely liberates the story of the third world from the grasp of the narrative of transition, a narrative in which is rooted not only the traditional Marxist analysis but also the non-Marxist modernization theory associated with the name of, among others, Durkheim, Max Weber, and structural–functionalists such as Talcott Parsons. I have already critically discussed at length the historical materialist perspective deployed by the Marxists. Central to this perspective is the notion of transition, an irreversible macro-level change from pre-capitalism to capitalism. It is a discrete change in the order of things in all spheres of society—economic, political, and cultural/ideological—that identifies a "before" and an "after", separated by "transition". In short, pre-capitalism in its entirety is replaced by capitalism. The Marxist attempt to understand capitalist development in the third world has been deeply embedded in this narrative of transition and, as I have already argued in the preceding chapter, this embeddedness has led to the reduction of the third world to a case of failure, especially to accomplish the macro-level transformation.

It is not only the Marxist theory of historical materialism but also the notion of transition that stubbornly resides at the core of the liberal, modernization theory presented by the sociologists. For example, Emile Durkheim's work seeks to explain the change from agrarian societies to the complex society of industrial capitalism. For Durkheim, what is important for any society is a moral and ethical order that acts as social cement binding its members together. Humankind is born in an established social world and the individual has to conform to the moral order constituted by that society. Modern industrial capitalism differs from the traditional agrarian society, according to Durkheim, in terms of the extent, complexity and intricacy of division of labor, and therefore it requires functioning a different moral and ethical order. Modernization is a process of evolutionary shift whereby the moral and ethical order of the traditional society rooted in religion is replaced with a different order based on individualism that reintegrates the individual into the social totality.

Despite their fundamentally different analysis of the modern, industrial capitalist society, both the traditional Marxist and liberal theories see such a society as having a unitary character with the subjectivity and behavior of the actors determined by a single systemic logic. For the Marxists, the unitary character is grounded in the capitalist mode of production, while the liberals see the unity as constituted by self-seeking rational individuals operating in a competitive environment. The difference lies in the fact that while the liberals view the modern, capitalist society as a harmonious whole, for the Marxists, it is a system fraught with conflicts and contradictions between social classes. The conflicts, however, result from the same form of rationality exercised by groups inhabiting different positions within the same system.

Implicit in this common belief held by the traditional Marxists and the liberal theorists in a unitary, single, homogenous systemic rationality of the capitalist industrial society is the shared notion of transition, the notion of a discrete all encompassing change based on the traditional/modern dichotomy. It is a change whereby the pre-capitalist/traditional order completely gives way to a capitalist/modern system, a change that irons out all discontinuities and differences, and highlights the systemic oneness of the capitalist order. While the Marxists see history as a linear trajectory of transition from one mode of production to another, the modernization theory views the shift from the traditional to the modern society as a transition from the traditional, moral and ethical order to a radically different one that is consistent with the complex nature of modern industrial capitalism. And much like the Marxists, the theorists of the modernization school also view the third world experience as one in which the transition from the set of institutions embodying the traditional moral order to those constituting the new modern moral codes has failed to take place—a case of failure to bring about the radical change from one order to the other.[7]

In the post-colonial *economic* I have described, non-capital is caught up in the parallel process of dissolution and recreation: it is annihilated by primitive accumulation but resuscitated by development interventions. This process of recreation wrenches it free from its historicist moorings and the "pre" gives way to "non". It is no longer pre-capital: a remnant of the past; an entity belonging to a hierarchical relationship with capital; a hierarchy rooted in the historicist notion of progress. It belongs to the capital–non-capital complex as an inescapable aspect of capital's post-colonial form and in effect extricates the narrative of post-colonial capital from the narrative of transition.

The important aspect of the post-colonial *economic* is that the complex formed by capital and non-capital resides in the commodity space. The need economy constituted by non-capital is implicated in the network of market relations and non-capitalist production processes are engaged in commodity production, i.e., production for the market. A clarification is due at this point. My usage of the term "need economy", in a sense, sharply differs from what it has meant for the transition theorists. In analyzing capitalist penetration into pre-capitalist formations, the term subsistence economy has been generally used to characterize a system based on production of use value for immediate consumption by the producers. In other words, it is a system in which the purpose of production is to satisfy need; it is not meant for the market and therefore products are not commodities. And capitalist penetration has been seen as a process of invasion of the subsistence economy by commodity relations. Thus, the opposition between capital and the subsistence economy is primarily posited as one between a commodity economy and a natural economy (Bradby 1975). In fact, this view of the subsistence economy as an economy based on self-provisioning is not restricted to the transition theorists; analysts of fully developed capitalist system have also used the term to describe an economic space marked by production of use value for self-consumption. For example, certain feminist critics of the Marxian value theory have focused on the various kinds of labor that women perform in the household and have argued that the Marxian value theory refuses to recognize these labors. And in doing this, these feminist theorists have characterized the space in which such labors are performed as the subsistence space, a space not implicated in the network of commodity relations (Bennholdt–Thomsen 1981).[8] In other words, the subsistence economy is a private space of production as distinct from the public space where commodities are produced.

In contrast to this understanding of the subsistence economy as a non-commodified production space, I am using the term need economy to describe an ensemble of production activities in which producers are engaged in commodity production. But this production space is fundamentally different from the space of capitalist production in that while the products of these activities are sold in the market, the purpose of production is to acquire money that will enable the producers to have access through the market to a bundle of goods and services that will satisfy their needs. We can describe it by the Marxian commodity–money–commodity (C~M~C) circuit or what Marx called the simple commodity production, although production in the need economy involves non-capitalist forms of organization other than self-employed individual producer. The point is that instead of immediate consumption of use value, production in the need economy is production of exchange value with the purpose of acquiring the required consumption basket through the *mediation* of the market. For example, a peasant engaged in cash crop production to earn a certain required level of income, according to my definition, belongs to the need economy. This conceptualization of the need economy as embedded in the network of commodity production is essential for describing the post-colonial *economic* because the economic landscape of the third world is marked by a huge informal sector—both rural and urban—constituted by people living on what may be described as petty commodity production.

Thus, capital and the non-capitalist need economy articulated through the network of market is what constitute the post-colonial economic formation. While critiquing Gibson–Graham's representation of the economy in Chapter 1, I claimed that capitalist development in the third world inevitably produces non-capitalist sites of production, and this calls for a conceptual distinction between capital and capitalism. My conceptualization of the post-colonial economic clears the space for such a distinction: the structural articulation of capital and non-capital residing in the commodity space is what I call post-colonial capitalism within which capital exists as a particular, and my purpose in the rest of the book will be to demonstrate that it exists as dominant particular. I will confront Gibson–Graham's claim that recognition of economic heterogeneity in the representation of capitalism necessarily contests capital's hegemony and argue that post-colonial capital's hegemony is to be understood as its dominant existence as a particular in a world of difference.

Dependency Once Again

The post-colonial *economic* as a complex of capital and non-capital linked through the network of exchange surely reminds one of the dependency theory which we dealt with at the beginning of our journey into the Marxist theory of capitalist underdevelopment in the preceding chapter. Dependency theory, especially the work of Gunder Frank, argued Brenner and others, displaced the definition of capitalism to the sphere of exchange, (i.e., circulation) thereby pushing the question of mode of production and class transformation out of sight. As we scanned through the Marxist literature on under-development, we came up with a series of attempts to explain why the transformation from pre-capitalist to capitalist mode of production remained unattained in the third world. With our conceptualization of the post-colonial capitalist *economic*, it seems we have come full circle. We are back to a representation of capitalist development in the third world in which the capitalist *economic* itself is constituted by an array of different modes of production contained within the network of market relations. Although this theorization differs from Frank's in a very fundamental way, it owes an intellectual debt to his work, a debt that I feel I must acknowledge. If read from our vantage point of the early 21st century, it is possible to discover an important insight in what Frank called "*development of underdevelopment*", an insight that critics like Brenner or Laclau driven by their obsession with the concept of transition failed to decipher. Throughout his work, Frank relentlessly argues that under-development must be seen, not as a set of initial conditions that capitalist development is meant to transform, but as an outcome of the very process of capitalist development itself:

"… Because underdevelopment, as distinct perhaps from *un*development, did not pre-date economic development; nor did it spring up of itself; nor did it spring up all of a sudden. It developed right along with economic development—and it is still doing so. It is an integral part of the single development process. (1967: 242)

In this assertion, there is an explicit rejection of the historicist notion of underdevlopment that lies at the heart of the narrative of transition. It is somewhat ironic that the Marxist debate on mode of production used Frank's work as a launching pad, in the sense that it was by critiquing his conception of capitalism as a system of exchange that a space was cleared for the analysis of modes of production. The critique of Frank fashioned by these theorists presumed that his conceptualization of capitalism was based on a total lack of awareness of the historical materialist framework and the trajectory of modes of production associated with it. For instance, the nature of the critique offered by Robert Brenner who labeled Frank's work neo-Smithian (discussed in detail in chapter I) gives the reader the impression that Frank's failure to see that the specificity of capitalism emanated not from the sphere of circulation from the sphere of production was rooted in a more fundamental failure to recognize capitalism as a particular moment in the sequence of modes of production in the historicist trajectory of progress. But a differently motivated reading of Frank reveals that all through his work, he was at pains to situate his story in opposition to the very idea of transition in terms of modes of production. His main purpose was to insist that underdevelopment was endogenous to the process of capitalist development, and to the extent that pre-capitalist and archaic organizations of productions inhabit the space of underdevelopment, they are to be seen as structured by capitalism to form an integral part of it rather than as a past that capitalism fails to transform. The thrust of Frank's work, in my reading, lies not so much in his emphasis on the global structure of accumulation and the related metropolis–satellite relationship as in his insistence on the need to liberate the experience of capitalist development in the third world from historicist stereotypes.[9]

My conceptualization of post-colonial capitalism is driven by the same concern and it is here that I wish to record my debt to Frank. In my situation, the need economy, as a site of non-capital, is a result of capitalist development rather than a residual of the past that stubbornly resists transformation. But I hasten to add that my post-colonial *economic* differs in a fundamental way from Frank's metropolis–satellite structure. Coexistence of different modes of production in Frank is characterized in terms of a metropolis–satellite relationship and it is a relationship based on transfer of surplus: development of the metropolis is fueled by economic surplus extracted from the satellite. It is in this sense that the process of development, Frank asserts, in its own course produces underdevelopment:

"Indeed, it is this exploitative relation which in a chain-like fashion extends the capitalist link between the capitalist world and national metropolis to the regional centers...., from those to local centers, and so on to large landowners or merchants who expropriate surplus from small peasants or tenants...At each step along the way, the relatively few capitalists above exercise monopoly over the many below, expropriating some or all of their economic surplus.."(1967: 7–8)

In sharp contrast to this extractive relationship, my conceptualization of the post-colonial economic is one in which capital and the need economy (the site for non-capital) are not locked in a relation in which economic surplus flows from the latter to the former. On the contrary, renewal of the subsistence economy necessitates an inflow of resources from the capitalist sector, a reversal of primitive accumulation. Capital's expansionary thrust works to annihilate non-capital, but the latter is then resuscitated by taming the predatory face of capital. It is a relationship based on exclusion and formation rather than inclusion and extraction.

From the Politics of Transition to the Politics of Exclusion

In keeping with this understanding of the post-colonial economic, how do we reconceptualize the politics of the post-colonial formation? Unmooring the *economic* and its dynamics from the historicist notion of systemic transformation, for sure, simultaneously unsettles the orthodox conceptualization of the spheres of politics. In particular, it calls for a rethinking of the question of actor and agency, especially the role of the so-called national bourgeoisie in relation to the project of capitalist transformation. In the orthodox Marxist rendition of the political economy of development, the possibility of capitalist transformation in the third world hinges crucially on the political and ideological agency of the bourgeoisie. The bourgeoisie is assigned the historical role of being the harbinger of the new order, and this role encompasses two distinct fronts. On the one hand, the bourgeoisie has to emerge as the political and ideological leader of the entire society, establish its dominance over the institutions of civil society and the state, and thereby supplant the pre-capitalist order by the new bourgeois order. In other words, it is under the leadership of the bourgeoisie that the "democratic revolution" has to be accomplished. Inability to assume this leadership role signals a historical insufficiency of the bourgeoisie; it is a case of failure in which the strength of the bourgeoisie fails to match the task assigned to it by the grand narrative of history.

The other sphere in which the role of the bourgeoisie is crucial is the sphere of external relations, i.e. the network of colonial relations or the neo-colonial world order, within which the economy finds itself implicated. The bourgeoisie must assert its independence vis-à-vis the external imperialist powers and the control they exercise over the national economy. The orthodox Marxists have seen the anti-imperialist thrust of the national bourgeoisie as an important condition for capitalist transformation in the imperialized economy. Traditional Marxism has always reminded us how important it is for the nationalist struggle against imperialist domination (of colonial or neo-colonial variety) to have at the forefront an independent bourgeois class aspiring to be free from the fetters of foreign capital and its economic and political domination. And failure on the part of the bourgeoisie to show its radical face has led to its characterization as comprador/collaborator, and again it is a case of historical insufficiency of the bourgeois class.

Thus the Marxist orthodoxy first posits a historical task for the bourgeoisie—a task defined in relation to the lineal trajectory of modes of production—and then judges its adequacy/inadequacy as a class in terms of whether it is up to that task. Gramsci's concept of passive revolution—we have already discussed it extensively—is an attempt to further problematize the question of sufficiency by arguing that a bourgeoisie, apparently incapable of ushering in a full-scale democratic revolution, can be seen as being engaged in an indirect, circuitous way of achieving the same goal by getting into the state first and then transform the economy in "small doses", in a reformist manner. The underlying assumption however is that these small doses of change will add up and ultimately bring about a full-scale transformation of the economy. In other words, the question of political agency of the bourgeois class remains deeply rooted in the concept of an all-encompassing transformation in which the pre-capitalist modes of production are supplanted in their entirety by the more progressive capitalist mode.

It is this pre-assigned role in transition that has served as the Marxist Procrustian bed—a criterion for measuring the historical sufficiency/insufficiency of the bourgeoisie.[10] But what if, instead of judging success and failure in terms of a pre-given task related to systemic transformation, we redefine the task itself? Can we then see the post-colonial bourgeoisie in a different light? Our characterization of the post-colonial economic has totally dispensed with the idea of transition and therefore the question of success or failure in relation to the story of transition does not arise. It is primitive accumulation that the bourgeoisie is engaged in, and its strength/weakness is to be judged in terms of its ability to usurp the economic space that lies beyond the domain of capital. In other words, seen in this perspective, the strength of the bourgeoisie lies in its success in carrying out the primitive accumulation. The fact that this process is accompanied by exclusion, marginalization and the creation of redundant, surplus labor power, and the emergence of a need economy constituted by non-capitalist production does not mark any failure on the part of the bourgeoisie in the historicist sense, i.e. failure to "create a world after its own image". On the contrary, non-capital is the inescapable consequence of post-colonial capital's successful primitive accumulation.

And this story of primitive accumulation calls for a reconceptualization of the realm of politics in the post-colonial context. Rejection of the historicist paradigm for sure closes the space in which the politics of a macro-level transformation is defined. But in a double gesture it simultaneously opens up a new political terrain—one that makes visible a politics centered on the question of exclusion, marginalization, and the constitution and renewal of the need economy. This new vision of politics unyokes the question of political agency from the imaginary of a big bang transition and displaces it onto a terrain defined in terms of the articulation of capital and the need economy, its inherent contradictions and the process of its reproduction. My central purpose in the rest of the book is to foreground this politics—I call it the politics of exclusion—as distinct from the politics of transition.

Globalization

It has already been argued that the existence of the need economy serves to legitimize the expanded reproduction of capital, i.e., it ensures capital's political and ideological conditions of existence. I must further probe the nature and complexities of this legitimization process. In other words, I must situate my narrative of post-colonial capitalism within the problematic of hegemony. It is in terms of the hegemony process that we have to grasp the simultaneous process of exclusion of surplus labor power and their reintegration into the need economy. The characterization of the post-colonial formation in terms of a capital–non-capital complex radically departs from the Gramscian framework of passive revolution in two fundamental senses. First, as I have already argued, by breaking with the very idea of transition, it wrenches free the problematic of hegemony from the preordained sequence of modes of production and the presumed historicist necessity on the part of capital to supersede pre-capital. But before I get into the question of hegemony, I should highlight the second departure that is no less fundamental than the first. The process of primitive accumulation and its reversal that lies at the heart of the post-colonial economic, I argue, is to be seen as a global process. When post-colonial capital engages in primitive accumulation it does so as an integral part of global capital. The question of legitimation therefore refers to the political conditions of existence of global capital as a whole, and creation of those conditions requires a global management of the wasteland by creating and sustaining a need economy. The Gramscian analytical framework on the other hand posits the nation state as the reification of the surrogate universal that constitutes the hegemonic unity strictly on the national level. The hegemony process is seen as completely insulated from the process of political and ideological reproduction of capital on the global scale. For Gramsci, modes of production, classes, civil society, and the state together define the hegemony process, but the process is strictly bound by the concept of the nation where the economic, political or ideological effectivity of the global capitalist order is not allowed to work.

The claim that the post-colonial formation is to be understood in relation to the ongoing process of primitive accumulation on the global level extricates the problematic of hegemony from the Gramscian nation-centered framework and redefines it in the context of global capitalist processes, global poverty and the supranational global institutions through which the conditions of existence of the global capitalist order are secured. What we are witnessing over the last decade is the emergence of one single global capitalist order within which capital, commodities, and information are supposed to freely circulate across national boundaries; and it is also an order which the third world countries have no way to escape but integrate.

Several analysts have challenged the claim that the globalization we are experiencing is unprecedented in terms of the volume of trans-border flow of capital or goods and services. These observers of globalization have argued that the volume of commodity trade and the flow of investments between the developed and developing countries far from increasing have actually declined in comparison with the 1950s and 1960s (Hoogvelt 1997, Thompson and Hirst 1996). In so far as trans-border flow of real resources are concerned, these studies assert that the MNCs over the last decade have shown no discernable tendency to increase their investments in developing countries; they have largely remained tied to their home base, and the trans-border flows of capital have remained confined within the triad block consisting of North America, Europe, and Japan. Thus globalization, according to these observers, is to a large extent a myth.

Granted that the extent of integration of the developed and developing economies in terms of commodity trade and direct investment flows hardly signals globalization of an unprecedented degree, there is however one strong sense in which what is being witnessed is indeed unprecedented and we are steadily and irreversibly moving towards a more globalized world. And that is in terms of assimilation of developing countries within a uniform and universal regime of property rights and mode of power. The entire third world is doubtlessly being brought within the purview of bourgeois property rights and its attendant technology of surveillance with international organizations, especially the WTO as the vehicle of this process of assimilation. Capital may not be footloose between the developed and developing economies, but post-colonial capital and post-colonial nation states are increasingly finding themselves subjected to an as–if inescapable "logic of the global market and capital". Although confined within the national boundary, post-colonial capital has to operate within the disciplinary regime effected by that logic. Thus, the national identity of post-colonial capital may not have dissolved into a global identity, its existence however is being redefined as an inextricable moment of a single global capitalist space.

On the other hand, the universal regime of property rights and market rules (e.g., TRIPS and TRIMS) enforced by the WTO is severely circumscribing the post-colonial nation states by denying them the space in which they could engage in the politics of passive revolution. Strait-jacketed within the global logic of capital and market and the global regime of property rights, these states can no longer act as developmental states and engage in the management of poverty on their own. Legitimation of global capital—reproduction of its politico-ideological conditions of existence—through poverty management is now a global project to be undertaken, planned, and executed by global developmental organizations and footloose NGOs. In other words, primitive accumulation by global capital produces a wasteland in the third world and legitimation of capital requires the creation and renewal of a need economy through a global discourse of development. [Post-colonial states are now actors in the globally instituted management of poverty only as a vehicle of that discourse]—they are now instruments of global governance.

This vision of post-colonial capital as embedded in a global capitalist space also forces us to rethink the distinction made in the Marxist theories of development between the external and internal constraints on capitalist transformation in the periphery. I have already dealt with it in the preceding section. In the traditional Marxist perception, the two barriers to be overcome in order to have capitalist development are feudalism/pre-capitalism and imperialist domination; the former is characterized as the internal constraint while the latter as the external constraint on capitalist transformation. There have been long and involved debates within the Marxist discourse on the relative importance of these two types of constraints as the explanation of capitalist underdevelopment. In my conceptualization of post-colonial capitalism as a globalized process of primitive accumulation and poverty management, a scenario in which a full-fledged capitalist transformation is ruled out even as a theoretical possibility, the distinction between the "internal" and the "external" dissolves in favor of the global process of the arising of capital and the creation of a post-colonial wasteland. Rejection of the notion of an all-encompassing capitalist transformation in the third world thus simultaneously renders several received ideas and categories of the traditional Marxist repertoire irrelevant.

What I want to emphasize is that these twin processes—assimilation of post-colonial capital into a global capitalist space and displacement of poverty management onto the global level—in my interpretation, constitute the current phenomenon of globalization as a truly unprecedented experience. And once globalization is interpreted in this way, we find ourselves far beyond the Gramscian nation state-centric framework of hegemony and passive revolution. For now, the question of hegemony, in its simple or complex form, has to be posed on the global level as the hegemony of global capital (of which post-colonial capital is an important moment), and the complex of capital and the need economy has to be seen as resulting from that hegemony process. The Gramscian surrogate universal that maps the hegemonic space is now reified in the body of not the nation state but the supra-national global organizations from which the discourse of development is disseminated.

Thus, our task is to grasp the process whereby the hegemony of global capital engaged in primitive accumulation in the third world, is constructed by the creation of a need economy. Central to this hegemony process is the relationship between the post-colonial *economic* and developmental interventions. I must first explore this relationship by asking how non-capitalist forms of production in the need economy are created, renewed, protected, and fostered by these interventions, and how they articulate with capital to constitute post-colonial capitalism as a distinct formation. In order to do this, I will, following Arturo Escobar, adopt Michel Foucault's theory of discursive formation to understand development as a discourse.

Among Foucault's theoretical contributions, the concept of discursive formation is probably the one that has been most influential in the field of social theory. Widely and effectively deployed in diverse areas such as anthropology, sociology, cultural studies, literary criticism, and gender studies, it has provided a theoretical strategy for understanding in a radically new way the complex relationship between reality and representation, institutions and the effects of truth, between power and knowledge. But its application to political economy has been scarce, and therefore a few words delineating the outline of the theory of discursive formation, I believe, would be helpful for those who are happily confined within the four walls of the traditional political economy.

In *The Archaeology of Knowledge* (1972) Foucault defines a discursive formation as a structured ensemble of statements made from institutional sites producing the effects of truth. The unity of a discourse, he argues, cannot flow from the stability of either the object or the thinking subject behind the statements because both the object of a discourse and its subject undergo transformation, substitution, and displacement within the space of the discourse. The unity, according to Foucault, is provided by the rules of formation that govern a discourse—rules that ensure a regularity in the dispersion of the object, subject and concepts within the formation. In other words, a discursive formation is a space that ensures conditions of emergence of objects and concepts, their displacement and transformation. The statements that constitute a discourse, Foucault claims, acquire their legitimacy from the institutional sites from which they are uttered and also from the status of the speaker, and it is through this legitimacy that a discourse produces its truth effects. What is important is that Foucault sees production, differentiation and transformation of objects of a discourse as practice: he calls it discursive practice, and this enables him to talk about modalities and strategies that this practice involves.

Put differently, a discourse is a structured ensemble of statements seen in terms of the exact specificity of their occurrence, and the theory of discursive formation seeks to determine their conditions of existence, wonder why certain statements come together and form a unity, while excluding others, to produce the effects of truth. Seen thus, a discourse, as Foucault emphasizes in *The Archaeology of Knowledge*, is different in a fundamental sense from the history of thought/ideas. The history of thought assumes behind the statements the presence of a speaking subject with intention, and it is this invisible speaking, thinking subject that provides the totality of the discourse. "But this totality is treated in such a way that one tries to rediscover beyond the statements themselves the intention of the speaking subject, his conscious activity, what he meant..." (p. 27). In contrast, the concept of discursive formation dispenses with the idea of a thinking subject hidden behind the statements; it is the statements themselves, as related utterances subjected to rules of formation, supported by extra-discursive institutional power that constitute the discourse as a totality. And the assumed continuity implicit in the history of thought is supplanted by the idea of discontinuity, heterogeneity and break to enable one to see the utterances forming a discourse in their historical specificity.

Development as Discourse

The Foucauldian concept of discourse points to a space where the will to truth and institutional power implode, and this implosion of knowledge and power is what has drawn development theorists toward the theory of discursive formation. For, development involves a particular way of knowing the reality, making statements about it from institutional sites, producing and disseminating effects of truth and bringing into play agents who intervene and act. Development as practice can thus be seen as deeply implicated in the knowledge–power of the discourse.

Novelty of the discursive approach to development becomes visible when contrasted to the way in which the "development of the idea of development" has been traditionally dealt with. Take for instance, the well-known book by Gerald Meier titled *Emerging from Poverty* (1984) that seeks to trace the genesis and evolution of development economics. In the first part of the book dealing with the beginning of developmental thinking, Meier identifies underdevelopment as an object of development economics in terms of a set of characteristics. It is followed by a section exploring how the idea of economic development has developed over time. He starts with the early growth theories of classical economists such as Adam Smith, Ricardo, and Malthus, and against that backdrop locates the 1950s, the period of decolonization of Asia and Africa as the beginning of development economics. He then traces the evolution of that economics by identifying a series of successive theoretical attempts to cope with the complexities of the development process, such as the theory of balanced growth, low-level trap and big push, and of the dual economy. These are presented as responses to the problems that the development process posited in its own course. The final section points to the need to develop a more purposeful and appropriate development economics and more imaginative ways of its application.

Thus the object of development economics, i.e., underdevelopment, is first posited and then the "development of development economics" is understood as a series of attempts to produce knowledge about that object. The presentation of a specific body of writings as development economics is predicated on the existence of a thinking, speaking subject hidden behind the trajectory of developmental thought, and shifts in the conceptual field of development economics are seen as responses of that subject to the problems encountered in the domain of developmental practice. In other words, the unity of development economics is sought here in a stable object of knowledge defined *a priori* and also in the intention of a stable subject with concern about development.

In contrast, a discursive approach would deal with statements made on development in their specificity, see how they are structured, and framed, and how the very object of discourse, i.e. underdevelopment/development is constituted and differentiated, in short, produced by the statements themselves. Makers of these statements would be seen as the vehicle of the discourse rather than thinking subjects located outside, and the institutional sites from which the statements are made (i.e., the state, international developmental organizations, universities, and research institutes) as the source of legitimacy and power of the discourse.[11] In Meier's approach, development is an idea that is used to arrive at policy prescriptions and their implementation, but the idea itself is devoid of any materiality. The discourse analysis, on the other hand, tries to grasp the idea of development as inseparable from the actions it produces, their modalities, and the apparatuses it calls into play. It is the material effectiveness of the idea of development that the concept of discourse tries to capture. And it is in this sense that discourse analysis understands development as practice, and statements on development as events.

Unmaking the Third World: Post-Development

Several attempts in this direction have been made (Ferguson 1990, Sachs 1992). Ferguson dissects the experience of development in Lesotho and brings to visibility how World Bank sponsored developmental interventions have in effect constructed the very reality of rural Lesotho as "primitive, underdeveloped and backward". In a collection of essays edited by Wolfgang Sachs (1992), critical theorists of development have sought to unsettle the conceptual foundation of the dominant developmental thinking by tracing out the archaeology of basic concepts such as, to name a few, poverty (Rahnema), need (Illich), resources (Shiva), environment (Sachs). In their concerted effort, they succeed in demonstrating that these concepts that serve as the basis of developmental practices, far from having any foundational fixity, are products of the development discourse itself. They are constituted and transmuted with the dynamics of the discourse, and in this process a dominant regime of knowledge is produced that constricts our thinking to an unconscious structure. In an act of discursive violence, the dominant form of knowledge obliterates many alternative ways of interpreting and relating to the world around us, many alternative forms of "beings and doings".

While these attempts are important in that they invite us to perceive development as a discourse, Arturo Escobar's *Encountering Development* (1995) is the pioneering one in the sense that it offers a full-fledged discourse analysis of development as a regime of representation and power. Escobar's project is partly inspired by Edward Said's *Orientalism* (1978) in which Said deconstructs the concept of the Orient produced by the European thought. He demonstrates that it is a cultural construct that represents the Orient as the "other" of the West by making statements about it and authorizing views of it. It is a discourse that "produced" the Orient, and it is the power of this discourse that allowed Europe to rule over the Orient politically and culturally. In a similar vein, Escobar argues that development as a discourse, by adopting a particular representational strategy, has produced "underdevelopment" as a reality to act upon, and the dominance of the discourse has ruled out the possibility of imagining reality in the third world in any other way. His deconstruction of development seeks to encounter this "colonization of imagination" to make visible how the interplay of knowledge and power makes it possible for development to act as an elaborate mechanism of control. The purpose, in other words, is to understand development

> ".. as a historically singular experience, the creation of a domain of thought and action, by analyzing the characteristics and interrelations of the three axes that define it: the forms of knowledge that refer to it and through which it comes into being and is elaborated into objects, concepts theories, and the like; the system of power that regulates its practice; and the forms of subjectivity fostered by this discourse, those through which people come to recognize themselves as developed or underdeveloped. The ensemble of forms found along these axes constitute development as a discursive formation giving rise to an efficient apparatus that systematically relates forms of knowledge and techniques of power."(Escobar 1995: 10)

Escobar identifies development not as an epistemological break in a process of unfolding of knowledge but as a historically specific construct by referring to the global configurations of power in the post world war II context. It was a construct that sought to establish the hegemony of the West in general, and the US in particular, by representing the rest of the world as "underdeveloped and poor", waiting to be changed after the image of the West. Thus the third world was produced as the "other" of the "modern and advanced" societies of the West, as "traditional and backward", as the space of underdevelopment inhabited by people characterized solely in terms of deficiency, absence, and lack. This identity of being "underdeveloped and backward" was inscribed on the third world and the possibility of constructing any other identity based on what its inhabitants thought of themselves and their own lives, and how they related to the immediate environment in which they lived, was completely ruled out. And with this representation emerged an entire body of knowledge pertaining to development, encompassing such diverse areas as economics, health, demography, and education, to be applied systematically to this discursively produced space of underdevelopment and thereby place the third world in a new and complex field of power.

With these particular forms of knowledge, the development discourse simultaneously brought into existence an elaborate apparatus of development, and together they defined a technology of power, a mechanism of control, to which the entire underdeveloped world was to be subjected. Escobar describes the process of deployment of the development discourse in terms of professionalization and institutionalization of development. The particular forms of knowledge produced by the discourse reduced development to a set of technical problems to be solved by experts and professionals, and the axioms that served as the basis for these solutions were seen as rational, scientific therefore universal, without any historical and cultural specificity. The professionals "sought to devise mechanisms and procedures to make societies fit a pre-existing model that embodied the structures and functions of modernity."(p. 52) The process of professionalization also brought into existence an elaborate network of institutional sites—such as research institutes, academic departments in universities, international organizations like the World Bank, IMF and the ILO—where developmental knowledge was to be produced, recorded, stabilized, modified, and then disseminated. And the task of concrete interventions into the third world on the basis of this body of knowledge was left entirely to the development bureaucracy—both national and international. Professionalization, institutionalization, and bureaucratization together, Escobar argues, constituted a mechanism of control and surveillance that sought to subject the third world to the discipline of the discourse, thereby making the discourse a real force with material effectiveness.

Escobar's highly imaginative attempt to provide an understanding of development as a regime of discursive power undoubtedly clears a space that allows radically new ways of conceptualizing the postcolonial experience. His book has provided theoretical underpinning to an emergent political position that celebrates the idea of "post-development", a position I must critically engage with in order to assert the nature and specificity of my own theoretical project. Post-developmentalists claim that development has failed hopelessly to deliver to the poor of the third world, and therefore the entire paradigm of development must be abandoned in favor of radically new imaginaries of human possibilities produced from the grassroots level. As Majid Rahnema, an advocate of post-development writes:

> [F]or all the victims of colonial rule, [development] did appear for a while as a promising mirage.... But the mirage ultimately transformed into a recurring nightmare for millions. As a matter of fact, it soon appeared to them that development had been, from the beginning, nothing but a deceitful mirage. It has acted as a factor of division, of exclusion and of discrimination rather than of liberation of any kind. (1997: x)

And hence what is needed is not alternative development but an alternative to development, that is, the rejection of the entire paradigm altogether.

As I have already stated, central to my own characterization of post-colonial capitalism is the relation between primitive accumulation on one hand and developmental interventions on the other. And the discursive approach to development offers an attractive and powerful framework to theoretically capture the mutuality and contradictions between the two. But although I will deploy the idea of development as a discursive formation, I must at the very outset emphatically distance my own project from that of post-development. The purpose of my theoretical search for a new conceptualization of the post-colonial formation is fundamentally different from the concerns that animate the post-developmentalists. In fact the specificity of my theoretical project, its exact points of departure from the received theories of political economy of development, becomes apparent once the story of post-colonial capitalism I am trying to tell is situated in relation to a critique of the way Escobar attempts to "unmake" the third world. Let me explain.

Politicizing the Economy: Encounter of a Different Kind

Escobar understands development, and so do the post-developmentalists, as embedded in a narrative of transition based on the tradition–modernity dichotomy. For him, development means modernity and what the development discourse strives to do is trans-form the "traditional" into the "modern". His critique of develop-ment is, in a broader sense, an encounter with modernity and its project of transformation. But in fashioning his critique, Escobar completely leaves out of his theoretical purview the other narrative of transition involving modes of production and class, thus fore-closing the possibility of asking the question: What is the relation-ship between the post-colonial capitalist formation and the regime of development? How do they articulate? Certain critics have found Escobar's depiction of development "capital-ocentric" (Gibson–Graham 1996: 42, Gibson–Graham and Ruccio 2001). There is a sense in which it is, because he uses modernity, development and capitalism interchangeably. But by reducing capitalism to develop-ment, with the latter seen entirely in terms of the tradition–modernity dichotomy, Escobar rules out any possibility of further problem-atizing capitalist formation in the third world and therefore, of ex-ploring the nature of its articulation with the discursive construct of development. Thus by conflating development and capitalism, Escobar leaves no space where the relationship between the dynamics of the post-colonial capital and the dominant imaginaries of de-velopment can be addressed. In order to be able to deal with this question of articulation between the regime of development and capitalist formation in the third world, we must reinscribe the nar-rative of modes of production and class into the discursive field of development, and posit the space mapped by development and the space of capital as two distinct yet inextricably related spaces and then try to grasp their mutuality and contradictions.

In other words, to understand the complexity of the structure and modalities of development's discursive power, we must locate the economy as a politically contested space and then see how it articulates with the developmental regime. The claim that Escobar's discursive approach to development and its application to the Columbian case—and Ferguson's analysis of the experience of de-velopment in Lesotho (Ferguson 1990) as well—persistently makes is that the primary purpose of the development discourse from the very beginning has been to exorcise the concept of development of its political contents, of the conflicts and contradictions emanating from economic and social relations that lie at the heart of the process of change that is supposed to be brought about by development. The discursive formation seeks to depoliticize the term "development" reducing it to a set of mere technical problems of capital accumulation, economic growth, and the distribution of its fruits among those who are underdeveloped and poor. It is the responsibility of experts (e.g., economists, agronomists, nutritionists, and ecologists) to adopt methods that are "rational and scientific", and therefore "politically and ideologically neutral", to arrive at a solution to these technical problems. Politics has no role to play in determining the content of development, nor does the implementation of the solutions prescribed by the experts require resolution of any political question. Development means a discrete change in the way society and the economy are organized, and in the way they function, but the process whereby these changes are brought about does not involve any political subjects, any agency of social groups or classes; the process is unleashed, monitored, and managed by a supposedly apolitical network of bureaucratic apparatuses.

Both Escobar's and Ferguson's deconstructive efforts are animated by the same urgency to assert the political dimensions of development, the conflicts and contradictions that inhere in the very idea of development, the contradictions that the techno-scientific vision of development keeps out of sight. The purpose is to challenge the truth effects produced by the discourse by making visible subject positions and actors who can politically contest the regime of power that the discourse defines. But in politicizing development, Escobar's deconstructive approach does not make any attempt to extricate the economy from the depoliticized space of development and displace it onto a politically contested terrain. On the contrary, he identifies the economy as serving as the foundation of the modernizing project of development and anchors his opposition to the discursive power of development in an explicit cultural critique of the economy. As a result, the possibility of restoring the political dimensions of the economy and mapping a space from which the developmental regime could be encountered on politico-economic terms is subverted.[12]

Although I immensely enjoyed being with Escobar in his novel attempt to deconstruct "development", it is at this point that I part company with him. My project, as distinct from and in a sense opposed to Escobar's, is to politicize the economy by representing the depoliticized narrative of economic transformation as a process fraught with political contradictions. By inscribing the narrative of primitive accumulation within the field of development, I want to make visible an entirely different terrain of contestation and negotiation in which the political contradictions and conflicts that inhere in the dynamics of post-colonial capital keep coming to the fore, and the discourse of development relentlessly tries to negotiate these contradictions to reproduce the narrative of economic development as a depoliticized process.

And this brings us to the second point of my departure from post-developmentalism. Once the question of articulation between development and post-colonial capital is brought to the fore, we inevitably find ourselves in a position where we must break with the paradigm of transition to which Escobar confines his view. The main thrust of my view of post-colonial capitalism, as I have already emphasized, is to displace the articulation of capital and non-capital that constitutes the post-colonial *economic* onto a non-historicist terrain. If now the process of the reproduction of the post-colonial economic formation is to be seen in relation to the development discourse, the conceptualization of development itself must be liberated from the grasp of the narrative of transition. Escobar's preoccupation with the tradition–modernity dichotomy, and his vision of development as a regime of power of which the sole aim is to transform the "traditional" into the "modern", makes it impossible for him to locate a fundamental shift that occurred within the development discourse since the early 1970s. It is a shift from the earlier notion of "development as a systemic transition" to one of "development as improvement". The earlier claim was that development necessarily means a process of capital accumulation through industrialization accompanied by disintegration of pre-capitalist/premodern economic organizations and social institutions, bursting of the bonds of caste, creed, and race, and their replacement by capitalist/modern economic, cultural, and social institutions. In the early 1970s, this view of development as an all-encompassing, macro-level transformation yielded place to a different notion of development that aimed at meeting the needs of the poor of the third world—needs defined in terms of nutrition, shelter, health, and education—in direct ways that are not necessarily mediated by a program of overall "transformation" of the traditional order. It is an eclectic approach that sets "improvement of the conditions of the poor" as the developmental goal to be achieved by direct inter-ventions and recognizes that the strategies adopted to achieve the goal may involve deployment of traditional institutions and forms of economic organizations as instruments. In other words, develop-ment as capitalist transformation through accumulation was to a large extent supplanted by an approach that emphasized the pos-sibility of uplifting the conditions of the poor by "ensuring and im-proving" the conditions of existence of their familiar ways of life and activities they have been traditionally engaged in. And this shift was the result of the attempt by the development discourse to nego-tiate the political contradictions posed by post-colonial capital's primi-tive accumulation.

It is this shift that I want to foreground: I will demonstrate how in response to the question of absolute poverty at a specific moment of the rise of post-colonial capital, the development discourse distanced itself from the narrative of accumulation-based capitalist transformation, restructured itself, redefined its object, and changed the modalities of its interventions. One may even step a little further and claim that development as a discourse, in the true sense of being a discourse distinct from the narrative of capitalist transformation, emerged with this shift, i.e. when it emerged as a network of inter-ventions aimed at the "management of poverty" in the wasteland produced by the primitive accumulation of post-colonial capital, rather than an all-encompassing "transformation" of the third world from a state of being "backward and poor" into one that is "modern and rich".

A differently motivated deconstruction of development can fore-ground this shift within the discursive space, a shift that marks fundamental changes in the regime of power that development is. These changes are to be seen in relation to what I have characterized in the preceding section as "rehabilitation of the dispossessed" of the wasteland created by primitive accumulation. In other words, the changes are inextricably related to the process of creation and renewal of the need economy that I have identified as an inescap-able moment of post-colonial capitalist formation.

The sole concern behind Escobar's attempted deconstruction is to see development as an encounter between modernity and tradition—or to put it differently, between capitalism and what pre-cedes it. Whatever structural changes the dynamics of the discourse might have involved, for him, modernity and tradition are two strictly separable spaces, and development remains a project of modernity that seeks to systemically transform what it sees as its "other", i.e. tradition. He is concerned with the space of development as a whole, and these shifts within that space are of little interest to him. He writes:

[A]lthough the discourse has gone through a series of structural changes, the architecture of the discursive formation laid down in the period 1945–55 has remained unchanged, allowing the discourse to adapt to new conditions. The result has been the succession of development strategies and substrategies up to the present, always within the confines of the same discursive space.' (p. 42)

Here Escobar identifies the paradigm of development as an oppressive space and looks for an exit from that space to contest it from outside. That leads him to embrace the idea of post-development and to valorize the anti-developmentalist politics constituted by the new social movements. And I want to highlight precisely these "structural changes" and "succession of strategies and substrategies". The purpose is not merely to trace out the evolution of the idea of development within the discursive formation since its emergence, but to see the transformation and reconstitution over time of the object of the discourse as inextricably linked with the process of arising of post-colonial capital. A process that is caught up in an endless struggle on the part of capital to cope with an outside that perpetually frustrates its aspiration to be universal and self-subsistent resulting in a complex of capital and non-capital that the development discourse must create, renew, and sustain.

And it is here that I locate the third and the most important difference between the post-developmentalist project and mine. In order to grasp how development helps reproduce the post-colonial capitalist order, the question of their articulation, I argue, must be situated within the *problematic of hegemony*. Escobar seeks to contest the "hegemony of the development discourse" but he seems to use the term "hegemony" in the sense of its everyday use: dominance. He deals with the hegemony of development without making any reference to the literature produced within the Gramscian tradition that already exists, especially that which deals with the concept of hegemony and its relation to the question of agency and subjectivity in the context of politics and social change. As a result, his rendition of the hegemony of development cannot escape questions such as:

What does it mean to say that a discourse is hegemonic? Under what conditions does it become hegemonic? How do we characterize the hegemony of the development discourse? Is the structure of hegemony simple or complex? These are questions that I find inescapable in trying to explain my understanding of post-colonial capitalism. In what follows I will go beyond Escobar and situate the writing of capitalist transformation in the third world, and its relation to the imaginaries produced by the development discourse, within the problematic of hegemony. My purpose is to further complicate the sense in which development can be understood as hegemonic practice because it is only in relation to an understanding of hegemony as a complex structure that, I argue, it is possible to delineate the contours of the post-colonial economic formation and its dynamics.

The project of unmooring the space of development from the paradigm of systemic transition, and of seeing development in terms of a complex form of hegemony, also distances itself from the post-developmentalist position in terms of the political possibilities it opens up. Escobar's reluctance to problematize hegemony does not allow his encounter with development to go beyond the dichotomy between modernity and tradition inscribed in a story of transition; the sole aim of his counterhegemonic politics is to mobilize the possibilities that lie outside the space of modernity and to pit them against the regime of development. This politics is predicated on the belief that an original and authentic "tradition" exists in the form of an unadulterated, pristine "indigenousness", and one can locate in this indigenousness potential subjects that can be posited in radical opposition to the modernizing project of development. The new social movements that figure so prominently in the post-development scenario are seen as the vehicle of these subjectivities that seek to inscribe the social space of the third world with identities that are radically different from the ones produced within the development discourse. Post-colonial theorists have already critiqued this view of indigenousness as the "other" of modernity on the ground that it fails to capture the complexities of post-colonial development. They argue that in order to understand the post-colonial developmental experience, one has to explore how "tradition" negotiates "modernity" and in the process produces a "hybrid" space, a space that displaces both the "traditional" and the "modern" and lock them in a relation of mutual constitution (Gupta 2001).[13] But one can also approach the question from the other side and explore how the development discourse allows modernity to appropriate, rather than annihilate tradition by censoring and reconstituting it, by inserting elements of the "modern" within the structure of "tradition", and turning it into an instrument to be deployed for achieving developmental goals. My rendition of development as a complex hegemonic space, in which tradition and modernity, capital and pre-capital, converge, coalesce, and constitute each other, makes visible a terrain of counterhegemonic politics within the space of development itself. The aim of this politics is not to look for an exit from "development" and contest it from outside, but to contest and subvert the hegemonic order from within by inscribing new identities and demands into its discursive field.

Our post-developmentalist claims that with the advent of development "a merciless war was waged against the age-old traditions of communal solidarity. The virtues of simplicity and conviviality, of noble forms of poverty ... and the art of suffering were derided as signs of underdevelopment."(Rahnema 1997: x) But today's postcolonial world is replete with instances in which the castaways of development, those left out, are increasingly asserting their demand to be included into the ambit of development in terms of access to education, health care, social security, nourishment, and above all to means of livelihood. They seem to think that they have had too much of the "noble forms of poverty" and the "art of suffering". The inhabitants of the wasteland are invading the space of development to inscribe their presence into it. In view of this, I find the politics that strives to radically intervene into and reconstitute the development discourse itself in terms of new imaginaries of development far more attractive than the one that aims to pit a "lost paradise" against the developmental regime. The development discourse with all its material effectivity is ubiquitous to the extent of being inescapable, but this is not to be seen as the reflection of the "colonization of imagination". What has colonized our imagination is not development as such but specific imaginaries of development that, as part of a hegemonic construct present themselves as the "true" and "universal" mode of thinking. To "decolonize" imagination, these dominant imaginaries have to be radically contested, and their hegemony unsettled, without trying to abandon the space of development itself.

Even after having understood development as a regime of power that reduces the third world to an object of knowledge–power and techno-bureaucratic intervention, as a panoptic gaze that allows no aspect of the life process to remain invisible, I find it pointless to look for an original and authentic space entirely outside the reach of development. Valorization of indigenousness in fact can be as oppressive as the subjectivities produced by development's discursive power, especially when the inhabitants of the wasteland are voicing their demand to be in the interior of development rather than remain its castaways. And at the same time, I claim that the hegemony of the development discourse is not as total and powerful as the post-developmentalists think it is; there are cracks and fissures on its surface. A meaningful oppositional politics, I would argue, should look for its radical subjects not in an originary, pristine "outside", but in those cracks and fissures, in the interstices of the hegemonic order woven by development. And mobilize those subject positions to unsettle the order by inscribing into its field radically new imaginaries.

It is a politics fundamentally different from the one associated with the post-development scenario. The significance of Escobar's theoretical intervention, however, remains constant because contestation of the dominant imaginaries of development is possible only if development is understood as a discursive formation, a regime of truth. For, it is only by contesting and unsettling the truth effects of the structured ensemble of statements that constitutes the dominant discourse and its material effectivity that a counterhegemonic space can be posited, a space in which a new representation of the economy and the political subjectivities associated with it can be inscribed. The discourse theory provides an immensely powerful framework that allows for an understanding of hegemony as a discursive construct and at the same time makes visible the possibility of mapping a terrain of oppositional politics that seeks to subvert the hegemonic construct by exposing gaps and holes on its surface.

In sum, my approach to the post-colonial experience of development departs from the post-developmentalist position in that it: (a) reinstates the political economy of post-colonial capitalism involving the story of modes of production, accumulation, and class, and sees development as a discursive formation within which the conditions of post-colonial capital's reproduction are created, (b) discerns in the space of development a paradigmatic shift from a historicist notion of transition to a notion of development as management of the wasteland created by primitive accumulation of capital, and (c) interprets the development discourse as a *complex* hegemony of post-colonial capital and maps a counterhegemonic space within the field of development itself.

But in order to be able to do that, I must displace the Gramscian notion of hegemony onto the terrain of the Foucauldian analysis of power and reconceptualize it in terms of the theory of discursive formation. The discourse interpretation of development asserts that development is the product of a particular representational strategy, and developmental practices derive from that regime of representation. In other words, the discourse represents the reality in a particular way by allowing each entity to have a specific meaning and in effect produces a regime of truth grounded in those meanings. It is in this sense that the discourse is hegemonic. The entities have complex and multiple meanings, and what the discourse does is arrest their floating character by asserting one meaning while keeping the multiplicity of meanings out of sight. And in order to do this, the discourse privileges certain entities by placing them at the center and then organizes all other entities in relation to that centre. Borrowing a term from Ernesto Laclau and Chantal Mouffe, I call this center *nodal point*.[14] The (set of) nodal point(s) allows the discourse to arrive at a closure by "fixing" the meaning of every entity and also of the relation between entities. Hegemony is an articulatory practice that successfully constructs nodal points and thereby the dominant regime of meaning.

The hegemonic closure, however, is ultimately contingent and provisional; Laclau and Mouffe describe it as "sutured totality". It is susceptible to subversion in the sense that the totality can be unsettled by positing alternative (set of) nodal point(s) thus bringing to visibility the other meanings that were kept out of sight. In the Gramscian formulation, hegemony is a state where the elite successfully projects its sectional interest as the universal interest. In our new interpretation, a particular set of meanings is projected through discursive articulation as the universal one to constitute hegemony. And given its contingent nature, it can be contested by articulatory practice that pits alternative system of meaning against the dominant one.

Now I have to further complicate matters to make room for complex hegemony. The notion of complex hegemony was introduced within the traditional Gramscian framework in the preceding chapter. A quick recap: simple hegemony means rule by thesis, i.e., the elite rules with its own agenda. In other words, the subaltern identifies herself/himself with the essence of the elite space, forgetting its own essence. Hegemony has a complex structure when it is based on a surrogate space from which both the elite and the subaltern spaces are seen as flowing. In terms of the Hegelian triad, here thesis incorporates a part of the antithesis to produce a surrogate synthesis. Can we conceive of a similar distinction in the Foucauldian framework where the nodal point fixes meanings through discursive closure? If we consider two such closures constituted by two different (sets of) nodal points, then how are we to see the interaction between the two discursive spaces thus generated? In other words, how are we to theorize interaction between different hegemonic formations produced by different (sets of) nodal points? The concept of hegemonic closure around a single (set of) nodal point(s) corresponds to the Gramscian notion of simple hegemony. The definition of hegemony can be stretched further to capture its complex form, for that is essential for an understanding of development as a hegemonic discourse in the post-colonial context.

Let us consider within our framework two (sets) of nodal points, A and B, each privileging certain entities around which other entities are organized to produce a hegemonic closure. And the discursive space produced around B engages in contestation with the space produced by A. Now we can think of a third (set of) nodal point(s), C, which creates a third space that accommodates A and B. Here privileging of entities involves two steps. C constitutes a discursive closure by being a privileged entity, fixing the meaning of A and B; and then A and B, each as privileged entity within the space constituted by C, further create discursive closures within the original closure. Thus the spaces produced by A and B are turned into two subspaces, two moments, flowing from the original space created by C. This would be the complex form of hegemony in the Foucauldian framework.

The complex form of hegemony thus conceptualized will allow us to understand the post-colonial capitalist formation as a hegemonic order that is necessarily heterogenous. As I discussed at length at the beginning of the preceding chapter, J.K. Gibson–Graham views the centered representation of the economy as "capitalistic" as the "prevalent hegemonic practice" and argues that deconstruction of the economy with the aim to rehabilitate/foreground the non-capitalist economic sites within the representation maps a counter-hegemonic space. In Chapter 1, I have fashioned my critique of Gibson–Graham in terms of the notion of "complex hegemony" and argued that hegemony in its complex form can be seen as expressing itself through difference rather than monism. Now having displaced the concept of hegemony onto the terrain of discourse theory, I will demonstrate that decentering and de-essentialization can be moments of the hegemonic construct itself; that the hegemonic power does not necessarily posit itself as a stubbornly rigid entity that all other entities must identify with; it also allows itself to be represented as decentered, fragmented and diffused, while insidiously working its dominance behind this malleability and open endedness. I share Michael Hardt and Antonio Negri's concern when, in expressing their skepticism about the efficacy of a postmodernist politics in the era of globalization, they warn us about the anti-foundational, anti-essentialist strategy in global capital's self-representation

> The affirmation of hybridities and free play of differences across boundaries .... is liberatory only in a context where power poses hierarchy exclusively through essential identities, binary divisions, and stable oppositions. The structures and logics of power in the contemporary world are entirely immune to the "liberatory" weapons of the postmodern politics of difference. In fact, Empire too is bent on doing away with those modern forms of sovereignty and on setting differences to play across boundaries. (2000: 142)

Thus, in order to delineate the contours of a counterhegemonic politics, there is a need to problematize hegemony in a way that enables us to recognize that it can work through difference and hybridity rather than unity and monism.

In the following chapters, I will see development in relation to the hegemony process. If, as the post-developmetalists claim, the development discourse is hegemonic, then we must understand its hegemony in terms of construction of nodal points and production of meanings. Applying the Foucauldian framework, I will characterize the development discourse as a hegemonic construct based on specific nodal points, producing a particular representation of the economy within which the meaning of economic entities—such as capital, non-capital, the state and the market—are provisionally fixed. The provisional totality, and the system of meaning associated with it, is posited as a regime of truth. The truth effects produced by the construct are however susceptible to subversion and different meanings of the economic entities come to the fore and engage in contestation with the hegemonic construct of development. In the face of this, new nodal points are constructed to restore hegemony as a new, provisionally sutured totality. This process of subversion and reconstitution of meanings is what constitutes the dynamics of the discourse, and it is in this sense that I understand hegemony as a process rather than as a static construct.

I will identify three moments of this dynamic. Chapter 3 describes the *first moment* of this hegemony process as one in which *accumulation* serves as the nodal point for the development discourse, and the process of development is identified with the process of *primitive accumulation of capital.* In the provisional totality thus produced, development is identified with the expansion of capital, and pre-capital is posited as the "other" of accumulation, an entity located outside the totality and one that the development process seeks to annihilate. This is the case of simple hegemony where capital rules by its own agenda and hegemony expresses itself as violence against non-capital backed by persuasion.

Primitive accumulation and the annihilation of pre-capital produces a wasteland inhabited by the excluded surplus population that creeps in through the sutures and subverts the totality. This is where I locate the *second moment* of the development discourse. In Chapter 4, I argue that the legitimation crisis posed by the continued existence of absolute poverty necessitates a *de-essentialization* of development. The development discourse seeks to reorganize itself and produces a new system of meanings of the economic entities on the basis of *need* as a new nodal point. By foregrounding concepts such as "basic needs", the discourse shifts away its focus from capital and thereby distances itself from the notion of development as transition.

The tension between need and accumulation as the two contending nodal points remains at the heart of the development discourse until they both are turned into parts of a new *complex* totality produced by *the market* as the master nodal point. With the rise of neo-liberalism, post-colonial capitalist development is now being posited as a market driven process within a system of meanings that can accommodate accumulation and need as two apparently non-contradictory nodal points residing within a single space defined by the market. It signals a regime of capital that requires a need economy inhabited by non-capital to rehabilitate the victims of accumulation. This is the *third moment* of the discourse, described in Chapter 5, where a complex form of hegemony is discernable within which the reproduction of post-colonial capital, and its dominance, are ensured.

In terms of these three hegemonic moments I construct my narrative of post-colonial capitalism. It is a narrative on the one hand of representing the post-colonial world as the site for the re-enactment of the Western drama of capital's arising, and on the other, of the emergence of the army of surplus labor produced by the arising of post-colonial capital, and of how the wasteland unsettles the trajectory of capital's immanent history and condemns post-colonial capital to a perpetual state of *becoming*; a state in which it must learn to live with non-capital in a world of difference and assert its dominance through heterogeneity and pluralism.

I trace out the dynamics of the discourse from a symptomatic reading of the mainstream academic discourse of development economics and the idea of development produced by and disseminated from the international developmental organizations such as the World Bank and the ILO. And to grasp the material effectivity of the discourse—how it brought into play specific interventions and "produced" the very reality it sought to transform—I use as an illustration of my story the specific case of post-colonial India since the 1950s by subjecting the profile of her developmental experience from the paradigm of development planning to the current regime of globalization and the New Economic Policy to a "retrospective gaze". The Indian case seems to fit in well with the sequence of hegemonic moments that I have described, but my narrative, I would claim, goes beyond the specificity of the Indian experience and offers the contours of a more general framework for understanding the structure and dynamics of post-colonial capitalism.

Notes

1. The concept of primitive accumulation is conspicuously absent in Adam Smith's analysis of the emergence of the capitalist commercial economy.

Nowhere in *The Wealth of Nations*, nor in the *Lecture on Jurisprudence*, does Smith refer to the process of dispossession of the peasantry and destruction of self-provisioning leading to the creation of proletarianized wage-laborer. Regarding the emergence of the initial stock of means of production, Smith vaguely mentions previous accumulation apparently referring to savings out of what the potential capitalist produced with his own labor. Both Ricardo and Malthus are concerned with the working of a fully developed capitalist economy in which the initial capitalization of means of labor has already been completed and a working class has already emerged, and they do not find it necessary to address the question of transition and therefore of transformation of direct producers to dispossessed wage-labor. Thus in the development of the classical political economy as a discourse, inaugurated by Smith and consolidated by Ricardo and Malthus, the story of primitive accumulation signals an act of forgetfulness, of discursive violence. For an interesting account of how the architects of the classical political economy suppressed the issue of primitive accumulation, see Perelman (1983).

2. In *Capital*, Volume I, Marx identifies three forms of surplus population: floating, latent and stagnant, apart from the unemployment that results from periodic crisis and fluctuations in capitalist accumulation. Capitalist industry attracts and repels laborers at the same time, creating an army of unemployed in floating form. As distinct from this, surplus laborer in its latent form is created by the falling demand for an agricultural laboring population associated with the capitalist transformation of agriculture. With the expansion of the manufacture, these people are to be transformed into a manufacturing proletariat, but until the opportunities in manufactures grow sufficiently, and the channels of outlet from country to town opens up to make such a transformation possible, they remain as latent surplus population in agriculture. Finally, "[t]he third category of the relative surplus population, the stagnant, forms a part of the active labor army, but with extremely irregular employment. Hence it furnishes to capital an inexhaustible reservoir of disposable labor power."(p. 602)

3. In an article, written more than a decade ago, on the theories of development from a post-modern perspective, David Slater expressed, although in passing, skepticism about the adequacy of the Marxian concept of the reserve army to capture the nature of the marginality and exclusion in contemporary third world economies. "To what extent", he writes, "was it possible and desirable to apply the concepts of an industrial reserve army.... to societies that had not undergone a thoroughgoing process of capitalist transformation? ... How were these other people who did not easily fall into the customary categories of traditional Marxian class analysis to be explained?"(1992: 302) Slater does not pursue the question any further but I found in this comment a glint of the awareness that the phenomenon of marginality in the third world has to be distanced from the Marxian concept of the reserve army and situated in the context of the *becoming* of capital, rather than its *being*. Later, I came to know about a literature on the Latin American economic formations that presented the concept of the "marginal mass" to question the relevance of the reserve army in the Latin American

context (Nun 2000, Quijano 1983). This literature, however, has remained marginalized in the radical political economy of underdevelopment.

4. Balibar (1970) offers an interpretation of primitive accumulation as a genealogy, rather than a history, of capital. The initial conditions of capitalist mode of production (money in the hands of the cpaitlaist, free wage-labor and means of labor), Balibar argues, do not necessarily emerge through one structured process of change. Each one of them can be fulfilled in a variety of ways depending on the specificity of historical conditions within which capital arises.

5. For the implications of bringing the household to the fore for the Marxian value theory, see Folbre (1982).

6. In his well-known book, *Free To Lose* (1988: 134–135), John Roemer offers an interesting example of how the Marxist idea of exploitation based entirely on extraction of surplus may lead to paradoxes. He considers a situation in which some people who have no access to means of production are also unable to find a job in the capitalist production process. They receive unemployment benefits from the welfare state that are a transfer from the surplus value produced by the workers engaged in the capitalist sector and collected by the state in the form of taxes. Here the unemployed people are exploiters in the sense that they live on the surplus labor of others. But if these people find jobs in the capitalist sector as wage-laborer, they no longer receive any unemployment benefits but now have a wage-income that is higher than those benefits. According to the Marxian notion of exploitation, although better off in terms of income, they are now producers of surplus value and therefore belong to the class of the exploited. Roemer's purpose is to call attention to exploitation resulting from unequal access to means of production, a form of exploitation that the Marxian surplus-based definition fails to capture.

   Marxists have strongly critiqued Roemer's analytical framework and his interpretation of exploitation and class, and I do share the view that his analysis of class exploitation based on methodological individualism betrays a total failure to grasp the specificity of the Marxian method. However, I do also think that the Marxian framework must stretch itself beyond the notion of exploitation as necessarily a relation based on extraction/appropriation and negotiate the idea of exclusion and marginalization as exploitation. If dispossession is seen as an inescapable moment of post-colonial capital, any attempt toward a Marxist analysis of the post-colonial form of capitalism must engage with the non-extractive forms of exploitation.

7. In the context of advance capitalist economies, Berger and Piore (1980) offer an interesting story of how a "traditional sector" has stubbornly existed as an integral part of those economies. Existing alongside a high-tech, modern, capitalist sector, this "artisan sector" has shown remarkable resilience and has been able to reproduce and renew itself economically and politically. Berger and Piore characterize this as discontinuity and duality in the modern industrial societies and pose their observation in opposition to the vision of transition based on the traditional/modern binary.

8. For a critique of Bennholdt–Thomsen on this line, see Custers (1997).
9. The orthodox Marxist theory of imperialism has focused exclusively on the imperial economy—on the causes of export of capital—the imperialized economy is not dealt with except in terms of superficial statements on how imperialist penetration thwarts indigenous capitalist growth and reinforces pre-capitalist modes of exploitation. The only exception is dependency theory; if imperialism is to be seen as a constraint, then one has to abandon the historical materialist framework.
10. The traditional Marxist discourse further complicates the question of leadership in the process of transition by asserting that if the bourgeoisie is proved to be inadequate for the role assigned to it, an alternative way to accomplish the transition is to have a mobilization of the peasantry, which constitutes the majority of the population of underdeveloped economies, and the petit bourgeoisie under the leadership of the working class. Here the agency of the working class, instead of the bourgeoisie, is seen as the key to the transition process. Nonetheless, the idea that a full-scale transformation of the economy from pre-capitalism to private/state capitalism is possible remains at the heart of this strategy. Any other outcome of this process in which the project of an all-encompassing transition is not realized has been seen by the Marxist discourse as a case of failure. Listen to Ranajit Guha, an eminent Indian historian and the guru of the subaltern studies school, interpreting the colonial history of India:

> It is the study of this historic failure of the nation to come to its own, a failure due to the inadequacy of the bourgeoisie as well as of the working class to lead it into a decisive victory over the traditional Marxist discourse further complicates the question of leadership in the process of transition by asserting that if the bourgeoisie is proved to be inadequate for the role assigned to it, an alternative way to accomplish the transition is to have a mobilization of the peasantry, which constitutes the majority of the population of underdeveloped economies, and the petit bourgeoisie under the leadership of the working class. Here the agency of the working class, instead of the bourgeoisie, is seen as the key to the transition process. Nonetheless the idea that a full-scale transformation of the economy from pre-capitalism to private/state capitalism is possible remains at the heart of this strategy. Any other outcome of this process in which the project of an all-encompassing transition is not realized has been seen by colonialism and a bourgeois democratic revolution of either the classic nineteenth-century type under the hegemony of the bourgeoisie or a more modern type under the hegemony of the workers and peasants, that is, a new democracy—it is a study of this failure which constitutes the central problematic of history of colonial India. (1982: 7)

This tendency to interpret any outcome other than a full-scale transformation as failed capitalism continues to inform the Marxist analysis of post-colonial India. In explaining the post-colonial experience, the Marxists argue that India has failed to repeat the trajectory of the Western experience of development because of the failure on the part of the bourgeoisie to show its radical face against the neo-colonial domination that characterized the second half of the 20th century, and also the failure of the working class to become a class for itself and lead the rest of the toiling masses to the same end. Post-colonial development continues to be characterized as case of failure.

11. Several years before, the theory of discursive formation started being applied to the idea of development, Diana Hunt in a relatively less known book titled *Economic Theories of Development: An Analysis of Competing Paradigms* (1989), made an attempt to understand different theoretical frameworks within the literature on development in terms of the concept of paradigm offered by Kuhn. She strove to identify different schools of developmental thought not as competing claims within a common theoretical framework but as claims made within what she called competing paradigms. Kuhn defines a paradigm as the constellation of values, beliefs and perception of empirical reality, together with a given set of fundamental concepts and a distinctive methodology, which scientists accept, and within which they carry out their scientific enquiry. The paradigm is constituted by a specific set of key variables and their relationships that are accepted as fundamental to the particular field of scientific enquiry. The statements made by scientists are governed by a particular use of language specific to that paradigm. And there can be competing paradigms with their specific and distinct key variables and relationships.

A discursive formation, it should be emphasized, is not a paradigm. The concept of discursive formation is fundamentally different from that of paradigm in at least two respects. First, a paradigm emerges once the members of the scientific community agree upon a certain framework with specific concepts and methodology, and once the paradigm is formed, scientific enquiries can be carried out as long as they satisfy the requirements of the paradigm. In the case of discursive formation, every time a statement is made, the rules of formation of the discourse are invoked to judge the validity of the statement. In other words, it is a continuous process of surveillance, rather than an initial specification of rules, through which the discursive policing makes itself effective.

Second, and more fundamentally, the paradigm as defined by Kuhn does not address the relationship between the formation and stability of a paradigm and the structure and modalities of power: it does not explore the power–knowledge nexus. But for Foucault, the concept of the discursive formation is inextricably related with the problematic of power. The discourse is rooted in power while power expresses itself through the truth effects produced by the discourse. It is this implosion of power and knowledge that radically distances a discourse from a paradigm. However, Hunt's book is in my knowledge the first attempt—published almost five years before Escobar's—to understand theories of economic development in terms of competing systems of knowledge.

12. The story of capitalist transformation involving modes of production, class and the state, its historical materialist framework and the critique of colonialism/neocolonialism, is virtually absent in Escobar's encounter with the discourse of development. It is interesting to note that Escobar does not even mention the enormous literature on radical development theory (dependency, world system). In his analysis of capital accumulation as development and the role of development planning in that context, he conflates the structuralist, neoclassical and Keynesian perspectives and then critiques the centrality of the economy in the development discourse.

13. Gupta (2001) is an imaginative attempt to characterize this hybrid space in terms of the story of agricultural transformation in modern India. He argues that in the encounter between tradition and modernity in the third world, modernity is reinvented, reconstituted, and refigured according to the historical and social/cultural specificity of different locations. Thus, the non-modern aspects of these realities are to be seen not as the residual traces of tradition that resist the invasion of modernity but as inescapable constitutive moments of a hybrid space. By "post-colonial condition" Gupta means this complex space where tradition and modernity negotiate and constitute each other, a space that is not to be seen as a transitory moment in a teleological metanarrative of modernity and progress. Gupta illustrates this concept of post-coloniality with the story of how traditional Indian farmers in post-colonial India have negotiated modernity in the form of advance technology, use of fertilizers and techniques of irrigation in terms of their traditional perception of nature, land and ecology, producing in the process complex cultural, ideological and political identities. Thus Gupta's interpretation of post-coloniality is fundamentally different from Escobar's characterization of underdevelopment based on the tradition–modernity binary. Gupta's focus is on how tradition "reinvents" modernity, but if approached from the other side, post-coloniality can also be interpreted in terms of how modernity "reinvents" tradition. This is precisely what my purpose is: to understand this reinvention by locating the question of post-coloniality within the problematic of hegemony.

14. Ernesto Laclau and Chantal Mouffe, in *Hegemony and Socialist Strategy*, explore the question of construction of political identities and subject positions, and in doing that they conceptualize hegemony within a post-structuralist framework. For Laclau and Mouffe, society with its floating signifiers and their meanings overflowing, does not allow itself to be characterized as a centered totality. Every entity within a particular relational structure always carries a "surplus of meaning", i.e. the traces of other meanings possessed by the same entity within other relational structures. Thus there is a limit to all objectivity and this limit signals the impossibility of their self-constitution. Hegemony is an articulatory practice that produces the *social* by temporarily fixing the meaning of the floating signifiers and thereby turning the elements into moments of the construct. The totality thus produced discursively is "sutured", in the sense that the meaning of an entity or subject position within that totality is *provisionally* fixed by suturing the gaps and cracks through which other meanings seep

in. In other words, identities are contingent and negotiable but they are given a provisional fixity within a sutured totality produced by hegemonic practice.

The temporary fixity of meaning of the floating signifiers produced by the discursive closure requires what Laclau and Mouffe call the *nodal points*. These are defined as privileged signifiers, i.e., privileged discursive points, that fix the meaning of other signifiers in a signifying chain and constitutes the hegemonic articulation. For them, the nodal points serve to arrest the flow of differences within the discursive field and thereby constitute the discourse as a unity.

Thus in Laclau and Mouffe's rendition of hegemony, essence is dispensed with and identities are not grounded in any innate essence but are constituted by the outside. Hegemony is a discursive practice that provisionally fixes these identities.

Chapter 3

Accumulation as Development: The Arising of Capital

Making Development Happen

It was H.W. Arndt who first made this illuminating observation. In exploring the semantic history of the term "development", he observed that the publication of the British Development Act of 1929 marked a radical change in the perception of development (Arndt 1981). Instead of a concept capturing the process of economic transformation that a society undergoes (the economy develops), the Act posited development in the colonial context as a discrete structural change in the economy to be brought about by purposeful intervention (the economy has to be developed). In Arndt's apt characterization, development was now derived not from the intransitive but the transitive verb.

For the classical political economists, development was an all encompassing, macro-level process of change that an economy experiences—a process to be described, analyzed, dissected, and studied, and its implications investigated, enumerated, and evaluated. Adam Smith located this process of change in the new order that was emerging in Europe and portrayed it as an order organized around contractual relations between self-seeking individuals with a passion for material wealth. It was also an order that constituted the economy as a disembedded, autonomous domain of social life with internal laws of its own. He saw the network of markets regulated by the working of the invisible hand as creating an environment that encouraged productivity-enhancing division of labor. The expansionary thrust of the new system came from the class of manufacturers who invested their surplus as capital to set *productive labor* in motion rather than traditionally using it like the feudal lords to maintain an army of unproductive laborers. However, the process of change that Smith was trying to describe—the process of economic growth resulting from the shift from unproductive to productive labor—was for him a process that was already at work; he sought to comprehend the dynamics of the process, describe, and analyze it, highlight its immense potential and identify possible hindrances that might impede it.

In Ricardo, the story of economic growth was further consolidated in terms of social classes (capitalists, workers, and landlords) and their distinct roles in the accumulation process. Ricardo was mainly concerned with the constraints on this process, and he located the inelastic supply of land as the ultimate factor in setting a limit to capitalist accumulation. Scarcity of land, he argued, would ultimately lower productivity and therefore the rate of profit in capitalist agriculture. That in turn would cause the terms of trade to move against industry, reducing the overall rate of profit on capital and therefore dampening the accumulation process. But like Smith, Ricardo also viewed economic growth through capitalist accumulation as a process that was at work out there, waiting to be described, analyzed, and investigated.

The classical economists, it is true, also dealt with the question of intervention. Although they understood economic growth as a process that the society was experiencing, they were aware of the need for intervening into the process in order to facilitate it by removing the factors that might act as impediments. For Smith, the most appropriate form of intervention was non-intervention into the working of the market. His advocacy was for a minimalist state that, instead of meddling with the free market, would confine itself to law and order, defense, and essential public works. Ricardo went a step ahead and saw the need for the state to act directly and take measures that would enhance capitalist accumulation. His strong advocacy against the Corn Law in the British Parliament was premised on the claim that free import would cheapen corn in the domestic market, which in turn would reduce the product wage-rate the industrial capitalists had to pay, and thereby jack up the rate of profit and therefore the rate of accumulation. But for both Smith and Ricardo, not to mention Malthus, Sismondi, and a host of other classical political economists, the interventions were nothing more than piecemeal social engineering. Put differently, in the view of the classical economists, the process of economic growth could be influenced, facilitated, and enhanced by appropriate interventions, but the systemic shift from stagnation to growth was perceived as a transformation that was independent of the intention of the subject who intervened. Thus, the role of the political economist as a mere observer and analyst of the development process was deeply inscribed in the theoretical field of the classical political economy.

Marx's theoretical system was rooted in a fundamental departure from the classical political economy. Yet in a broad sense, he shared the classical view of development as being derived from the intransitive verb: development and progress is a process that a society undergoes. But unlike that of his predecessors, Marx's vision of social transformation was premised on the working of the inexorable Hegelian dialectic. History is the journey of the *spirit/consciousness* toward *freedom* as its destination, a process of dialectical unfolding in which the lower moments of the idea are superseded by its higher moments. Marx departed from Hegel by characterizing the successive moments of history not as stages in the development of the *idea* but in terms of the materiality of the modes of production, and by locating the source of the dynamics in the contradictions inherent in them. Social classes and conflicts, among them, are central to the Marxian understanding of progress—progress as freedom from both scarcity and domination—but economic and social transformation, in the Marxian paradigm, from primitive society to socialism and communism, is ultimately grounded in a logic of inevitability of historical change with class struggle as nothing more than the vehicle of that inescapable trajectory of development.[1]

It is true, as Arndt argues, that this notion of development underwent a change in the colonial context and the term development came to be understood as a process that had to be introduced/initiated: the colony had to be developed. But it was not until the emergence of the development discourse after the formal decolonization of Asia and Africa in the late 1940s and 1950s that development in the sense of being derived from the transitive verb became universally established with all its material effectivity. It was only then that the classical notion of development as a process of change that the society inevitably passes through was entirely replaced by the claim that development was the result of conscious, rational action on the macro level, rather than piecemeal intervention into an ongoing process. It was no longer a process to be observed, described, and analyzed, it was a process to be initiated, sustained, and monitored. *Development was perceived as a systemic change that was to be brought about by purposeful, rational action, a task to be performed, a goal to be achieved and a mission to be carried out.* It was posited as a task for which plans had to be prepared, programs designed, and calculations made. And finally, the programs had to be implemented to radically transform the conditions that constituted underdevelopment.

There is however a crucial difference between the conceptualization of development in the colonial context and development as a discursive construct that emerged in the 1950s. In the case of colonies, development was seen as purposeful action to change the material conditions of life, but the responsibility of bringing about the change lay with the imperial power and its agencies. Development of the colonies was presented as a concern of the colonizer, as a mission to change the life of the native, and as a specific domain of exercising the colonial power. Backwardness of the colony was, of course, a part of the discursive construct produced by the colonizer but the materiality of that discourse, the interventions that it called into play, flowed from the agency of a concrete, centered, and visible form of territorialized, imperial political authority and its attendant organs of power. The post-colonial development discourse differs fundamentally from its colonial precursor in the strong sense that its materiality does not emanate from the political authority of the state. Development is a body of techno-scientific knowledge, produced and disseminated from specific institutional sites such as universities, research institutes, and developmental organizations. Although these institutional sites legitimize the statements made about development, the real power of the discourse derives from the supposed neutrality and universality of knowledge itself. The interventions and actions that it brings into play are part of the discursive practice whose practitioners are "experts and professionals", acting as trustees of rationality rather than agents of political power. It is true that post-colonial states are often significant actors in developmental programs, but what is important is that their role as an agent of change derives not so much from their political authority as from the truth effects produced by the discourse. The realm of development is the realm of reason, a realm beyond and above the state as a political authority. It is in this sense that development in the post-colonial scenario is truly a discursive formation with its own specific and unique technology of power. It is a technology of power that works, not through the political authority of the state and its attendant institutions, but through the material effectivity of the discursive formation. The relations of power that the technology produces "cannot themselves be established, consolidated nor implemented without the production, accumulation, circulation and functioning of [the] discourse". (Foucault 1980: 93)

The most important effect produced by this technology of power is the depoliticization of development. The technology of power, and the modalities in terms of which it works, requires, as Escobar has forcefully argued, that the development process be professionalized and beaurocratized; in other words, depoliticized. The specificity of development as a discourse in the post-colonial context lies not merely in the shift from the classical idea that *the economy develops* to the claim that *the economy has to be developed;* the uniqueness of the discourse derives also from the representation of development as a politically neutral process of social change.

A comparison with the classical vision of development brings out this point sharply. Adam Smith (1975) locates at the core of the process of economic transformation the drive to amass wealth, a drive whose root he argues is in the human psyche, in the desire of bettering our condition. But in his depiction, the process of development is ultimately a political process, a process fraught with conflicts between social groups. For him, the feudal order is an encumbrance on the pursuit of wealth and he sees the commercial society as the outcome of social conflicts between the merchants and the feudal lords. The dominance of the manufacturing class as employers of productive labor—and of competition among them that spurs investment and accumulation—is established only after winning the battle against the mercantile oligarchies. Thus development as envisaged by Smith is a process that involves contradictions and conflicts, and the agent of change at a particular stage has to win the political battle to successfully bring about the new order. And even after the manufacturers have emerged as the dominant class, their confrontation with the landlords in the domain of politics continues to be at the heart of the growth process, as Ricardo's battle against the Corn Law demonstrates. Although Ricardo was not concerned with the question of transition from the pre-capitalist to the capitalist system of production, the political dimensions of the capitalist accumulation process are far more explicit in the Ricardian story than in Smith's in the sense that it seeks to describe the process entirely in terms of social classes (capitalists and landlords) as actors with specific class interests and the conflicts that arise between them. Ricardo's capitalism is a class divided system in a far more direct and concrete sense than Smith's commercial society, and seen in this light, Ricardo, not Smith, was the true precursor of Marx.[2]

The political nature of the development process and the role of class contradictions are far more fundamental in Marx than in either Ricardo or Smith. In the Marxian view, each epoch of the development trajectory is characterized in terms of the dominance of a specific mode of production, i.e., a specific articulation of productive forces and relations of production. The specificity of the articulation implies a particular mode of generation and distribution of surplus and therefore of a given configuration of social classes with their definite positions in the matrix of social production. Although the process of change from one mode of production to another is the outcome of the contradictions inherent in the articulation itself, conflicts between social classes and the dynamics of class struggle is seen by Marx as a crucial factor precipitating those contradictions and influencing the trajectory of change. Transition from one mode to another is facilitated or held back by the relative power of different social classes and their ability to act as agents of change at that particular juncture. Thus, class politics is an inescapable moment of the inexorable dialectical process of unfolding of the consciousness through the successive stages of history.

The post world war II discourse turned development into a matter of rational planning, appropriate programing and efficient implementation, and in doing this it also purged development completely of its political content. It adopted a representational strategy in which development is understood as a matter of economic and social engineering, as a process governed by, as it were, the politically and socially neutral laws of mechanics; it involves no political and social conflicts, contradictions or active agency. It is these twin aspects—understanding of development as a change to be brought about by purposive action rather than as an ongoing process to be analyzed, and stripping development of its social and political dimensions by reducing it into an engineering exercise—that mark the radical departure of the post-colonial development as discursive construct from the classical approach to the question of social change.

Different Stage but the Same Script

Writing on the early post world war II theories of modernization and development, B.S. Cohn remarked:

"These theories say to Asians, Africans or Latin Americans: what you are today we have been in the past; you may become what we are today, but by that time we, of course, will be something else because we will have gone on. The modern developmental model as it was worked out by economists and political scientists in the 50s borrows this structure by trying to identify or scale aspects of third world societies in relation to the history of Europe. It assumes a lineality in European history.... That is both a prerequisite for modernization and an indicator of change." (1980: 212 quoted in Rosen 1985: 229)

The early development discourse was premised on this lineality of European history and it inscribed onto the third world a specific identity: that of being behind the West, an undeveloped form of what developed West was. And development meant that the third world would have to chase the West, follow the same trajectory of change and traverse the same route to the same destination. Thus, the notion of development around which the discourse in its early stage organized itself was one of a systemic transition: transition from the traditional to the modern, from the stagnant to the dynamic, but at the very core of it was inscribed the idea of transition from pre-capital to capital. This idea of transition and change was totally divorced from the possibilities that the economic, social, and cultural formations of the third world might have carried within themselves possibilities that could point toward an entirely different imaginary of economic and social change. It was not an idea of transition in the sense of being an open ended set of alternative possibilities, a space in which different ways of actualizing human potentialities could be mapped. On the contrary, it was a predetermined, unidirectional trajectory derived from the ex-post, immanent history of capitalist development in the West and its presumed lineality.

In the specific domain of economic transformation, the discourse saw the third world as the stage on which the drama of capital's arising in the West was to be acted out once again. In order to develop, the underdeveloped economies will have to experience the process of transition in which pre-capitalist economic forms will wither away, and the post-colonial capital will arise, be self-reproducing and *become* in the Hegelian sense. "On approaching development problems," writes Gerald Meier, "the early development economists first thought of what 'obstacles' to development had to be overcome …. If the underdeveloped economy bore some resemblance to the classical stationary state, then the positive forces that classical economists had emphasized as delaying the advent of the stationary state—namely, capital accumulation and technical progress—could now also be emphasized as forces to accelerate development. From the classical tradition, a major obstacle to be overcome was capital deficiency" (1984: 135–36).[3] A program of rapid capital formation was prescribed for the third world and the discourse structured itself around the single question of accumulation. What I seek to demonstrate in the following sections is that underlying the narrative of development produced by the discourse—a narrative of how an underdeveloped economy by engaging in the process of capital accumulation gradually develops—is the case of primitive accumulation creating the initial conditions of the self-sustained process of capital formation. It is a narrative of estrangement of direct producers from their means of production and of appropriation of the latter within the system of capitalist production. Put differently, what lies invisible in the early discourse of development is how the unity of labor with the means of labor within the pre-capitalist system is destroyed and the means of labor are transformed into *capital, an alien power confronting labor*—a narrative so vigorously told by Marx.

The early vision of accumulation-based development, I shall argue, is a depoliticized narrative of primitive accumulation. It extricates the Marxian account entirely from the political terrain of conflicts and contradictions among social classes, and displaces it onto an "as if" politically neutral field of developmental planning. A process involving the onslaught launched by a rising bourgeoisie on all pre-capitalist forms of production, the exercise of coercive power through the state as well as through the institutions of civil society, the legitimized violence, and the usurpation of the entire economic space within the expanded reproduction of capital, is thus exorcized of all its political dimensions, sanitized and disinfected, and then presented as a process defined solely in terms of the saving–investment–accumulation sequence; a sequence that can be planned for, programed and then triggered.

In what follows I shall offer a reading of the early texts of development economics with Marx's narrative of primitive accumulation in mind. It is a symptomatic reading that deconstructs the discourse to make visible what it keeps in the dark; to make explicit, loud and clear what it leaves unsaid; to reclaim what it expurgates. The purpose is to unsettle the construct by delineating and foregrounding the contours of a narrative that remains repressed, stifled, and hidden in the imaginary of development the discourse disseminates. *And demonstrate that the representation of the economy and the development process in that imaginary constitutes a specific form of post-colonial capital's hegemony. In short, the purpose is to politicize development.*

But in order to do that we first have to grasp the structure of the process of primitive accumulation and the specific modalities of power that are associated with it. While in *Grundrisse*, Marx offers the concept, in *Capital* Volume 1, he provides a detailed account of primitive accumulation in England. It is the last part, part viii, of the volume, and it is interesting to note that he discusses the conditions of capital's emergence at the end, rather than in the beginning, of a volume devoted to the analysis of the capitalist mode of production. But the logic of the order follows from the very concept itself, that it is the immanent history, a past flowing from the present that can be grasped only from the structural logic of full-fledged capital after it has *become*. And it is only after arriving at an understanding of its *being* that we are in a position to probe the *becoming*, the arising, of British capital. In the following section, I delineate the dynamics of the relation between capital and pre-capital in the process of primitive accumulation from Marx's discussion on the specific case of England.

Structure of Primitive Accumulation and the Modalities of Power

"In the history of primitive accumulation," writes Marx, "all revolutions are epoch making that act as levers for the capitalist class in course of formation; but, above all, those moments when great masses of men are suddenly and forcibly torn from their means of subsistence, and hurled as free and "unattached" proletarians on the labor market. The expropriation of the agricultural producer, of the peasant from the soil, is the basis of the whole process...... In England alone has it the classic form." (1954: 669)

Three interrelated aspects of the process can be identified from Marx's detailed account of the English case:

(1) Accumulation of money by merchants;
(2) Conversion of the accumulated money into capital (means of production) and transformation of direct producers into free wage-laborers; and
(3) Creation of an external market for the product produced under the capitalist mode of production.

Mercantile Accumulation

In order to understand mercantile accumulation, we need to consider the two forms of circulations—of commodity and money—and their interrelation. The circulation of commodity takes the form of $C \sim M \sim C$ where commodities are exchanged for money (M) in the market which in turn is used to purchase commodities. An independent producer who owns his means of production produces C as use value but in the presence of division of labor, his consumption bundle is different from the one he produces. Exchange with the mediation of money is the means with which the first C is transformed into the second C. Thus the circuit of commodity begins and ends with use value.

The flip side of the circulation of commodity is the circulation of money. The circuit $C \sim M \sim C$ implies the corresponding circuit $M \sim C \sim M'$ of the merchant. While the producer sells in order to buy, the merchant buys in order to sell. The merchant spends M to purchase C with the sole aim of selling it for a larger amount of money, M' (M' minus M is greater than zero). Unlike the producer's circuit that has use value at its two ends, the merchant's circuit begins and ends with money. When one round of circulation is completed, the initial quantity of money increases which then is used to purchase commodity for the next round. Mercantile accumulation is entirely in the form of money; its source lies in the sphere of circulation. The merchant buys cheap and sells dear and therefore his profit arises from unequal exchange, what Marx calls a *profit on alienation*. The producers receive the full value of their product in the form of M, but the merchant sells the product to the buyer at a higher price.

The question of merchant's capital has received very little theoretical attention in the Marxist analysis—Kay (1975) being to the best of my knowledge the only exception—and as a result there is a certain amount of confusion about the specific nature of mercantile accumulation. Therefore an elaboration on the accounting side of the two circuits of commodity and money may be rewarding. Imagine a community of direct producers where the means of production are owned either by the individual producers or by the community as a whole. Producers in the community produce goods for subsistence consumption and also a luxury good (muslin!) denoted by C. The merchant buys C from the producers for M, and this M in turn is used by those producers of C to obtain their subsistence consumption and raw materials for production from the rest of the community. Suppose C* is the amount of consumption goods and raw materials produced by the rest of the community. A part of this C*, call it S*, is purchased with M by the producers of the luxury good as raw materials and goods for their own subsistence consumption. The surplus S* is the same as the C at the end of the C ~ M ~ C circuit. So, the surplus of consumption goods and raw materials produced in the community is exactly equal to M. Thus the community as a whole has produced C and C*, but it has consumed only C*, and there has been an inflow of money, M, into the community from outside. We could also say that the community has been monetized to the extent of M. The total production therefore is equal to the total consumption plus the inflow of money implying that the exchange between the community and the merchant is an equal exchange, and the merchant's profit arises from the fact that the buyer is made to pay a price that is higher than the price (that is equal to the value of the product) received by the producer. It is in this sense that the mercantile profit (i.e., the difference between M' and M) is entirely a profit on alienation.

The point to be noted here is that exploitation of the direct producer is *not* the source of mercantile accumulation: producers get full value of their product and there is no unpaid labor. And here lies the distinction between merchant's capital and industrial capital. In the capitalist mode of production, the producer sells his labor power to the capitalist and the quantum of labor extracted from labor power is larger than its cost of reproduction. The worker does not receive any payment for this surplus labor, and therefore it is unpaid labor. This excess of labor performed over and above the necessary labor is the source of the capitalist's profit. In contrast, the merchant's profit does not arise from any unpaid labor in the sphere of production; it arises from unequal exchange exclusively in the sphere of circulation.

From Money to Capital, from Direct Producer to Wage-Laborer

Accumulation by the merchant is the first condition of primitive accumulation. But mercantile accumulation is in the form of money, and to become capital the money must be transformed into means of production. This constitutes the second aspect of primitive accumulation. Under the capitalist mode of production, circulation of money takes the form of $M \sim C \sim C' \sim M'$. Although this circuit begins and ends with money, it is different from the circuit $M \sim C \sim M'$ in that here M is used to purchase means of production including labor-power (C) which then is transformed into C' within the sphere of production, and finally sold in the market to obtain a larger amount of money (M').

Thus the circuit of money in the case of capitalist production, instead of being confined within the sphere of circulation as in the case of mercantile accumulation, penetrates the sphere of production. In order to understand clearly the difference between the two circuits, let us consider once again the community of direct producers described in the preceding section. The community produces a surplus S^* consisting of consumption goods and raw materials for the producers of C, and within the community there is a unity of labor and means of production in the sphere of production. Circulation of money as capital requires that this unity be broken and labor be estranged from the means of production in the activity in which the luxury (C) is produced. Once laborers engaged in the production of the luxury good are divorced from the raw materials and consumption goods that served as their means of labor, the circuit of capital now begins with M purchasing S^* and labor power of those separated from their means of labor. The materials and labor-power are now brought together within the capitalist mode of production to produce C' which is finally sold in the market for M'. (The C in the second step of the circuit M ~ C ~ C' ~ M' is not the same as the C in the merchant's circuit M ~ C ~ M'; in the circuit of capital C consists of S* and labor-power that is sold as a commodity.) It is in this sense that capital moves beyond the domain of circulation and penetrates the domain of production. Labor power receives its subsistence but more labor is extracted from labor power in the interior of production than is necessary to produce the subsistence basket, and it generates a surplus of labor for the capitalist which is reflected in the difference between M' and M. In other words, unpaid labor in the interior of production is the source of capitalist's profit, and it is fundamentally different from the merchant's profit on alienation arising from unequal exchange in the sphere of circulation.

Therefore the condition under which merchant's accumulation can be transformed into capital is the separation of labor and means of labor in the sphere of production. The unity of labor and the means of labor in the pre-capitalist system must dissolve to create the conditions of emergence of the circuit of capital. Primitive accumulation is the story of this process of dissolution. The process on the one hand frees the means of production so that they can enter the circuit of money and turn into capital; on the other hand, it turns direct producers into wage-laborer who have nothing but their labor power to sell to the capitalist.

> The capitalist system presupposes the complete separation of the laborers from all property in the means by which they can realize their labor. As soon as capitalist production is once on its own legs, it not only maintains the separation, but reproduces it on a continually expanding scale. The process therefore .... can be none other than the process that takes away from the laborer the possession of his means of production; a process that transforms .... the social means of subsistence and of production into capital [and] the immediate producers into wage-laborers. The so-called primitive accumulation is, therefore, nothing else than the historical process of divorcing producers from their means of production. (Marx 1954: 668)

What is important is that it is not a natural or evolutionary process but one that is marked with the exercise of coercive power in a variety of forms. In the case of the arising of the English capital, the eviction of the peasantry from land resulting from the enclosure movement served to divorce direct producers from their means of production. The peasantry was forcibly driven by the feudal lords out of the land to which they had enjoyed the same feudal rights as the lords, and the common lands to which they had access were usurped, creating a vast army of proletariat with nothing to sell other than their labor-power (Ashton 1948, Hill 1985). The laborers became "free" in the double sense that they were no longer considered as a part of the means of production as in the case of slavery, nor were they the possessors of the means of production as in the case of peasant proprietor; they were "therefore, unencumbered by any means of production of their own."[4]

While peasant cultivators were driven out of their land, in a parallel process in England, a class of capitalist farmers emerged that were eager to produce a surplus of agricultural product for the market. What had earlier been produced by peasant cultivators and used as means of production by them was now generated by capitalist farmers and sold in the market to become capital on which the "free proletariat" could be made to work as wage-workers within the capitalist enterprise. "The spindles and looms, formerly scattered over the face of the country, are now crowded together in a few labor-barracks, together with the laborer and the raw material. And spindles, looms, raw material, are now transformed from means of independent existence for spinners and weavers, into means of commanding them and sucking out of them unpaid labor."[5] (Marx 1954: 698)

Agriculture as a Home Market

The third aspect of primitive accumulation is the emergence of agriculture as a home market for the products of the capitalist industries. In the pre-capitalist system, the surplus of materials and means of subsistence produced remained with the peasant cultivator that they worked upon to produce goods for their use-value. When peasant cultivators are expropriated from their land, these materials, produced by large farmers, are sold to the capitalist industry as commodity. Seen from the other side, capitalist industry now finds a market for its product in agriculture.

The emergence of capital through the process of primitive accumulation thus inevitably results in the destruction of rural industries and handicrafts. For example, the raw cotton and wool were earlier used in activities of spinning and weaving within agriculture carried out in peasant households. In terms of our example in the preceding section, the surplus produced by the community, S^* was used by the members of the community to produce C within the communal system of production. The non-agricultural, petty manufacturing activities were thus embedded in the agricultural sector constituting an integrated system of production of use value. The agricultural surplus, S^*, now flows to the capitalist manufacturing centers to be used as capital, and the activity in which C was produced earlier withers away. Instead, C' is now produced within the capitalist sector a part of which finds a market in agriculture where it is sold for S^*.

In other words, primitive accumulation results in the separation of industry and agriculture. The separation, an inevitable consequence of primitive accumulation, however is not brought about once and for all. Until the capitalist sector comes entirely on its own, it has to rely from time to time on rural handicrafts and petty production for processing the raw materials up to a certain point. "If it destroys [the handicrafts] in one form, in particular branches, at certain points, it calls them up again elsewhere, because it needs them for the preparation of raw material up to a certain point."[6] Only when industry is sufficiently modernized that it is capable of bringing about the entire transformation of raw material within the system of capitalist production, that the rural domestic industry finally disappears and the industry–agriculture separation is completed.

The point that we need to take note of, and this is in a sense the central message of the discussion on primitive accumulation, is that primitive accumulation refers to the process of capitalization of the means of production. There is a tendency among both political economists and the historians of capitalism to interpret primitive accumulation solely as the process of expropriation of the peasantry from land. But that process alone is not what constitutes the idea of primitive accumulation. It is the loss of access suffered by the peasantry to means of production other than land (i.e., means of subsistence, raw materials)—an estrangement that results from their expropriation from land—that the idea of primitive accumulation tries to grasp. It is a process that alienated producers from the entire set of conditions within which they had existed as direct producers.

Modalities of Power

The primitive accumulation is a process marked with the exercise of power in its various forms and strategies; an inquiry into the history of the process brings them within sight. As stated in the preceding section, my purpose is to interpret development as a regime of power and the early phase of development as a depoliticized version of primitive accumulation. In order to do that, it is essential to delineate the forms and modalities of power that are integral to primitive accumulation.

In the entire process of dispossession of the peasantry and capitalization of the means of production, the state acted as an explicit power organ of capital. The juridical power of the state—the power to restructure property relations and entitlements, and to act as the fiscal authority—was deployed to bring about the structural changes that were necessary for the inauguration of the capitalist system of production. In the sphere of fiscal policy, the state exercised its power in terms of three instruments that served as the levers of primitive accumulation: taxes, public debt, and protection provided to the domestic capitalist sector. The structure of taxes imposed by the state was biased against the pre-capitalist sector, which undermined its economic viability, leading to its bankruptcy. Public debt promised annuity that was financed out of the revenues of regressive taxation and the consequent redistribution of income in favor of the new bourgeoisie led to further dissolution of the artisan sector. And finally, the state provided protected markets to the domestic capitalist industry by using tariffs and other import restrictions to keep the foreign competitors away. Put together, these three instruments created the conditions for estrangement of labor and capitalization of the means of production.

In the sphere of property relations, it was by using the juridical power that the state restructured rights and entitlements to create the new regime of private property. Not only was the peasant denied the right over land that he had traditionally enjoyed, the state sanctified the private property right over the means of production by explicitly exercising its coercive power against encroachment. While it helped to establish the regime of bourgeois property as the precondition for the system of capitalist production, at the same time, it served another important purpose: by ruling out the various ways people could acquire subsistence in the earlier regime, it created conditions under which they could subsist only within the capitalist system of production. The newly emerged proletariat had double freedom: freedom from feudal bondage and freedom from property. But while the first was a real freedom, the flip side of the second was unfreedom: subjugation to capital.

Destruction of all forms of self-provisioning was as important a purpose of primitive accumulation as the capitalization of the means of labor. In the *Ancien Régime*, there were common properties to which people had right of access (right of free pasture, wood-collecting, hunting) and these accesses allowed the poor to provide for themselves and their families for subsistence. In addition to this, property rights were somewhat fuzzy at the borderline and there was a certain degree of non-applications of rules and non-observance of legal rights at the margin. In other words, there was a certain degree of "tolerated illegality" that was a condition for the "political and economic functioning of the society" (Foucault 1979: 82). The space provided by this illegality of rights allowed the lower strata of the society to acquire subsistence by transgressing the rights to property.

The new regime of property rejected all these illegal practices, viewing them simply as theft and therefore punishable crimes. Protection of private property—with its clearly defined boundary and the right to exclude—by the coercive power of the state now meant the usurpation of the entire space of self-provisioning by transgression and encroachment. Foucault in *Discipline and Punish* offers a fascinating account of this restructuring of the economy of illegality with the emergence of the capitalist production economy.

The story of primitive accumulation in England is usually told against the backdrop of the Enclosure. However, it was not the eviction of the peasantry from their land that alone constituted the process of primitive accumulation. It was a process in which an entire ensemble of structural changes, encompassing every sphere of the economic and social life, was brought about by the systematic exercise of the juridical power of the state with the aim of positing capitalist production as the only sphere where the material conditions of life could be reproduced. In other words, it was a process of ruling out the myriad ways of ensuring subsistence that the pre-capitalist order permitted.

An interesting example of this application of the juridical power to rule out alternative ways of self-provisioning is the case of game laws in England. Hunting had always been a source of food for people and their families, but in the middle of the 18th century, England made the then existing game laws more severe, and their enforcement harsher. The new law prohibited everybody except the nobility—which accounted for only one percent of the population— from hunting and thus denied people an important means of subsistence. The bourgeoisie too, despite its wealth, was subjected to the same prohibition, but the new law ultimately served the purpose of the bourgeoisie by negating one of the conditions of acquiring subsistence outside the sphere of capitalist production. As Perelman puts it:

> Although their(*sic*) origin of the game laws was indeed feudal, they evolved with the changing class structure of British Society. In the end, one of the most hated institutions of feudalism, long remembered in the legend for leading Robin Hood onto a path of crime, became an important ingredient of capitalist development. (1983: 52)

The Poor Law was another example of entitlement to subsistence that allowed the poor to a certain level of consumption if his income fell short of the standard that was considered the minimum. The Law was now seen as a fetter on the movement of labor because each person was entitled to the assistance only within the parish he/ she was domiciled in. If he/she was absent for more than a year, he/ she was to lose his entitlement in the old parish and to claim it in the one he/she had moved in. This acted as a disincentive on the one hand for the worker to leave his/her own parish, and on the other for the employer to employ someone for a year or more. The Law was changed to severely restrict those entitlements and the austerity of the new Poor Law forced workers to move in search of employment.[7]

An entire system comprised various forms of entitlements to subsistence, both legal and illegal, was thus withdrawn to goad people towards wage-employment for capitalist production. Primitive accumulation is not the story only of driving direct producers out from their land. It was a process that extracted people, through the coercive power of the state, from their life-world. It was the world, the known environment, in which they had traditionally lived and subsisted, not merely by producing articles of use value but also by gleaning and garnering in the fuzzy zone of law and property right. In this process, the character and modality of the sovereign power also underwent a fundamental change, from its pre-capitalist form to a new form of control and punishment that was in consonance with the emergent bourgeois order. In the old regime, power exercised by a multiplicity of authorities was marked with inertia, and punishment of violation of property and rights was spectacular but at the same time selective, discontinuous, and haphazard. With the emergence of the new regime, " [it] became necessary to define a strategy and techniques of punishment in which an economy of continuity and permanence would replace that of expenditure and excess" (Foucault 1979: 87). In other words, it was a new technology of power based on continuous policing and surveillance.

Destruction of the entire structure of pre-capitalist entitlements and closing of the channels through which people could gather subsistence were, however, not enough to ensure that the dispossessed of the earlier regime would turn into wage-laborer. Although bereft of all means of subsistence other than the sale of their labor power, the dispossessed refused to surrender to the rule of capitalist production by shunning wage-employment, and instead resorted to beggary, crime, and vagrancy. It was a peculiar but an extremely powerful form of resistance to the rule of capital. The shadowy and fearsome figure of the tramp, the vagabond and the beggar, who lived on the borderline of casual employment and petty crime, invaded the social space that the new bourgeois regime was seeking to organize, structure, and bring under its own command. It constituted a distinct domain for the deployment of the juridical power. Nowhere were the coercive instruments of the state more explicitly and more brutally used than in the case of coercing these inhabitants of the fringe of the economy and society, the limbo space between the old and the new regimes. A series of draconian laws were passed in Europe, that Marx termed "the bloody legislations against the proletariat", prohibiting beggary and vagrancy and subjecting those engaged in them to severe punishment. According to a legislation in England under Henry VIII in 1530, beggars unable to work received a beggar's license but "sturdy vagabonds" were to be whipped and imprisoned and forced to put themselves to labor. In 1572 during Elizabeth's reign, unlicensed beggars were to be severely flogged unless someone was willing to take them into service for two years. "Thus were the agricultural people, first expropriated from the soil, driven from their homes, turned into vagabonds, and then whipped, branded, tortured by laws grotesquely terrible, into the discipline necessary for the wage system".[8] Capital's claim that it liberated these people from feudal bondages and opened for them the doors of the "free world of capital" sounds ironic in view of the fact that they were literally whipped into the that new world of "freedom".

Of no less importance was the fact that there was also an ethico-moral justification of this coercive power of the state. The violence of the state against those who refused to accept wage-slavery was sanctioned by a new discourse that extolled "labor" and berated "idleness". Work, in the sense it is understood in today's modern society, was an invention of this period, an invention of capital; it was the new ideology of the bourgeoisie and its ethic of work that posited labor as the expression of a man's worth and honor, and idleness as degrading and demeaning (Gorz 1989). Never before capital's emergence had labor been given the status of being the center of social integration. It was the bourgeoisie that sought social integration around the concept of labor—the capacity of the human body to produce goods by acting upon nature—that at the same time was the source of profit for capital. Thus idleness was the negation of the very basis of capital, and it had to be demolished ideologically by positing labor as moral in opposition to indolence as immoral. The role played by the houses of confinement was primarily one of inculcating this ideology. The houses, apart from suppressing beggary, idleness, and vagrancy, also forced the confined to work, to engage in manufacturing activities such as weaving and knitting, although it was in most cases economically unprofitable. But despite the lack of economic viability, it served to establish a certain ethic of work.

> ...[In] this very failure, the classical period conducted an irreducible experiment. What appears to us today as a clumsy dialectic of production and prices then possessed its real meaning as a certain ethical consciousness of labor, in which the difficulties of the economic mechanism lost their urgency in favor of an affirmation of value. (Foucault 1988: 55)

This ethical consciousness of labor was central to the ideology of the ascending bourgeoisie, of the capital in arising. Viewing labor not merely in terms of the wealth it produced but in terms of an ethical transcendence actually served to establish the conditions of capitalist production by providing an ideological justification of the coercive methods adopted to turn the dispossessed into wage-laborer for the capitalist system of production. The ideology of work espoused by the bourgeoisie was an integral element of primitive accumulation.

The state power in its juridical form, however, was not the only form of power that made primitive accumulation and the emergence of the capitalist mode of production possible. Parallel to the coercive power of the state, a regime of what Foucault calls the "capillary form of power" was at work that sought to discipline the society by subjecting the human body to a network of continuous surveillance at various micro sites: school, hospital, and workshops. It was a non-sovereign, disciplinary power that operated outside the domain of the sovereign–subject relation, and this disciplinary mechanism combined with legislations and juridical controls to form the entire field where power was to be exercised for ensuring the conditions of the emergence of capital and produce "docile bodies" as the source of surplus value.

In sum, the entire process of primitive accumulation and the emergence of capital in England in particular and Europe in general was marked with the explicit and brutal exercise of power in both its macro-juridical as well as its micro-capillary forms. An array of instruments of coercion were deployed to divorce direct producers from their means of production and entitlements to subsistence, and to force them into the space of capitalist production as wage-laborer, as producers of surplus value. The nature and modalities of power were essentially prohibitive and restrictive: it excluded, suppressed, silenced, and denied. It was power in its negative form, power that worked by saying "no".

An understanding of the nature and forms of power associated with primitive accumulation is particularly important for us. When I presented the contours of my story of the third world capital and the trajectory of its post-colonial developmental experience—a story that I seek to unfold in the rest of this book—I claimed that there has been a shift in the development discourse since the 1970s that can be interpreted as *a strategy of political management of the wasteland by having recourse to a reversal of primitive accumulation.* I will detail it in the following chapters but what I want to take note of at this point is that the notion of development as provision of basic needs involves the deployment of a form of power whose techniques are fundamentally different from the ones that primitive accumulation was based on. It is a different mode of power that does not operate in terms of denial and suppression; it is a power that is productive and creative, it constructs and enlivens subjectivities rather than impede them. This is a mode of power that Foucault in his *History of Sexuality* calls "bio-power". It operates in terms of two modalities. The first modality, the capillary form of power that we have already mentioned, disciplines human multiplicities through their spatial distribution and continuous surveillance at micro-sites such as prison, hospital, etc. And the second modality involves governmentalization of the social life by bringing the entire population under the panoply of disciplinary techniques and production of subjects that interiorize the disciplinary mechanism and rearticulates it from within, animating thoughts and practices that conform to the socially sanctioned norms. In other words, bio-power is a form that applies itself on life in its en-tirety, organizing, and reproducing it from within.

The basic need-based approach to development rests on this productive mechanism of power in contrast to its prohibitive and restrictive mechanism. The purpose of developmental interventions in this case is to create and extend, rather than destroy and withdraw as in the case of primitive accumulation, entitlements outside the capitalist space for the excluded and the marginal. For example, efforts on the part of the international developmental organizations to partially revive subsistence farming for the African peasants, which shrank in the face of cash-crop production, are aimed at ensuring food security and self-provisioning where capitalist development fails to deliver in terms of employment and entitlements. Similarly, the employment strategy currently promoted by these organizations is highlighting the prospect of "self-employment" as distinct from wage-employment in the capitalist sector, and the dominant argument is in favor of providing resources to the unemployed in order to enable them to "fend for themselves". While the "bloody legislations" forced the dispossessed into capitalist production by denying him any other subjectivity or means of subsistence, here in the post-colonial scenario, power is operating in terms of the elaborate apparatuses of development management to keep the poor away from the factory gate by producing the "self-employed" and "subsistence peasant" as the subjects of bio-power. And here lies the complexity of development as a regime of power. It is productive in that it produces subjectivities, but at the same time it confines these new subjects to a peripheral space outside the space of capital. It is a regime constituted by an implosion of the restrictive and productive forms of power. But let us postpone this discussion till Chapter 5 and get back to the story that we are trying to build up step by step.

In what follows, I engage in a symptomatic reading of the core of the literature on economic development produced in the early phase of the emergence and consolidation of the discourse. As I said at the beginning of this chapter, my purpose is to interpret the initial moment of the discourse as an attempt to de-politicize primitive accumulation and present it as the development process. Despite their many differences in emphasis and orientations, the entire body of writings by the early architects of development economics in the 1950s and 1960s, I argue, converged to exorcise the process of capitalist accumulation of the conflicts and contradictions that inhere in it, to obliterate from the discursive field the fierce political battle that must be fought to clear the space in which the initial conditions for sustained capitalist accumulation can be ensured. In other words, the early vision of development sought to efface the stamp of power and coercion that the Western capital carried in the era of its arising and re-inscribed the same story in the third world landscape as a politically neutral project for the latter's emergence from economic backwardness and poverty. I will interpret the early form of the development discourse as a hegemonic articulation, in the sense of Laclau and Mouffe (discussed in Chapter 2), with surplus, accumulation, and growth as the chosen set of privileged nodal points. In terms of these nodal points, the meaning of the otherwise decentered and floating elements that constitute the economy (labor, production, market, the state, etc.) are provisionally arrested to produce the "economy" as a contingently stable totality. Our purpose is precisely to demonstrate that the notion of the economy, of under-development and of the development process in the early development literature are all products of a particular discursive articulation, a hegemonic representational strategy, and it is this very strategy that depoliticizes primitive accumulation and presents it as a politically neutral process of developmental planning.

Inauguration of the Discourse:
De-politicization as a Political Strategy

Development as a Political Project

Escobar asserts at the beginning of *Encountering Development* that the development discourse that emerged in the 1950s was not a moment of an epistemic trajectory but a historically specific project of the Western powers in general and the US in particular in the post world war II scenario. The aim of the project was to once again establish the dominance of the developed capitalist countries of the West over the once colonized regions of the world after their formal decolonization. The discursive constitution of the third world and the idea of development marked a "cognitive colonization" of imagination about society and change, a novel form of control very different from what the colonial world had experienced. The inauguration of the discourse of development was in this sense a political project of extending the dominance of the West over the non-Western world, and also an important constituent of the Cold War politics.

If we take a quick look at what was happening in the green room before the curtain was raised for the development drama, we would see that the discourse of development was driven by concrete and explicit political concerns of the Western powers at the particular historical conjuncture of the 1950s. George Rosen in his *Western Economists and Eastern Societies*, a documentary history of the Ford Foundation's role in inaugurating development planning in South Asia in the period spanning 1950 to 1970, brings to our notice the report of the committee formed in 1949, headed by Rowan Gaither. The purpose of the committee was to examine what the Ford Foundation could do in the interest of the underdeveloped regions of the world. The report in its introduction expressed deep concern about the threat of another world war and suggested that the US must act to eradicate the widespread poverty and deprivation in those regions, the factors that constituted the threat.

> Half the people of the world are either starving or lack adequate food.... Such conditions produce unrest and social instability, and these, when aggravated by ignorance and misinformation, produce acclimate conducive of conflict.

The comparative good fortune which favors this country enables it to help mitigate these conditions. (Quoted by Rosen 1985: 3)

More specifically, the purpose of developmental intervention was to fight the spread of communism:

As the tide of communism mounts in Asia and Europe the position of the United States is crucial. We are striving at great cost to strengthen free people everywhere. The need of such people, particularly in underdeveloped areas, are vastly and seemingly endless, yet *their eventual well-being may prove essential to our security.* To improve their living standard they must import and use knowledge, guidance and capital. The United States appears to be the only country able to provide even a part of the urgently needed assistance. (Quoted by Rosen 1985: 4, my emphasis)

This is an unconcealed, overt admission that the concern about development of the third world stemmed, not so much from an altruistic, humanitarian concern, as from the urgency to launch a battle against communism and establish political control over the newly decolonized countries. If President Truman's speech at the UN inaugurated the discursive construction of the third world as "poor and underdeveloped", and prepared the conditions for its subjugation to a network of developmental interventions brought into play by knowledge–power, there is little doubt that this inauguration of development as a regime of power was animated by a historically specific, concrete political concern. It was primarily driven by the political imperatives of the struggle for dominance, given the international configuration of power at that particular historical juncture. In short, developmentalism was a political project from the very beginning.

To avoid misunderstanding, let me clarify here that the understanding of development as a political project does not mean that purposeful interventions in the economic sphere for the betterment of people's lives are any less desirable. The point that is being made here is that developmental practices cannot be separated from the logic of the politics in which they are embedded. If this "embeddedness" is kept out of sight, and the practices are posited as an independent object of analysis, we cannot grasp the dynamics of the development discourse because the shifts within the discourse—the changes in the statements made about development and the practices they animate—are inextricably related to the question of power, dominance, and hegemony. It is only by locating development, however benevolent and welfarist it may be, in the political terrain that we can understand why developmental practices are what they are. That precisely is our purpose.

The idea of strategically deploying the paradigm of development in the struggle for global hegemony, however, did not dawn on the architects of the international capitalist economic order until the beginning of the 1950s. Only a few years earlier, in 1944, the Bretton Woods Conference had been organized by the US and Britain, under the intellectual leadership provided by Keynes, in which the three international organizations—the International Monetary Fund, the World Bank (then known as the International Bank for Reconstruction and Development) and the International Trade Organization—were proposed, and their modalities and areas of operation deliberated. These organizations were conceived by both the US and Britain entirely as ones that would ensure smooth functioning of a world monetary system and the availability of finance for post war reconstruction. And development was nowhere on the agenda of the two organizations. As Gerald Meier (1984) informs us, Keynes vehemently opposed the inclusion of twenty-one less developed countries among the invited because in his opinion they had "nothing to contribute" and would "merely encumber the ground" (p. 11). Not surprisingly, no attention was paid to the issue of development in the discussions on the role of the Bank and its areas of operation. The Mexican delegation was the only one to strongly argue in favor of having a developmental perspective in the Bank's agenda and, with the support of Cuba and Columbia, submitted a draft amendment to the Bank's charter; it included the amendment but only after watering it down to the point of insignificance. "For those providing the major contribution to the Bank", writes Meier, "the immediacy and urgency of reconstruction effort clearly dominated the more distant vision of development" (p. 14).

It is interesting to note that even Lord Keynes with his proverbial wisdom and foresight failed to anticipate the shape of things to come; in only five years following the conference, the priorities for the architects of the international economic order changed radically. In President Roosevelt's Bretton Woods, concern for reconstruction of the war ravaged Europe stubbornly prevailed over the urgency of development of the LDCs, but one only had to wait until 1949 to hear President Truman reversing the priority by placing development at the center of the agenda with all the international organizations perceived as vehicles of the development mission. The story of Ford Foundation told by George Rosen was not an exception; it was the general trend.

The inauguration, consolidation, and dissemination of the development discourse were thus deeply implicated in the global politics of power from the time of its very inception. Although it seems somewhat paradoxical, the primary concern of this political project was to present development as a totally depoliticized process. It is this attempted depoliticization of economic and social transformation in the third world that constituted the very politics of global hegemony throughout the entire period of the Cold War. In the following sections, I will critically engage with the early theories of development economics with the aim of demonstrating how the discourse exorcized economic development of its political dimensions to reduce it almost to a problem of classical mechanics to be solved by the "politically neutral" apparatuses of planning.

Capital Formation and the Mechanics of Development

The emergence of development economics in the early 1950s as a distinct field of inquiry was premised on the consensus among economists about the inadequacy of the then existing framework of economic theory for grasping the phenomenon of underdevelopment. It was widely felt that the mainstream theories of micro and macro-economics, public finance and economic growth, designed and developed to address problems of developed economies, lacked explanatory power when faced with the task of characterizing economic formations of the less developed countries. A different theoretical framework with its own set of concepts and categories was needed to analyze the state of underdevelopment, identify its structure and the elements that constitute it, and to formulate strategies for triggering off the process of economic growth to enable the underdeveloped economies to break with their present state.

Among the early architects of development economics were Nurkse, Rosenstein–Rodan, Hirchman, Leibenstein, and Lewis; they together produced a body of writings that constituted the early discourse.

Although there were differences in their approaches and emphases, their writings on development shared one common characteristic: extrication of the process of development from the problematic of power, i.e. the political process in which it is embedded. This embeddedness was something that the classical economists were deeply aware of and which they in fact highlighted. In contrast, the early development economics portrayed economic development as a politically neutral exercise of rational calculation and planning. Leibenstein introduces his book *Economic Backwardness and Economic Growth*, by stating that his purpose is:

> "[To] look at the matter as a purely intellectual problem .... This approach may lead not only to a formulation in highly abstract terms but also to one that *abstracts the intellectual problem from its broader social and political setting.*"
>
> "The abstract, non-empirical and non-historicist approach is specially congenial to the individual worker who is interested in the development problem as a whole. The problem of explaining the disparities in per capita income is an historical as well as an analytical one. [It] would certainly be convenient if we could frame our problem in such a way as to *take intellectual question out of its historical context*" (p. 3, my emphasis)

The early theories strove to understand economic backwardness in terms of a "low level equilibrium trap" or "vicious circle of poverty" in which low income generates low savings and investment, which in turn reinforces low productivity and therefore reproduces the initial low income. The state of underdevelopment is the result of this circular causation. The argument that follows is that only a "critical minimum effort" or a "big-push" in terms of a massive dose of investment can extricate the economy from the bog of backwardness and place it on a path of self-sustained growth (Leibenstein 1957, Rosenstein–Rodan 1943). The root cause of underdevelopment therefore is the lack of capital and the only solution to the problem is rapid capital formation.

It is interesting to note in this context that Rosenstein–Rodan's seminal article addressing the question of industrialization in Eastern and South Eastern Europe was written in 1943, in the middle of the world war II and several years before the Warsaw Pact. It began with the explicit recognition of the need to chalk out a strategy for industrialization for those regions, a strategy that would be fundamentally different from the Soviet model of self-sufficient, heavy industry oriented growth. More specifically, the purpose was to integrate the Eastern European economy into the global capitalist order dominated by the US because "the existing heavy industries in the US, Great Britain, Germany, France, and Switzerland could certainly supply all the needs of international depressed areas" (p. 247). The urgency to posit a development trajectory that was not only an alternative but actually opposed to the trajectory followed by the Soviet Union only betrays the political nature of the development discourse. Its primary purpose was to resist the spread of communism, and development economists, as the vehicle of the discourse, in effect acted as functionaries of this political project.

Let us return to the notion of the "low-level trap" and "big push" and the need for rapid capital formation. In this formulation, the entire problem is reduced to relations among quantitative variables such as income, consumption, saving, investment, and the growth rate of population. The forces that result in economic backwardness are represented solely in terms of a set of relationship among these variables, and self-sustained economic growth is a matter of an arithmetic involving saving, investment, and the capital–output ratio (Singer 1952). The mode of production, distribution, and utilization of economic surplus in the underdeveloped economic formation, and the configuration of property and power relations on which it rests, appear nowhere in this formulation. Almost in the spirit of classical mechanics, development economics focused on a set of apolitical, asocial, as if natural forces, acting against each other, producing a state of stagnation as a self-perpetuating equilibrium. And only an exogenous force, a big-push, from outside could unsettle the inertia generated by the existing constellation of forces and catapult the system onto a trajectory of self-sustaining economic growth. The task of development economics was to calculate the size, intensity, and the mode of application of the exogenous shock. It is almost like calculating how much force is required, and how to exert it, to provide the push to a spaceship in order to enable it to escape earth's gravitational pull.

The "shoe factory problem", presented originally by Rosenstein–Rodan (1943) and later by Nurkse (1952), now a part of the folklore of development economics that can be seen as an illustration of the exorcism of development of its political content. An entrepreneur decides to set up a shoe factory by hiring wage-laborers, and he/she faces a problem. The problem is that the workers will naturally spend an insignificant fraction of their wage-income on the shoes they produce, spending most of it to acquire other articles of consumption. But the owner of the factory must be able to sell the entire output if he is to realize the profit. Therefore, the factory can be set up only if there is demand for shoes from people who do not earn their income from the shoe factory. In other words, a fraction of the income generated in the rest of the economy must be spend on shoes produced in the factory to make the factory a viable project; it can not emerge in isolation entirely on its own. The inevitable conclusion then is that investment decisions must be made simultaneously in different industries so that they can act as complements of each other by mutually providing each other's market. Thus there is a strong case for "balanced growth".

Development economists have spent a significant quantum of analytical energy trying to characterize the shoe-factory problem as a case of "no–industry–Nash–equilibrium", an explanation of continued reproduction of the state of underdevelopment. We have already discussed in the preceding sections how the destruction of direct production and self-provisioning served as the precondition for the emergence of the social division of labor associated with the capitalist mode of production. In an economy inhabited solely by direct producers who can produce their own consumption articles, there can be no capitalist production because the value produced in the capitalist enterprise will remain unrealized. No capitalist factory, shoe or umbrella, is viable under this condition. Proletarianization of the direct producers, their estrangement from the conditions of production, rules out self-provisioning and creates the market for the capitalist sector. In the case of Russia, this precisely was the issue, i.e., the decline of petty production in the old *obschina* in the face of capitalist development over which Lenin and the Narodniks so fiercely debated.

Of course, once a capitalist sector has already emerged, a problem of disproportionality can arise within the capitalist sector itself due to over-investment in one branch of production and under-investment in another. Rosenstein–Rodan's shoe-factory problem can be interpreted as referring to such disproportionality.[9] But it cannot serve as an explanation of underdevelopment and the non-emergence of the capitalist system of production. Development means the initiation of the self-reproducing and self-expanding process of (private/state) capitalist production. It requires as a precondition the reconfiguration of the relations of power that constitutes underdevelopment and restructuring of its property relations so that capitalist production becomes viable, and these are the inescapable political conditions that must be met if the development process is to be unleashed. The formulation of the development problem in terms of the forces of mechanics and their static and dynamic balances and coordination keeps the politics of systemic change completely out of sight and presents it as a problem to be solved by "experts". No political or social agency has any role to play in this project.

However, it is precisely these formulations of the development problem that underscore the point that we are sparing no pains to make. The construction of development as a discourse began in the middle of the last century and development economics served as the center around which the discourse organized itself. The discourse was animated by the political imperatives of the Cold War, by the need to subject the "third world" to the control of the developed West. But the strategy adopted in this game of power was to present developmental interventions as benign, apolitical, and ideologically neutral. The stated purpose of the discourse was, as indicated at the beginning of this chapter, to re-enact the development trajectory that the West had already experienced, but with a crucial difference. Capitalist development in the West, its journey from the *Ancien Régime* to an industrial society, from tradition to modernity, was to be purged of its political dimensions and presented as a matter of techno-bureaucratic planning exercise. The depoliticization of development was the very strategy of the new regime of power, and a reading of development economics as a discourse brings this new modality of power into visibility. In what follows, I am going to concentrate on Arthur Lewis' seminal article of 1954, titled *Economic Development with Unlimited Supply of Labor*—which probably is the most celebrated and frequently cited article in the writings on economic development—interpret it as a discursive construction and then interrogate its representation of the economy.

The reason I choose Lewis is that in his work one gets a fully-blown picture of the early vision of economic development as a process of transformation and my purpose is to demonstrate that the Lewis model is a discursive construction with *accumulation* as

nodal point (in the sense of Laclau–Mouffe) that produces the economy as a contingent totality by provisionally fixing the meaning of
its instances and places capital and pre-capital in a hierarchy. And
we can characterize this as the first of the three moments, as stated
in the end of Chapter 2, of the hegemony of development as a discourse. An interrogation of his representation of the economy also
brings to light that the particular representational strategy adopted
by Lewis allows him to present the process of primitive accumulation
as a politically neutral process of development in a dual economy.
In short, the purpose of our discourse analysis is to politicize the
Lewis' narrative of (capitalist) development.

Accumulation as Development: the Dual Economy of Lewis and the First Moment of Hegemony

The vision of the economy marked by dualism can be traced back
to the writings of J.H Boeke on the colonial economy of the Dutch
Indonesia. Boeke (1953) observed that the Indonesian economy
consisted of two distinct sub-economies, with different structures,
organized by different calculations and motivations. There was a
modern Western economy driven by individualism, rationality, and
capitalist calculations, and a traditional economy characterized by
limited needs, backward bending supply curve of labor, and unre-
sponsiveness to market incentives. This dualism, Boeke argued, was
not so much a creation of colonialism *per se* as of capitalist penetration in a traditional economic formation.[10] On a more general
level, the concept of cultural and social dualism was quite prevalent
in the representation of the colonial history. As Meier informs us, a
history of nineteenth-century Jamaica, entitled *Two Jamaicas*, highlighted the simultaneous presence of two cultures, two ways of
life in the African Jamaica and the Western Jamaica (1984: 151).
Early reports by international developmental organizations also emphasized that the most important feature of the African economies
was the coexistence of a traditional economic system and a modern
exchange system. Development of these economies, the reports
stressed, meant an expansion of the "money economy", its encroachment on the traditional sector and the eventual withering away of
the latter.

The strength of Lewis' 1954 article, and the reason why it is still
regarded by development economists as the pioneering treatise on

economic dualism, consists in the fact that it offers a comprehensive and detailed description of the dual economy, theoretically far more rigorous than what these reports present. Instead of conceptualizing dualism in terms of the presence or absence of monetization and exchange, Lewis, in the spirit of Boeke's anatomy of the Indonesian economy, goes beyond the sphere of circulation and locates the basis of dualism in the sphere of production, in the forms, organizations and conditions of production. For him, the dual economy is marked by the simultaneous presence of a "subsistence/traditional" sector and a "capitalist/modern" sector. In his characterization,

> The capitalist sector is that part of the economy which uses reproducible capital and pays capitalists for the use thereof. This coincides with Smith's definition of the productive workers, who are those who work with capital and whose product can therefore be sold at a price above their wages..... [The] use of capital is controlled by capitalists, who hire the services of labour."
> (1954: 407)

The capitalist sector is thus one in which the capitalist, who controls capital, hires laborers to work with that capital and to him accrues the surplus, i.e., the difference between the value produced in the activity and the wage-bill. The surplus takes the form of profit and the guiding principle for this sector is the calculation of profit and its maximization. Labor is employed only up to that point where the maximum surplus (or profit) is obtained. The specificity of the capitalist sector lies, Lewis asserts, not just in the production of surplus but also in the mode of its utilization. The capitalist uses the surplus to create new capital, both of the fixed and circulating variety, so that a larger number of laborers can be employed in the next round of production. Put differently, production of surplus in the capitalist sector is for accumulation of capital and the specificity of this sector is grounded in the drive for accumulation.

Lewis' capitalist/modern sector thus has two distinct features that distance it from the rest of the economy: production of surplus by workers employed on the basis of capital, and utilization of that surplus to create additional capital. It is a sector defined in terms of wage-labor, profit and the expanded reproduction of capital.

Here we should also take note of the fact that by "capitalist" Lewis means not just private capitalist but state capitalist as well. When the modern sector is state-owned, profit takes the form of surplus generated in the state sector, however, the rationale and the dynamics of the sector remain the same. In fact, "[t]he state capitalist can accumulate capital even faster than the private capitalist, since he can use for the purpose not only the profit of the capitalist sector, but also what he can force or tax out of the subsistence sector." (1954: 419)

In contradistinction to the capitalist sector, Lewis posits the rest of the economy as the subsistence/traditional sector:

> "[the] subsistence sector is by difference all that part of the economy which is not using reproducible capital. Output per head is lower in this sector because it is not *fructified by capital*. This is why it was called 'unproductive' the distinction between productive and unproductive labor had nothing to do with whether the work yielded utility, as some neo-classicists have scornfully but erroneously asserted." (*ibid.*: 408, my emphasis)

The distinguishing feature of the subsistence economy is the absence of reproducible capital. This, however, does not mean that the producers use no instruments in their production activities. What is absent is capital as the basis of employment of wage-labor as in the capitalist sector. When Lewis uses the phrase "fructification by capital", he is referring to the production of surplus that capital extracts from wage-labor, and the subsistence sector is one in which such extraction is ruled out.

What then is the distinguishing feature of this sector? According to Lewis, it is the presence of *surplus labor*. A significant fraction of those inhabiting this sector, although apparently working, have no contribution to the production at the margin. Inhabitants of this sector share the total labor required for production and also the income that is generated. This means that every worker is underemployed, but he receives the average income that allows him to subsist, and if some of these underemployed workers are withdrawn from the sector, the remaining ones can work more and easily perform the same amount of labor so that the output will not suffer any decline. In other words, it is a sector marked by the presence of latent surplus labor that can be siphoned without causing any contraction of the sector in terms of output.

Thus, the dual economy, on the one hand, has a self-expanding, dynamic capitalist sector where accumulation of capital can continuously expand the employment of surplus-producing workers, and a subsistence sector serving as a pool of surplus labor that can potentially be transferred to self-sustaining, capital-based employment in the former. In this scenario, Lewis describes the process of development as one in which the capitalist sector expands, drawing labor, and resources from the subsistence sector. If capitalists offer a wage rate that is a little higher than the subsistence income, laborers will respond to it and move to the capitalist sector. The migration causes no reduction in the output in the subsistence sector, but since those who move had entitlement to their subsistence income, the transfer entails a marketable surplus of wage goods for those employed in the capitalist sector. The dynamic capitalist sector expands without causing any strain on the subsistence sector until the pool of surplus labor is exhausted.[11] However, the process of development is also the process of withering away of the subsistence sector. When the entire pool of surplus labor is withdrawn, the subsistence sector ceases to have the characteristics that distinguished it from the capitalist sector and ultimately gets transformed after the image of the latter.

Economy as a Provisional Totality

Having delineated the contours of Lewis' dual economy, we are now in a position to explore how his narrative of transition and development "produces the economy" through discursive articulation. We recall that in our conceptualization of hegemony, economic entities acquire provisional fixity only within a totality produced by discursive articulation around privileged nodal points, and the act of producing the contingent totality is what we have defined as hegemonic practice. Being contingent and provisional, the meanings and the hegemonic totality within which they are articulated, are always susceptible to subversion.

How is the *economy*, in which Lewis' development process occurs, constituted? The entire narrative of transition, of the process of transferring surplus labor from the subsistence to the capitalist sector, is presented around the notion of surplus, investment, and accumulation. Accumulation is the privileged nodal point around which the other elements of the economy are organized, and their meanings fixed. For example, *production* as such does not have one fixed meaning; it may be seen as an act of material transformation for the direct satisfaction of needs; it may also mean production for market where the sole purpose of exchange is consumption; and of course it may be seen as an activity with the purpose of producing a surplus for accumulation. When Lewis chooses accumulation as the nodal point and posits the capitalist sector as *productive* in contrast to the *unproductive* subsistence sector, the meaning of *production* is discursively fixed; it is understood as the activity in which a surplus is produced for accumulation. The other possible meanings are not entirely obliterated but devalued and demoted as characteristics of production in the subsistence sector. In a similar vein, *labor* is posited as productive only if it is estranged from the means of labor and produces an additional value, over and above its own maintenance, for the employer. Purposive labor-producing use-value is a feature of the subsistence economy and therefore associated with stagnation and underdevelopment. *Market* as a process through which labor, raw materials, and wage-goods are made to flow from the subsistence to the surplus-producing capitalist sector is accorded a privilege by the discourse while its role as a site where direct producers exchange their use-values is pushed out of focus.

The discourse thus organizes the *economy as a totality* around accumulation by positing the various instances of the economy in terms of their capacity to support and facilitate the accumulation process. It is a provisional totality in the sense that the other meanings of these instances are relegated to the subsistence sector that constitutes the outside of this totality. The representational strategy adopted by Lewis structures the space of development in a way that places capital and pre-capital in a hierarchy. Accumulation is seen as taking place only within the capitalist mode of production. The sole purpose of labor and production is to produce surplus (in the form of profit) for accumulation and therefore production activities undertaken, and labor performed, in the capitalist sector alone are in the interest of development. In short, capital is synonymous with development; it is the sector that contains all the developmental potentials. It is posited as a sector that is modern, advance, and dynamic, with an innate capability of expanding its ambit to ultimately subsume the entire economic space. Pre-capital, in contradistinction, is identified with underdevelopment; it is traditional, backward, stagnant, and incapable of retaining its own economic space in the face of capital's expansionary thrust.

Production in the traditional sector serves development only in so far as it makes available cheap wage goods for the advanced sector. The fact that non-capitalist production satisfies consumption needs carries negative implications for development since it does not generate surplus for accumulation. Exchange between the two sectors is only a channel through which labor and other resources can flow from the subsistence to the capitalist sector and also the product of the latter can be sold to the former for realization of the surplus as profit.

The identification of development with capitalist accumulation also fixes the meaning of the state, its role in the development process. A developmental state, Lewis argues, ought to use its instruments of coercive power for creating condition conducive to accumulation. For example, power of the state to create high-powered money is to be used to provide money capital to the organizers of capitalist production, or to create inflation that redistributes income in favor of profits, and therefore, of accumulation. With accumulation as the overarching logic of development, the discourse foregrounds the state as a facilitator of accumulation, and obliterates its other possible role as a provider of entitlements for consumption. In fact, systemic redistribution for the purpose of generating consumption entitlements is seen as a feature of the subsistence sector where the average subsistence income exceeds marginal productivity, and such redistribution is identified as unproductive utilization of surplus condemning the pre-capitalist economy to a state of stagnation.

The discursive articulation of the economy and the structuring of the space of development in relation to accumulation as the nodal point is what we can interpret as the first of the three moments of the hegemony process we identified at the end of Chapter 2. It is the case of simple hegemony in Gramscian sense when capital rules by its own agenda. When the development discourse conflates development and capitalist accumulation, the narrative of development coincides with the narrative of capital's arising, although the assumed political neutrality of the space of development depoliticized the arising of capital. The story of capital's arising is displaced from the politically contested terrain to the politically neutral terrain of development.

The hegemony in this case takes the form of explicit dominance of capital over pre-capital. In the discursive construct, capital and pre-capital are locked in a hierarchical predator–prey relation in which the former is strong, powerful, and permanent while the latter is its negation: weak, powerless, and transitory. Much like Edward Said's *orient* as the "other" of the *occident*, the pre-capitalist subsistence sector is constituted as the "other" of the capitalist sector, as what capital is not. The representation denies the subsistence sector any rationality of its own, subjects it to capitalist profit accounting and thereby renders a section of its inhabitants "redundant and surplus". The presence of surplus labor marks the "irrationality" of the subsistence sector, the reason why it is backward and stagnant. And development means the inevitable withering away of the stagnant and the backward in the face of the vigorous expansion and spread of the dynamics and the modern. The representation of development thus has a particular regime of capital inscribed in it—a regime in which the relationship between capital and pre-capital conforms to the notion of dominance that informs Gibson–Graham's work referred to in Chapter 1. It is a "capitalocentric" discourse in which the dominance of capital works through suppression, silencing, and demotion of pre-capital; capital here is characterized in terms of its strength and fullness in contrast to pre-capital's weakness and lack. (Gibson–Graham 1996)

The interpretation of capitalocentrism as hegemony calls for at least two clarifications. First, when we present the early development discourse as a hegemonic formation, we are interpreting hegemony as hegemony of a discourse and not of a class as in Gramsci. Chapter 1 began with the Gramscian notion of hegemony in which hegemony means persuasion as distinct from coercion. Let us recall that in the Gramscian conceptualization, the ruling class is hegemonic when it succeeds in projecting its own sectional interest as the universal interest and is able to elicit active consent of the subaltern classes; the ruler and the ruled are seen as particulars flowing from the same universal. Put differently, the Gramscian notion of hegemony is the dominance of one essence over another; the subaltern identifies with the essence of the ruler and sees himself after the ruler's image. And hegemony takes a complex form when the projected universal has to incorporate, besides the ruling class's own essence, some elements of the subaltern space. However, in both cases, hegemony serves to legitimize the order by hiding its inherent hierarchies. But in our framework, hegemony is a discursive practice that provisionally fixes the meanings of economic entities;

it is not the dominance of one essence over another as in Gramsci, but a provisional fixation of identities by arresting their floating character. It is by definition hegemony of a discourse, and not hegemony of any particular class with an essence of its own. But it is important to note that the hegemony of the discourse creates conditions within which a particular class-rule can reproduce itself. When we identify development as a hegemonic discourse, we do not reduce the space of development to the space in which the story of modes of production is inscribed. Development is an independent space and the structuring of that space around a particular set of nodal points allows capital to exercise its dominance over pre-capital. When the early development discourse articulates the economy in relation to accumulation, the two spaces apparently coincide and this is what we call the first moment of the hegemony process. But the implications of viewing development and capital as two distinct yet articulated spaces will be apparent as our analysis proceeds to consider the other moments of hegemony. We will then see that the conditions for capital self-reproduction can be ensured only if development asserts itself as an independent discourse with its own agenda.

Second, hegemony of the capitalocentric discourse of development does not hide hierarchies and dominance; on the contrary, it organizes the economy precisely in terms of the relations of dominance and subordination and legitimizes the hierarchy in the name of progress. Centrality of accumulation produces the economy as a provisional totality around the capitalist sector while the pre-capitalist subsistence sector is marked off as a dark zone that constitutes the outside of that totality—an outside that must be squeezed, bled, and ultimately allowed to wither away in the interest of capitalist accumulation. It is "simple hegemony" in the Gramscian sense since the dominance of capital is expressed in terms of its own agenda (accumulation) but hegemony here means legitimation of the predatory expansion of the domain of capital and the harnessing of the state and other institution of civil society for facilitating the process. Annihilation of the pre-capitalist formations is the goal that is set before the society and the discourse of development is hegemonic in that it is able to elicit consent to this project of annihilation. In other words, the first moment of hegemony is legitimized violence against pre-capital—violence backed by persuasion.

A specific technology of power, and an ideology legitimizing its deployment, accompanied the arising of capital in Western Europe, and the conditions of existence of the *Ancien Régime* were undermined in a systematic and concerted way. In the post-colonial context, the development discourse brings into play a similar technology of power to annihilate pre-capital, and the legitimation of this process of annihilation is ensured by truth effects produced by the discourse.

Dual Economy and Primitive Accumulation: What Happened to z-goods?

Although the representation of the economy posits the two sectors in terms of an explicit hierarchy, with one assigned the role of supplying resources and labor for the expansion of the other, the process of development in the dual economy as described by Lewis is a benign process in the sense that it involves frictionless transfer of "surplus labor" from unproductive to productive employment. When laborers in their present occupation contributes nothing to output are transferred to the productive capitalist sector, output in the latter increases with no concomitant reduction in output elsewhere. It involves no conflicts of interest, no political contradictions as long as the supply of labor at the given wage-rate, and of wage-goods and raw materials at given prices are unlimited. We will now interrogate this narrative of development to reveal the contradictions inherent in the process of industrialization in a dual economy, the politics of development that the narrative keeps out of sight. To do that, we first critically engage with the productive/unproductive binary used by Lewis.

Lewis is quite explicit about the fact that in envisaging the dual economy he is drawing upon his classical predecessors rather than the then prevailing neo-classical paradigm premised on efficient allocation of resources. More specifically, he invokes Adam Smith in making the distinction between the two sectors in terms of the concept of productive and unproductive labor. But while his modern sector is indeed "productive" in the sense in which Adam Smith used the term, his interpretation of the subsistence sector as "unproductive", despite the claim, is not exactly Smithian. And this is an important point that we should explore because it will provide us with the clue to an understanding of the specificity of the development discourse as distinct from the process Adam Smith described.

In *The Wealth of Nations*, Smith makes the distinction between productive and unproductive labor thus:

There is one sort of labour which adds to the value of the subject upon which it is bestowed; there is another which has no such effect. The former, as it produces a value, may be called productive; the latter, unproductive labour. Thus the labour of a manufacturer adds, generally, to the value of the materials which he works upon,......*[t]he labour of a menial servant, on the contrary, adds to the value of nothing*. Though the manufacturer has his wages advanced to him by his master, he, in reality, costs him no expense, the value of those wages being generally restored, together with a profit, in the improved value of the subject upon which his labour is bestowed. But the maintenance of a menial servant never is restored. (1975: 294–295)

Productive labor, for Smith, works on the basis of capital—but is alienated from it in terms of ownership and control—reproduces the conditions of production and produces a surplus. The surplus can be used to augment the initial stock of capital so that more labor can be employed in the next period. Thus productive labor is capable of self-expansion. In contrast, unproductive labor, the menial servant, is maintained out of revenue, therefore its employment cannot be increased unless there is an increase in revenue; in other words, expenditure on the menial servant cannot be restored from the labor performed by the servant. The distinction has nothing to do with the nature of the use value of what the two types of labor produce.

Productive labor, according to Smith, is the source of capital accumulation and growth, while unproductive labor, being a drain on revenue, is a drag on it. In Smith's vision of the pre-capitalist economy, the feudal landlords maintain an army of menial servants out of the revenue extracted from agriculture. The size of the unproductive employment cannot be increased unless there is an increase in the revenue. The process of capitalist transformation therefore is envisaged as one in which unproductive workers are transferred from revenue-based employment to capital-based employment and thereby transformed into productive workers. Capital sets productive labor in motion, and the surplus produced by labor is used to create additional stock, thus making accumulation and growth a self-sustaining process.

Lewis' capitalist sector is one in which labor produces an additional value over and above the wages paid, which accrues to the owner of capital as profit. This profit is used to create new capital, leading to expansion of output and employment. It clearly coincides with Smith's definition of productive labor. But his subsistence sector does not quite agree with what Smith called unproductive labor. The crucial difference is that for Smith, the phenomenon of unproductive labor maintained out of revenue is embedded in the feudal order of the economy, an order with its own structure of political authority. But Lewis' unproductive laborers reside within the peasant household, and who, despite the fact that their contribution to production is nil receive the average subsistence income as an entitlement ensured by the institution of pre-capitalist extended family. Thus, the transfer of these surplus laborers to the capitalist industry does not depend on the outcome of a political battle for radically altering the existing configuration of power and property. For Smith, transformation of unproductive labor into productive labor signified the transition from a feudal to a commercial society and the rise to dominance of the capitalist class against the feudal authority. By reducing the subsistence sector to self-employed peasant households, Lewis extracts the story of accumulation from the political terrain in which Smith located it. It is a passive sector, a reservoir of surplus laborers, and once the capitalist offers a wage that is a little higher than the subsistence income, laborers respond to it and, as if in a Newtonian frictionless world, move freely towards the capitalist sector. And those who remain in the subsistence sector happily put in more labor (since earlier there has been work sharing) and bring the surplus that accrues to them to the market so that it can be used as wage-goods for the capitalist sector. Once unleashed, the process will work itself out; the point is to give the ball the initial push.

Even if we take Lewis' characterization of the traditional, pre-capitalist sector on its own terms as a collection of passive, self-employed peasant households, one feature of this sector strikes us. It is a feature constituted by an absence rather than a presence. In describing the subsistence sector nowhere does Lewis mention even the possibility of non-agricultural production activities. Non-agricultural, non-leisure activities such as manufacturing or processing of agricultural raw materials always existed in backward agrarian economies and constituted an important aspect of their economic and social life. These are activities that Stephen Hymer and Stephen Resnick (1969) called z-goods: "We shall denote these non-agricultural activities", they wrote, "whether carried on in the household or in small scale service and artisan establishments in the village, as z, a purposely vague title to indicate the heterogeneity of the group."[12] (1969: 493) Lewis' dual economy does not recognize the existence of any such activity and therefore when the capitalist sector sells its product to the subsistence sector, it does not face any market problem caused by self-provisioning within the subsistence sector. In fact, the obliteration of non-agricultural production from the economic space of the traditional formations is a general feature that marks the entire body of writings of the early development economists. When Rosenstein–Rodan was referring to the existence of surplus labor in the agricultural sector of Eastern and South Eastern Europe, and formulating his program for planned industrialization, he was also silent about non-farm activities in the rural economy.

For us, this is a point of immense importance because by exploring the implications of this silence we can reveal how the development discourse sought to depoliticize the process of the emergence of capitalist production and present it as a process of development free from any contradiction. Once we consider z-goods production as an important element of the subsistence sector, we can interpret the development process in Lewis' dual economy in a very different way, as a depoliticized narrative of primitive accumulation. Production of z-goods is based on the unity of labor and means of labor, and as the development process begins, the very wage-goods and raw materials that served as the basis of z-goods production now flow out from the subsistence sector in the form of marketable surplus. The conditions under which z-goods were produced disappear and the means of labor are transformed into capital. On the other hand, laborers who had enjoyed pre-capitalist entitlements to subsistence are turned into wage-workers that sell their labor power to the capitalist employer. And they are made to work upon the means of production, which has now become capital through market exchange, to produce a surplus for the employer. Development in the dual economy thus entails an industry–agricultural separation, and the withering away of z-goods creates the market for the product of the capitalist sector within agriculture. This is precisely the process that Marx described as primitive accumulation. By effacing z-goods from the story of transition, Lewis (in particular and the early development economists in general) presents the development process as one in which the expansion of the modern capitalist sector does not cause destruction of any alternative forms of non-agricultural production. The process of capitalist industrialization, a process fraught with conflicts and contradictions, is thus presented as a politically neutral process of transfer of surplus labor based on "rational accounting" and laws of classical mechanics.

That the destruction of z-goods production is essential for the emergence of capitalist production has been widely recognized by the analysts of concrete cases of capitalist development. In the context of development of capitalism in Russia, when the Narodniks complained that capitalist industries were destroying small-scale manufacturing activities in the rural economy, Lenin celebrated the phenomenon and wrote:

> The growth of small production among the peasantry signifies the appearance of new industries, the conversion of new branches of raw material processing into independent spheres of industry, progress in the social division of labor, while the swallowing-up of small by large establishments implies a further step forward by capitalism, leading to the triumph of its higher forms. (quoted by Perelman 1983: 222)

For Lenin, the "swallowing-up" was an inevitable moment of capitalist development and he welcomed it as a change in favor of a "higher form" of production, a form that was more advanced in terms not merely of social division of labor but also of its innate potential for the development of productive forces. He even applauded the fact that the peasantry was switching its consumption from goods produced within the rural economy to better and more attractive commodities offered by capitalist industries. Let me quote at length:

> As industrial occupation spreads, intercourse with the outside world...becomes more frequent....They buy samovars, table crockery and glass, they wear neater cloths. Whereas at first this neatness of clothing takes the shape among men, of boots in place of bast shoes, among the women, leather shoes and boots are crowning glory.... Of neater clothing; they prefer bright, motley

calicoes and kerchiefs, figured woolen shawls and similar charms...

In the peasant family it has been the custom for ages for the wife to clothe her husband, herself and the children......As long as they grew their own flax, less money had to be spent on the purchase of flax, less money had to be spent on the purchase of cloth and other materials required for clothing, and this money was obtained from the sale of poultry, eggs, mushroom, berries, a spare skein of yarn, or a piece of linen. All the rest was made at home. (quoted by Perelman: 223)

Here Lenin sees the substitution of z-goods by products of the capitalist sector in a very positive light, as a sign of progress. The classical political economists, from Adam Smith to James Stuart, took the same view of this change (Smith described the small manufacturing units in rural areas as indolent and sauntering). It is even truer about Marx. In the discussion of primitive accumulation, Marx is at pains to draw our attention to the brutality and coercion associated with the process, but he is quite explicit in asserting that despite the pains and sufferings, it is an inescapable condition for capitalist transformation which for him is big leap towards progress from the "idiocy of village life". It is the same spirit in which he sees imperialism as the "unconscious tool of history' for the colonies.[13] The difference between Marx and his classical predecessors is that the latter underplay and gloss over the harsher aspects of the transformation and saw capitalism as the ultimate form of progress and freedom, while Marx relentlessly reminds us that capitalism savagely dismantled the old order and rose on its tomb, and it is an exploitative system which will eventually be superseded by socialism as the higher moment of progress. But the emergence of the capitalist system as a negation of the pre-capitalist order is for Marx, and also for Lenin, an unambiguous movement in the direction of progress. The dual economy model is premised on the same presumption of capitalist industrialization as progress; only by effacing z-goods from the discourse, it keeps the costs associated with transition, which Marx or Lenin explicitly, and the classical economists implicitly, recognized, out of visibility.

One however can argue that Lewis *et al.* were writing on industrialization in economies of Asia and Africa that were emerging from colonial rule, and their z-goods sectors had already been wiped out by penetration of commodities from the metropolis. The phenomenon of de-industrialization in the colonies, as economic historians prefer to call it, forced people previously engaged in rural non-agricultural production to go back to land for subsistence and thus created the army of the underemployed which Lewis' concept of surplus labor refers to. Therefore the question of destruction of the rural manufacturing sector in the face of industrialization in the post-colonial dual economy does not arise.

From our perspective, we can respond to this argument at two levels. First, despite de-industrialization to a considerable extent during the colonial period, many of the newly independent backward economies still had a significant level of traditional manufacturing activities (Ranis and Stewart 1993). When in the 1950s India was formulating plans for industrialization, planners kept referring frequently to the existence of what they called small and cottage industries in the rural economy as an important provider of employment. When Hymer and Resnick presented the concept of z-goods, it was based on the observations they made in the 1960s on the rural economies of Ghana and Philippines. Thus the absence of rural non-agricultural activities in the dual economy does not square with the facts.

On a different level, we can argue that even if we assume that non-agricultural activities are absent and conceive the subsistence sector as consisting only of peasant households engaged in agriculture, capitalist industrialization in this scenario means that surplus laborers and the means of labor (that flow to the capitalist sector as marketable surplus of wage goods and raw materials) can be united only on the basis of capitalist relations of production, where the means of labor turned into capital confronts labor as an alien power. This subverts any other alternative forms of unity of labor and means of labor. It is only by selling his labor power to the capitalist and producing a surplus for him that the worker can acquire the wage-goods necessary for his subsistence. In other words, the program of capitalist development in a dual economy rules out other potentially feasible forms for organizing non-agricultural production. The capitalist sector in this case emerges and expands by annihilating non-capitalist production in the sense that it prevents their possibility from turning into actuality.

The development discourse justifies the ruling out of non-capitalist production by the implicit assumption that the expanding capitalist sector will be able to absorb the entire pool of surplus labor. When Marx and Lenin welcomed capitalist transformation of the economy and the withering away of rural manufacturing, their enthusiasm was also premised on the same presumption: that the advanced and dynamic capitalist sector will eventually bring the entire economy within its own ambit. Our point of departure from the traditional Marxian imaginary of capitalist development, as explicated in Chapter 2, is the recognition of the existence of a wasteland of the dispossessed created by the arising of post-colonial capital—a space inhabited by those who are expropriated from their traditional activities and entitlement but not allowed entry into the space of capital. Seen from that perspective, legitimation of capital requires that the dispossessed be rehabilitated and non-capitalist forms of production turn out to be important and effective means for achieving that end. Fifty years after Lewis' work inaugurated the development discourse, a consensus now seems to be emerging that the trajectory of capitalist development envisaged by Lewis has failed miserably to transfer the entire pool of surplus labor to productive employment in the capitalist sector. The international developmental organizations that once embraced the accumulation-centric approach are increasingly recognizing the existence of production activities in the "informal sector" that constitutes an outside of the capitalist sector. ILO's insistence on the importance of the informal sector as a source of employment and on the need to provide support to it, and World Bank's concern about non-farm rural employment, are re-inscribing z-goods into the space of development, albeit in a displaced and reconstituted form. In the subsequent chapters we will explore in detail how the development discourse has struggled to negotiate the phenomenon of exclusion and reconstituted the discursive space to produce hegemony in its complex form.

Materiality of the discourse lies in the practices it calls into play; it is these practices that we must focus on if we are to understand how the discourse works. In the following section, I will consider the early experience of development planning in post-colonial India, a process that was animated by the then emergent discourse of development economics. I will now attempt to bring to visibility how the early moment of industrialization in post-colonial India served to accomplish the task of primitive accumulation in the guise of a depoliticized, be-nevolent process of development in a dual economy.

Industrialization in Post-Colonial India: Planning as the Realm of Reason

A long drawn and intense political battle against foreign rule made possible the emergence of India as an independent nation state and thus created the ground for planned industrialization; yet, curiously, the idea of planning from the very beginning sought to distance it-self from the world of politics by premising itself on a dichotomy between the "realm of politics" and the "realm of rational economic calculations". The nationalist movement saw a huge mobilization of the peasantry and other sections of the toiling masses behind the demand for the end of colonial rule, a demand that was based on the claim that the Industrial Revolution in England and the resultant dominance of the large scale machine-based production had led to the impoverishment of the Indian masses under the British rule. But immediately after decolonization, the newly born Indian state embarked on planning by extricating the question of industrialization from the rhetoric of nationalist politics in which it had been embedded earlier. The essentially political nature of the question was pushed out of sight and the regime of planning was presented as a politically neutral regime committed to rationality and progress.

Jawaharlal Nehru, the first Prime Minister of India and the chief architect of the Indian Planning Commission, was the personification of this new paradigm of development. In *The Discovery of India* written in 1946, he probed the causes of economic backwardness of colonial India and strongly recommended that modern industrialization was the only means to liberate the Indian economy from the bog of poverty and underdevelopment. His analysis shows that he was aware of the fact that capitalist development necessitates the withering away of the traditional economy, as it did in England, but he was also convinced that the dispossessed will ultimately find a place in the modern economy although the period of transition is marked with immense human suffering. India's poverty and economic backwardness, he argued, was due entirely to the fact that while import of cheaper manufactures from mechanized British factories had led to the destruction of the traditional handicrafts, the dispossessed Indian masses never had a chance to be rehabilitated in the new industrial economy that thrived in Britain. India had paid the price of capitalist development in Britain without the chance of enjoying its fruits.

> The transition from pre-industrialized economy to an economy of capitalist industrialism involves great hardship and heavy cost in human suffering borne by masses of people...... There was this hardship in England during the period of transition but, taken as whole, it was not great as the change over was rapid and the *unemployment caused was soon absorbed by the new industries.* But that did not mean that the cost in human suffering was not paid. It was indeed paid, and paid in full by others, particularly by the people of India.... It may be said that a great part of the cost of transition to industrialism in western Europe were paid for by India, China and other colonial countries.[14] (Nehru 1981: 300, my emphasis)

Clearly what Nehru here is referring to, although in a different language, is the process of primitive accumulation. He explicitly recognizes the possibility that the dispossessed may be permanently deprived of the benefits of capitalist industrialization whose foundation is laid by primitive accumulation, and locates the cause of India's poverty in this deprivation. But for him, it is the colonial relations that lie at the heart of the problem, producing this perverse outcome. Had India not been a colony, the process of primitive accumulation would have led to the development of modern industries in India. Industrial development would have encompassed the entire population and the price paid by the dispossessed would have been rewarded with the benefits flowing from that development.

The inescapable implication of Nehru's argument is that the Western experience can be replicated in post-colonial India. Now that India is an independent nation state in a position to build its own economy, it can have a program of massive industrialization that will transform the entire economy from a traditional to an advanced one. It would traverse the same trajectory of development that the West has experienced. "We are trying to catch up", Nehru said in his speech in Parliament on 15 December, 1952, "as far as we can, with the industrial revolution that occurred long ago in Western countries". And in this process of catching up, the specificity of the Indian situation demanded that the state play an active and decisive role in the economic sphere.

Thus in Nehru's vision, the arising of the Western capital can be acted out once again on the post-colonial Indian stage. We have already characterized, following Marx, the story of this arising as the immanent history of capital. The Western capital in its fully developed form has suspended in its *being* its immanent history, its *becoming*. For Nehru, the real history of post-colonial India will replicate the journey of the Western capital's *becoming,* with the active intervention of a "developmental state".

Nehru's vision, however, did not go unchallenged. Gandhi, the man who rallied the entire country behind the nationalist cause, had very different things to say about industrialization. "When I read", he wrote in *Hind Swaraj,*

"Mr Ramesh Dutt's *Economic History of India,* I wept; and as I think of it again my heart sickens. It is machinery that has impoverished India. It is difficult to measure the harm that Manchester has done to us. It is due to Manchester that Indian handicraft has all but disappeared."[15]

This apparently echoes Nehru's critique of the colonial rule and its devastating impact on the Indian economy. But Gandhi then takes the issue far beyond the question of colonial rule when he says:

"Mechanization is good when hands are too few for the work intended to be accomplished. It is an evil when there are more hand than required for work, as is the case in India..........spinning and weaving mills have deprived the villagers of a substantial means of livelihood. It is no answer in reply to say that they turn out cheaper, better cloth, if they do so at all. For, if they have displaced thousands of workers, the cheapest mill cloth is dearer than the dearest khadi woven in the woven in the village."[16]

Clearly, Gandhi here is holding machine-based large scale industrialization itself, rather than its form in the specific context of colonialism, responsible for dispossession, loss of livelihood and poverty. While Nehru was convinced that industrial development in independent India would encompass the entire toiling masses left impoverished by colonial rule, provided of course that the Indian state commits itself to social equity and justice, Gandhi was equally convinced that the impact of industrialization would be no different than what it had been during the colonial period. Seen from our perspective, Gandhi in his own way arrived at the conviction that the arising of capital inevitably causes permanent dispossession, irrespective of whether it is imperialist or national. And also, regardless of whether it is private capital or state capital in the form of public sector, the outcome will be the same.

Pandit Nehru wants industrialization because he thinks that, if it is socialized, it would be free from the evils of capitalism. My own view is that evils are inherent in industrialism, and no amount of socialization can eradicate it.[17]

And he further argues that

Industrialization on a mass scale will necessarily lead to passive or active exploitation of the villagers as the problems of competition and marketing comes in. *Therefore we have to concentrate on the village being self- contained, manufacturing mainly for use.*[18] (My emphasis)

Here Gandhi finds the solution in what we have already called z-goods: goods that are produced within the agrarian economy for satisfaction of local needs. While reading the Gandhi–Nehru debate, one does have a feeling of *déjà vu*, for despite fundamental differences both in the contexts and the ideologies in which they are grounded, the difference between Gandhi and Nehru on the question of industrialization reminds one of the Lenin–Narodniks debate we have already referred to in the preceding section. In both cases, the question is one of destruction of z-goods production and loss of entitlements resulting from the arising of capital. At this dawn of the 21st century, we can now see the irony that the past century held in store. Nehru's vision prevailed over Gandhi's concern, and Lenin's over the Narodniks', but by the end of the century the same concern seems to have returned with a vengeance, with governments and developmental organizations struggling to cope with problem of jobless growth and exclusion by carving out a space for z-goods production within the network of capitalist circulation and exchange.

The Gandhi–Nehru debate continued for quite some time, with followers on both sides, and generated considerable tension within the Indian National Congress until the formation of the National Planning Committee. The Committee was overwhelmingly dominated by experts, scientists and industrialists who shared Nehru's vision of a modern industrialized India. J. C. Kumarappa, a staunch Gandhian, tried to remind the Committee of the Gandhian position on the small versus large industries, but the Committee almost unanimously endorsed the view that planning in India must give highest priority to the program of large scale industrialization. And several years before the first Five-Year Plan started, a confident Nehru wrote,

Any argument as to the relative merits of small-scale and large-scale industry seems strangely irrelevant today when the world, and the dominating facts of the situation that confront it, have decided in favour of the latter. Even in India the decision has been made by these facts themselves, and no one doubts that India will be rapidly industrialized in the near future.[19]

The question that had energized the entire nationalist movement was finally "resolved" in favor of a modern, industrialized, independent India after the image of the West.

To follow the trajectory already charted by the West was only one part of the Nehruvian vision. There was another part that is important for us: the strict separation between the domains of developmental practices and politics. Our claim has been that the discourse of development in the post world war II period depoliticized development and presented it as a techno-bureaucratic project embedded in a power–knowledge nexus. And as a part of that project, development economics sought to portray primitive accumulation as an apolitical process of saving, investment and income growth. Nehru's vision of planned industrialization in postcolonial India from the very beginning surrendered to the hegemony of the development discourse and embraced the idea that the program of industrialization only involves making of plans by experts on the basis of "scientific and rational" calculations and their implementation by the bureaucratic apparatus of the state. The state was to take an active part in the industrialization process and exercise its power wherever necessary, but the legitimacy of these interventions was derived not from the claim that the state had its own justification for the use of its political authority and coercive power to achieve developmental goals, but from the universality of the "truth effects" produced by the development discourse—from a "regime of truth" grounded in the knowledge–power rather than in the centered authority of the state. The developmental state with its Planning Commission and techno-bureaucratic apparatuses was a vehicle of the discourse and its "politically neutral" practices.

The early 1950s witnessed the process of integration of the Indian planning into an international program of development; it was also the process of its acquiring the status of a discourse. Foucault has told us that whether an ensemble of statements can form a discourse depends on the status of the speakers, the sites from which they speak and the manner in which the statements are made. In those years, the discourse of development was consolidating itself on an international level in terms of these conditions and while the Indian economy was turned into an object of developmental knowledge, efforts were made to create the same conditions in the local Indian context. As described by George Rosen, the most important role in this context was played by the Center for International Studies at the MIT in the US.[20] It was established in 1951 as a place where experts, primarily economists, would engage in intensive research on the development prospects of South Asia, especially India and Pakistan. Although initially funded by the US government, the center soon distanced itself from the state by resorting to private funding from the Ford Foundation. Its stated purpose was to get involved in the Indian planning process with its experts providing advice to the planners. There were three important aspects of this involvement. First, they funded new research institutions in India— the Institute of Economic Growth in Delhi, the Delhi School of Economics and the Gokhale Institute in Pune—and closely inter-acted with the Indian Statistical Institute in Calcutta, so that these Indian institutions could emerge as sites, integrated into a network of Western institutions, from which experts would speak about de-velopment. Second, Indian students and researchers were encouraged to go abroad for training and return as experts with the stamp of a Western institution. And third, the Indian research institutes were persuaded to shun economics that was then taught in Indian universities—an economics that belonged, following the classical

British academic tradition, to the history–politics–sociology nexus—
and adopt a new vision of economics grounded in mathematical
techniques, statistical calculations, and econometric tests. These
three aspects together meant that authorized "experts" would now
make statements from recognized institutional sites on development
on the basis of inferences drawn from statistical and econometric
exercises. The way nationalist thinkers, from Bal Gangadhar Tilak
and Dadabhai Naoroji, or even Ramesh Chandra Dutt, to Gandhi
and Nehru, had spoken about the Indian economy in the colonial
period was no longer accepted as the manner of making meaningful
statements; the "idealist visionary" was now entirely replaced by
the "development professional", and the Indian economy was conceived as a knowledge object, a diseased body waiting to be cured
by doctors equipped with the modern science of medicine and techniques of surgery. In other words, with the creation of the conditions
from which flows the power of the discourse, Indian planning from
the very beginning found itself subjected to the discursive surveillance of "development".

The reason I want to highlight how the power of the discourse
was at work behind planning practices in India, or for that matter
in many other newly born nations after decolonization, is that it
allows us to have an understanding of the complex relationship between the notion of development and post-colonial capital in the
course of its arising. I will now demonstrate that the early Indian
plans took up the task of primitive accumulation—a task that the
Indian bourgeoisie was then not in a position to accomplish on its
own—in the guise of development in a labor surplus economy.

The Early Plans

Although the industrialization debate had already been resolved in
favor of large scale, modern industries, Indian planning had to wait
for a few years before it could bring large-scale industrialization to
the center of the agenda. Although it stated the creation of a modern
industrial base as the main objective of planning, the overall approach of the first Five-Year Plan was still dominated by the question
of employment, and the important role of the small scale and cottage
industries in that context. Out of a total plan outlay of Rs. 2356
crore, a meager 6 per cent was allocated to the large scale industrial sector in comparison with agriculture and rural development

(15 per cent), irrigation (16 per cent) and transport and communications (23 per cent).[21] The draft outline of the first plan is quite explicit in its recognition of mass unemployment as the main problem facing the economy, and the importance of small and cottage industries as the source of employment:

> In the reduction of unemployment and underemployment, cottage and small-scale industries have an important part to play. In a country where labor is plentiful relatively to capital, preference must be given, wherever technical conditions permit, to labor-intensive rather than to capital intensive processes. Cottage and small-scale industries have certain advantages. They do not involve the use of elaborate techniques; if raw materials are locally available, these industries can cater effectively to local markets. ...The individual worker is ... often unable to find the necessary finance to purchase the raw material or to adopt efficient techniques or to market his products on advantageous terms. These handicaps have to be removed through cooperative organization and well-planned state aid.[22]

The draft also makes an important distinction within the sector: between the part of the sector that can serve as an ancillary to large industries and the part whose products compete with the products of large industries. And it is recognized that when competition arises, the large is likely to compete out the small and therefore, those goods should be reserved for the small-scale sector in the form of quotas.[23]

Interestingly, here the planner recognizes that in the conflict between the small and the large, the Indian modern industry would have the same impact as Manchester and Lancashire had on the Indian handicrafts, and advocates measures to shield the small through reservation. This did not quite reflect confidence in the claim that those who would lose their livelihood as a result of the withering away of the small will find employment in the large-scale sector. This ambivalence—the drive for modern industries and reservation for the small on the employment ground—remains in the rhetoric of planning in its early years, although it started becoming clear from the second plan that there was a huge gap between the rhetoric and the actual allocation of outlays. One only had to wait till the third plan to see the planner ultimately identify the large as the "vehicle of progress" and the small as "transient".

The massive drive for industrialization began in second plan, with the allocation of outlay to industry jumping from 7.6 per cent to 18.5 per cent.[24] The plan was based on the well-known Mahalanobis model—inspired to a large extent by the success of the Soviet pattern of industrialization—that argued in favor of allocating the major part of the investible surplus to the capital goods sector. The attempt to strike a balance between the large and the small, however, continued for two reasons. First, it was admitted that the new large industries will not generate sufficient employment and the small must be allowed to continue as employment provider; and second, it was thought to be in a better position to mitigate the anticipated shortage of consumer goods resulting from the proposed pattern of investment, thus serving the twin purposes.

A closer look at the division of the total allocation for industry between large and the small, however, reveals a different picture: only 4 per cent of the total plan outlay went to the small-scale sector while the large-scale sector received 13 per cent.[25] In the third plan, the small's share further dropped to close to 3 per cent while the share of the large went up to more than 23 per cent.[26] Thus, far from reflecting the importance attached to the small in the planning rhetoric, the actual allocations demonstrate that in terms of resource flows, the large grew at the expense of the small.

The Indian planning ultimately resolved this contradiction when in the third plan our planner asserted, and I quote at length:

> The remedy [of unemployment] would be a continuing expansion of the national economy at a high enough rate to create adequate employment opportunities in the urban areas and to provide conditions for a continuing growth of agricultural production .... *Sustained programs over a period of years for the rapid development of agriculture and expansion of modern industries will be the only solution to the problem of unemployment. In the transitional stage,* it is necessary to maintain and indeed to promote labor-intensive methods of production to the fullest extent so long as this does not lead to a smaller aggregate production in the economy.[27] (My emphasis)

The phrases "expansion of modern industries" and "in the transitional period" are important. They suggest that in the ultimate analysis, the solution to the problem of unemployment and underemployment lies in the expansion of the modern industrial sector, and also in an expanding (modernized) agriculture. The entire production economy is thus divided between these two and whatever is there at present in the in-between space is transitory, it will disappear as the modernization process is completed. The planner must try "to maintain and indeed to promote" the activities that reside there, but it is a mere strategy to make the process of transition less painful.

Thus Indian planning finally frees itself from the ambivalence in its rhetoric and describes planned industrialization as the process that will ultimately bring the entire economy within the fold of the modern sector. The continued existence of the non-modern, traditional, labor-intensive sector is only a transient phenomenon, a moment of the trajectory of development, an object of strategic manipulation by the planner to generate employment in the period of transition. It will ultimately wither away, dissolving into the expanding modern sector of the economy. Although the process of reorganizing the economy to actualize this vision was already underway in the earlier plans, it is at this point that the discourse of planning—the representation of the economy adopted and the ensemble of statements made about its "development"—consolidates itself by coming in consonance with the planning practices. The realm of discourse and the realm of practice thus implode to produce a regime of truth in which planning becomes "discursive practice" in the Foucauldian sense.

Depoliticization

In 1987, Sukhomoy Chakraborty—an eminent Indian economist and an internationally acclaimed expert on development planning—in assessing the achievements and failures of planning in India, wrote:

> [I]t is quite inadequate to deal with the ....story [of Indian planning] in terms of the logic of primary accumulation of capital. ....Marx may have been justified in writing the history of the development of productive forces in seventeenth and eighteenth-century England as a story of *Ursprung liche Akkumulation,* misleadingly translated as 'primitive accumulation' ...... the post-independence experience of India has a basic structural difference. ....[Nehru] viewed planning as a way of avoiding the

unnecessary rigors of an industrial transition in so far as it affected the masses resident in India's villages. (Chakraborty 1987: 3)

We already know about Nehru's views on development, that he was convinced that industrialization was possible without going through the pains and sufferings of primitive accumulation. (I keep the issue of the quality of translation aside and continue to use the adjective 'primitive' rather than 'primary'). What I find interesting is that writing in 1987—after having witnessed the outcome of three-and-a-half decades of planning in which he himself had been actively involved for a considerable period of time, and more than fifty years after Nehru articulated his view, Chakraborty still affirms the Nehruvian claim that planning in India is to be seen as a way to achieve industrialization by avoiding the stage of primitive accumulation. He then interprets the Indian experience in the language of development of economics:

> From our vantage point today, the Indian development model of the mid-fifties is probably *better viewed as a variant of the Lewis model*. The variation relates to the two-sector disaggregation introduced by Mahalanobis, as well as to the active role allotted to the state. In the original Lewis model, the principal actors were the capitalists in the 'modern' sector, but in the Indian case a development bureaucracy was also assigned a major role. (*ibid*.: 14, my emphasis)

And he uses this interpretation to distance the Indian case from the Soviet experience in the 1920s. In the Soviet Union, he argues, the program of rapid industrialization required a transfer of surplus from agriculture. Soviet agriculture was still dominated by small and medium private producers, and in that context theorists like Preobrazhensky and Bukharin engaged in a debate over how best to ensure this surplus extraction. The idea of "primitive socialist accumulation", presented by Preobrazhensky, claimed that the maximum possible amount of surplus should be squeezed from the pre-socialist agriculture in order to finance socialist industrialization; and the coercive power of the Soviet state should be fully used to that end. Chakraborty acknowledges that the Mahalanobis strategy of industrialization was inspired by the Soviet experience but at the same time claims:

But I believe that Indian planners were not principally thinking in terms of extracting surplus from agriculture for financing investment in industry.

In actual fact, the [Indian] planners' strategy boiled down to the traditional thesis, upheld by several contemporary scholars of economic development, that during the early stages of industrialization it was necessary for agriculture to contribute to the building up of a modern industrial sector by providing cheap labor and also cheap food. (*ibid.*: 21)

Thus for Chakraborty, it is not extraction of surplus but supply of labor and wage goods from the traditional sector that created the conditions for the emergence and expansion of the modern industrial sector in India, and it fits in well to the Lewis scenario. Indian planners never sought to engage in primitive accumulation.

Nothing could serve as a better illustration of what I argued in my discourse reading of development economics in the preceding section. That the Lewis story keeps primitive accumulation out of sight and depoliticizes development by describing it as a process of frictionless transfer of surplus labor. Chakraborty here echoes the voice of the development discourse, the discourse that seeks to displace the question of transition from the terrain of politics and power to one of planning and management. And I would further argue that the obliteration of primitive accumulation from the discourse goes unnoticed because of a failure to grasp the nature of this accumulation, a failure that has profound implications. In Chapter 2, I had a brief section where I claimed, and let me iterate, that there is a widespread misperception about the concept of primitive accumulation of capital, a misperception shared by Marxists and non-Marxists alike: it is understood as a process of extraction of economic surplus (i.e., production minus consumption) similar to capitalist accumulation in the form of surplus value. Interpreted thus, primitive accumulation is the transfer of an excess of production over consumption from the pre-capitalist sector to the capitalist sector. The transfer, whether it is in the form of taxation or of a flow of savings from one sector to the other, must be reflected in a trade surplus between the two sectors: the pre-capitalist sector will inevitably run a trade surplus vis-à-vis the capitalist sector. The implication is that if the inter-sectoral trade is balanced, there is no extraction of surplus and therefore no primitive accumulation.

The claim that the Lewis story is not a story of primitive accumulation is rooted in this misperception. As I have demonstrated in the preceding chapters, the Marxian concept of primitive accumulation refers to the process of estrangement of labor from the means of labor and the transformation of money into real capital. The means of labor were previously united with labor; the unity dissolves and the same means of labor, used within the capitalist system of production, now confronts labor as capital, an alien power. In other words, it is a process that refers to the transformation of relations between labor and means of labor. The means of labor may flow to the capitalist sector through market exchange and the exchange may be balanced, but that does not mean that there is no primitive accumulation; all it means is that no surplus is being extracted. Put differently, there is no economic surplus in this case; there is only marketable surplus. But the fact that the constituents of this marketable surplus, i.e., the means of labor (wage-goods and raw materials) are extracted from their earlier unity with labor and made to flow into the domain of capitalist production, where they will relate to labor as capital, makes it a case of primitive accumulation of capital.

In the Lewis scenario, wage goods and raw materials flow from the traditional to the modern sector in the form of marketable surplus—it is not a transfer of economic surplus—but since this flow means the destruction of actual and potential non-capitalist production, primitive accumulation is, to be sure, at work. Chakraborty from his vantage point in the late 1980s claims that India's development strategy was significantly different from the Soviet model because Indian planners saw agriculture as a source of cheap labor and food, and not as a source of extractable surplus as the Soviet planner did; but from our early 21st century vantage point we can argue that he fails to see that despite the apparent differences both were instances of primitive accumulation. In the Soviet case the question of power was explicitly posited, the essentially political nature of development was recognized, and the project of economic transformation was placed on a politically contested terrain with the coercive power of the state seen as essential for bringing about economic transformation. In short, far from "depoliticized", development was an unambiguously and vibrantly political project in the Soviet Union. India, from the very beginning, embraced the Western discourse in which development was presented as a sanitized techno-bureaucratic project grounded in rationality, far removed from the messy world of politics. When the industrialization strategy of the early plans is identified with the Lewis model, and by that token posited in opposition to the Soviet model, it reflects how deeply our thinking about development is implicated in the knowledge–power of the discourse.

Once we see planning as discursive practice and go beneath its rhetoric, we find that whatever was done in the early years together constituted the conditions for primitive accumulation. The state's monopoly power of taxation, of printing money, and floating public debt ensured its access to money capital that was invested in modern industries. Means of labor, wage goods, and raw materials, had to be transferred from the agricultural sector and transformed into capital. From the allocation figures already cited, one can see that the first plan, when the emphasis on industry was yet to come, allocated a considerable amount to transport and communication, and it remained more or less the same in the subsequent plans. This paved the way for the movement of food and wage goods from rural to urban areas. As the means of labor took the form of marketable surplus to be channeled to the modern industrial sector, conditions of existence for manufacturing activities outside the modern sector were destroyed. Products of the modern sector filled the vacuum, providing further impetus to the process. And in sectors that enjoyed protection from reservation, the lack of access to the means of labor and credit severely constrained capacity expansion, condemning them to a state of atrophy. In sum, what the post-colonial Indian economy experienced in the first two decades was primitive accumulation under "non-coercive and politically neutral development planning".

But things did not exactly turn out the way Nehru had thought. The modern sector grew at an impressive rate and established itself as a technologically advanced, dynamic sector, but it also found itself surrounded by poverty and surplus labor. The outcome of planned industrialization in independent India turned out to be no different from the colonial experience, except for the fact that modern Indian industries had taken the place of steel and textile mills of Manchester and Lancashire. The story was more or less the same for the entire post-colonial world. Development sought to re-enact the drama of Western capital's arising on the third world stage—arise it did, but in its wake it produced a wasteland of the dispossessed. This wasteland was not so much a residue of the initial condition that development had failed to transform, as it was the result of capitalist development itself.

And the messy world of politics started encroaching upon the neat, orderly, and rational world of development planning. The issue of persistent absolute poverty made its way into the discourse of development and unsettled the centrality of "accumulation" in the representation of the economy. It questioned the conflation of accumulation and development and sought to invest economic entities with new meanings. A shift occurred within the discourse in the early 1970s, calling into play a different set of practices and interventions, and these new practices turned poverty into a direct target of techno-bureaucratic management, an object of governance. The realm of development embraced the realm of governmentality.

Notes

1. Marx's idea of transition is different from Smith's in that Smith was not dealing with transition and change in the dialectical sense.
2. Ricardo focused on the conflictual roles of capitalists and landlords, but he did not consider the possibility of any contradiction within the capitalist system, namely, between capitalists and workers, and its implications for the accumulation process. In contrast, Marx's emphasis was on the second contradiction and how it constitutes the dynamics of the capitalist system and the possibility of its supersession.
3. Although, as claimed by Meier in the above quote, the vision is informed by the classical tradition, it never refers to, or even mentions, the role of primitive accumulation in the context of capitalist transition. So far as its classical lineage goes, it is only Smith and Ricardo and none of them were concerned about question of origin of capital. Ricardo was dealing with full-fledged, self-reproducing capital, albeit with the issue of rent as a pain in its neck, and therefore the question did not arise for him. And Smith, although he was addressing the question of transition, was strangely silent about the source of early capital (Perelman 1983).
4. Marx (1954: 668).
5. *Ibid.*: 698.
6. *Ibid.*: 700.
7. Ashton (1948); Hill (1985).
8. Marx (1954: 688).
9. The shoe-factory problem has been stretched beyond what Rosenstein–Rodan and Nurkse meant it to be. When the shoe-factory problem is presented as a case of coordination failure and the consequent low-level–no-industry trap, we find underdevelopment represented in terms of a toy-economy and the multi-faceted, complex question of development reduced

to a mere riddle plaguing this caricature of an economy. The toy-land is inhabited by ahistorical, apolitical, omnipotent "entrepreneurs", fabricated within the development economics itself, whose decision to abstain from setting up factories is the outcome of a "game" defined solely in terms of calculations of atomistic individuals. And thus the need to understand development as an all encompassing, discrete systemic change, from a self-perpetuating stagnant state of the economy to a self-expanding, dynamic one, is sacrificed for the pleasure of playing with a toy-economy which in the ultimate analysis is little more than a barren pursuit of logical rigor.

10. See Bhattacharya (2002).
11. Average product in the traditional sector increases as labor moves to the advance sector. If the wage rate in the advance sector is set equal to the average product, then the labor supply curve becomes upward sloping from the very beginning. Lewis presented his story in flowing prose but later attempts at formalization of his story struggled with this problem. The problem in a way points to the fact that the source of unlimited supply of labor is primitive accumulation an dispossession rather than a reservoir of surplus labor within the family.
12. Hymer and Resnick's analysis, in terms of methodology, belongs to the mainstream development economics, in fact more to the neo-classical paradigm compared to Lewis' work. However, it is curious that it took more than a decade after the publication of Lewis' article for the question of z-goods to be raised. It is even more curious that the article was totally ignored in the subsequent writings on the dual economy; it does not figure in the bibliography of even the most comprehensive recent textbooks on development economics such as Ray (1998).
13. Marx however expressed skepticism about this view later in *Ethnographical Notebooks*.
14. Nehru (1981: 300).
15. Gandhi (1958: 18).
16. *Village Industries, ibid.* vol. 59, p. 356.
17. Interview to Francis G. Hickman, *ibid.* vol. 73, p. 29–30.
18. Discussion with Maurice Frydman, *ibid.* vol. 63, p. 241.
19. Nehru (1981: 408).
20. A detailed account of the MIT Center's involvement in the Indian planning process is available in Rosen (1985).
21. See Frankel (2005: 132).
22. *The First Five Year Plan: Draft Outline* p. 19–20.
23. *Ibid.*: 162–164.
24. Frankel, op. cit. p. 132. Table 1.
25. *Ibid.*: 132.
26. *Ibid.*: 188.
27. *The Third Five Year Plan, A Draft Outline*, p. 85.

Chapter 4

De-essentializing Development: Capital and Governmentality

If President Truman's speech in 1949 inaugurated the era of development, it was Robert McNamara's Nairobi speech in 1973 that marked the first shift within its discursive field. It can be seen as a turning point, the beginning of a new era in which the development project underwent displacement and transmutation bringing into operation an entirely new set of techniques and practices. In the two decades that followed, the received notions that had constituted the foundation of the project were subjected to intense critique and the idea of development was invested with new meaning; new goals were set, new strategies designed, and new practices defined. The realm of development increasingly embraced the realm of governmentality. The purpose of this chapter is to trace out and highlight this change and interpret it in terms of the dynamic of the discourse: how the discourse restructured its own space in response to the changing extra-discursive conditions.

The Nairobi speech was an address to the Board of Governors of the World Bank in which McNamara, the then president of the Bank, questioned the effectiveness of the accumulation-centric approach in eliminating poverty and deprivation, and stressed the need for an alternative strategy. He called attention to the fact that although many developing economies had grown in the preceding two decades at impressive rates, the growth process had bypassed a large section of the population of those countries, condemning them to a desperate state of poverty. There was therefore a strong case for redefining the objective of development by incorporating the alleviation of absolute poverty as the goal of developmental interventions. Instead of relying on the trickle-down effect—which evidently had failed—he emphasized the urgent need for designing policies to launch a direct assault on absolute poverty without the mediation of growth, and for redirecting the flow of development assistance for that purpose.

The speech was a turning point in the sense that this new orientation of development with alleviation of direct poverty as a goal distinct from accumulation and growth gained considerable ground within the Bank in the years that followed. The poverty-oriented approach defined two sets of new targets for the development planner. In so far as rural poverty was concerned, it focused on the different aspects of rural development including the productivity of subsistence farming. Alongside, the provision of health care, education and housing for the urban poor, and creation of productive employment for them, were seen as crucial for the alleviation urban poverty. Pursuing these targets meant a significant change in the priorities in the Bank's lending policy. In the preceding decades, its lending had been concentrated in infrastructure building—e.g., power plants, transport, and communications—primarily for modern industries in the urban areas. As these investments enhanced productivity in the modern sector, their economic returns were tangible and measurable, and therefore could serve as the criterion for the economic rationale behind the projects. The Bank cautiously distanced itself from the social sector and was explicitly reluctant to fund health or education programs because their links with productivity and growth, in its own perception, were remote, intangible, and unclear. In the 1970s—referred to as the McNamara years—there were significant changes in the Bank's lending policy with funds flowing to various anti-poverty programs. Robert Ayres, in his detailed study of the activities of the Bank in the McNamara period, highlights these changes by drawing attention to the fact that while in fiscal 1968 Bank lending for agriculture and rural development was only $172.5 million (18.1 percent of its total lending), by fiscal 1981 the amount had increased to $3.8 billion (31 percent of the total figure). What is more important is that the composition of lending within agriculture dramatically changed from irrigation and infrastructure-related investments to poverty-oriented rural development projects, the benefits of which were to accrue to the rural poor. It funded large rural nutrition projects in Brazil and Columbia. The new orientation was also reflected in the increasing concern with urban poverty: between 1972 and 1981, $1.6 billion were allocated to low-cost urban housing and slum rehabilitation. In a sharp contrast to the Bank's earlier approach, a significant amount of resources was also committed to primary education. (Ayres 1983: 5–6)

The recognition of poverty alleviation as a distinct and separate goal thus restructured and extended the space of development and defined new modes of interventions. The World Bank however was not the only institution that conceived the new perspective. In the early 1970s, several other international agencies critically engaged with the dominant discourse and expressed scepticism about the received idea of development. The ILO, with its focus on employment, had already begun to question the ability of the growth-centric model to absorb the entire pool of surplus labor. It argued in favor of treating employment as a separate objective of development and launched its World Employment program (WEP) to undertake extensive research on urban poverty. Several other forums held by the United Nations, the Tinbergen report and the report of the Dag Hammarskjold Foundation—all strongly emphasized the need to redefine the whole purpose of development and proposed an agenda with basic need satisfaction at its centre. Although the World Bank, given its greater access to resources and larger network of operation, acted as an important agent, the change in the perspective was the combined result of all these efforts. They all concurred at that particular juncture to bring about the shift within the field of development, constituting a new moment of the discourse.

This new orientation also altered the idea of the developmental state and its role in the process of economic transformation. The developmental state had been characterized earlier in relation to the program of planned accumulation: the task of the state was the promotion of capital formation by engaging in development planning, that is, by designing, implementing, and monitoring plans for the expansion of the modern industry. In the new perspective, the developmental state was now to address the problem of poverty in terms of direct interventions. Thus the space of development planning was now expanded to incorporate direct planned assault on poverty, bringing to the fore the state's welfarist role. In other words, the 1970s witnessed the process of what Foucault called the "governmentalization" of the developmental state.

Governmentality

What exactly is meant by the governmentalization of the state? I have already touched upon the concept in the preceding chapters, but at this point I must elaborate on it before I use it to describe the new face of development. Foucault's analysis of power refers exclusively to the advanced modern societies of the West, but I believe that the conceptual tools it offers can also be productively used for an understanding of some important aspects of the power-regimes in the third world. If the theory of discursive formation helps us to understand development as a regime of power, the concept of governmentality allows us to grasp the complexities of how that regime works.

In exploring the nature of subjugation and control in the contemporary Western societies, Foucault offers a diachronic account of power in these societies. The central point he makes is that power in the form of sovereignty has been supplanted in these societies by a new form he calls governmentality: that there has been a governmentalization of the state. Sovereignty in its macro-juridical form is premised on the concept of law and right, and when the sovereign power is exercised on the social body, it works in terms of restriction, prohibition, and denial. Governmentality, on the other hand, refers to the management of the social body in terms of interventions on the part of the state aimed at promoting the welfare of society. The purpose of these interventions is to activate and arouse the subjects, rather than constrict and repress them. While historically the state, Foucault demonstrates, has always performed these functions to a certain extent—he calls them "the pastoral functions of the state"—in the 20th century—the governmental role of the state has become the dominant form of power in Western societies.

The two paradigms of power, sovereignty and governmentality, are fundamentally different in their nature and modalities. While the sovereign power is repressive, governmentality as a form of power is productive. The subject of the sovereign power is the *citizen* with rights who participates in the sovereignty of the state, but in its governmental role the state views the social space as inhabited by a *population*. "Governments [perceive] that they [are] not dealing simply with subjects, or even with a 'people', but with a 'population', with its specific phenomenon and its peculiar variables: birth and death rates, life expectancy, fertility, state of health, frequency of illness, patterns of diets and habitations" (Foucault 1990: 25). This *population* is "constituted" through enumeration, quantification, and classification by censuses and surveys conducted by the government. On the basis of this information, "populations groups" are identified as targets of policies, as objects on which governmentality can be exercised. Thus with the rise of the governmental function of the state as the dominant mode of power, the citizens who were subjects of the sovereign dissolve into the *population* and become objects of governance.

Thus population groups are empirically identifiable entities—as opposed to the theoretically defined citizens—on whom the techniques of governmentality are to be applied. And their application has the precise aim of promoting welfare of the target group. What is important to the state is the efficiency of these techniques, judged by comparing the costs associated with them and the benefits—in terms of well being of the population group—they generate. In the words of Foucault,

> Government is defined as a right manner of disposing things so as to lead .... to an end that is 'convenient' for each of the things that are to be governed. This implies a plurality of specific aims: for instance, government will have to ensure that the greatest possible quantity of wealth is produced, that the people are provided with sufficient means of subsistence, that the population is enabled to multiply, and so on. Thus there is a whole series of specific finalities that become the objective of government as such.[1]

The logic of governmental technologies is thus grounded in a social cost-benefit analysis with the production of maximum benefits for the population at a given cost as its objective, a job to be done by experts and professionals. The criterion for identifying target groups can be economic conditions, ethnicity, caste, religion, age or gender—some characteristics that the members of the group share. The possible sites of governmentality are also varied and many: the family, the work place, the educational institution, the prison and so on. As population groups at which it is targeted, and sites where it is applied, are multiple, governmentality necessarily posits society as heterogeneous, consisting of a multiplicity of objects of welfarist interventions. Partha Chatterjee, in elaborating on Foucault, draws our attention to this heterogeneity of the *social*:

> All of this made governance less a matter of politics and more of administrative policy, a business for experts rather than for political representatives. Moreover, while the political fraternity of

citizens had to be constantly affirmed as one and indivisible, there was no one entity to be governed. There was always a multiplicity of population groups that were the objects of governmentality—multiple targets with multiple characteristics, requiring multiple techniques of administration....

[T]he classical idea of popular sovereignty, expressed in the legal–political fact of equal citizenship, produced the homogeneous construct of the nation, *whereas the activities of governmentality required multiple, cross-cutting and shifting classifications of the population as the targets of multiple policies, producing necessarily a heterogeneous construct of the social.* (Chatterjee 2004: 35–36, my emphasis)

In short, a governmentalized state addresses empirically constructed, multiple population groups, with the purpose of promoting their welfare, in terms of rationally designed efficient techniques of administration. Here power operates not from a centered notion of sovereignty that claims its legitimacy by referring to something internal to itself, but as a decentered system of bureaucratic administration whose legitimacy flows from its instrumental role in promoting social good.

Capital and Governance

What then is the relationship between governmentality and capital? Is the promotion of welfare an end in itself? Or does the state govern on behalf of capital? These questions become inescapable if we posit the problematic of power in the context of the political economy of capital and the logic of its reproduction. Foucault himself does not address these questions. In fact, he begins his exploration of power by rejecting the modern theories—the Marxist theory in particular—that have traditionally interpreted sovereignty and the macro-juridical forms of control as reducible to the logic of capital's rule. According to him, these theories are totalizing and reductionist, and therefore fail to capture the complex nature of power in contemporary societies. But after enunciating its decentered, dispersed, and heteromorphous character, he does not relate the new conceptualization of power to the question of the reproduction of capital's conditions of existence. Although scholars have drawn upon Foucault's analysis in many different contexts, none of them has thrown any light on this connection—Michael Hardt and Antonio Negri's *Empire* is probably the only exception. For example, in his otherwise highly imaginative work on third world democracies, Partha Chatterjee—I have already quoted him—explores the implications of governmentality in the realm of post-colonial politics but leaves the question of how his "politics of the governed" relates to the post-colonial capitalist formation unaddressed. The connection between governance and the hegemony of capital thus remains invisible.

One can search for this connection in the context of the advanced capitalist societies of the West, explore how governmental interventions in the sphere of health, education, employment, sexuality and so forth converge to consolidate the rule of capital. But that is not what we want to pursue here. We would rather place the idea of governmentality as a form of power in the context of post-colonial capitalist development and the hegemony process—the narrative we are trying to build in this book—to bring this connection into visibility. We have already seen how development depoliticized primitive accumulation and constituted the hegemony of capital vis-à-vis its outside. But the arising of capital leaves in its wake a surplus population—those who have lost their access to the means of labor but are unable to sell their labor-power as a commodity. They constitute a space outside capital's own realm, the space of poverty, and although capital is economically self-subsistent, its political and ideological conditions of existence depend on how this space is negotiated. The destruction of pre-capital as the necessary condition for capital's arising was legitimized in the name of progress, but now poverty is integral to capital's own existence, an "other" that it cannot escape. Development can now claim the legitimacy of capital's existence only by addressing poverty and deprivation in terms of governmental technologies with the aim of ensuring subsistence to the dispossessed, to the inhabitants of the wasteland that surrounds the world of capital. This requires that a part of the capitalist surplus be transferred from the domain of capital for implementing anti-poverty programs; development now means a reversal of primitive accumulation.

Thus there is dispersion within the discourse with its object undergoing transmutation. By shifting the focus from accumulation to eradication of absolute poverty, the discourse distances itself from the capital's own agenda, and the space of development emerges as a space distinct from the one in which the story of the modes of production and capital is inscribed. Development is no longer synonymous with the project of an overall capitalist transformation of the economy, a project that President Truman's 1949 speech described as one for which "ancient philosophies have to be scrapped; old social institutions have to disintegrate; bonds of caste, creed and race have to burst".[2] The primary concern of development now is the "improvement" of the conditions of the poor, who is located outside the domain of capital, with governmental technologies. The two spaces, however, are inseparable in the sense that each provides the condition of existence of the other. While resources flowing from the capitalist space allow the developmental state and other agencies to engage in anti-poverty programs, these interventions in turn legitimize the existence of capital by "taking care of its castaways". In order to grasp the post-colonial capitalist formation, it is essential that we recognize the distinction between capital and development and then focus on their mutuality and contradictions. Conflation of the two spaces completely keeps out of sight the complexities of the structure of power and hegemony within which the reproduction of capital takes place in the post-colonial context. Radical development theorists, Marxists in particular, have missed this crucial distinction and reduced development into capital and by implication, the international organizations into vehicles of imperialism. An eminent Indian Marxist political economist interprets the shifts in the World Bank's policies thus:

> In different phases of the Bank's operation in India, its policy package has been sold under different labels. Sometimes it has invoked the concept of 'efficiency' and 'comparative advantage' to support the argument. For a while, under McNamara, it professed concern about poverty .... [Its] profession of social concerns [has] often given rise to the illusion that the World Bank is an agency independent of imperialism......[No] matter what specific argument it has advanced.... and no matter what social concern it has professed, its basic policy prescription in favor of 'liberalization' has never changed.[3]

As the exclusive focus here is on the Bank's role as an "agent of imperialism", shifts in its priorities and strategies appear to be of little import. The fact that the changes in the priorities within the Bank's agenda are linked with capital's changing conditions of existence is thus completely missed. These simplistic interpretations pay no attention to the dynamics of the development discourse and therefore fail to see the complex relation between capital and governance on which the regime of accumulation is based. This reductionism surely has proved to be costly: in the face of the current phenomenon of capitalist globalization, Marxist orthodoxy is now either surrendering to the TINA syndrome or is adopting critical positions that it thinks are radically opposed to the regime of capital without realizing that they are in fact a part of capital's auto-critique. These reactions are rooted in the inability to grasp the complexities of the emerging order.

Need, Entitlement and Capability: Development as Governmentality

The concern about absolute poverty brought the concept of "basic needs" to the center of discussions. The concept referred to material needs such as food, shelter, clothing, health care, and access to safe water and also to non-material needs like education, human rights, and political participation. Throughout the 1970s the basic need approach dominated the discourse and determined the nature of policy interventions. The concept however was not rigorously formulated; it was rather a loosely defined set of ideas. The new approach to development had to wait till the early 1980s to find its theoretical justifications in the work of Amartya Sen and others who followed him in this area of research. In an article in 1983 titled *Development: Which Way Now?*, Sen interpreted development in an entirely new light, providing the crucial elements for the theoretical foundation of poverty oriented strategies. To appreciate the significance of Sen's intervention into the discourse, it is important to keep in mind the background against which it was made. The early 1980s was the time of the rise of the neo-liberal market ideology with Ronald Reagan and Margaret Thatcher in power in the US and Britain. There was an all out attempt to bring every social institution under the sway of the new ideology, including of course the academe. In the specific context of development studies, the existence of development economics as a separate field of study was increasingly being questioned. With the cases of East Asian economies such as South Korea and Taiwan presented as success stories of market driven development, the argument for development planning was already losing force. What justifications could there be, it was now asked, for having development as a separate branch of economics when all economic phenomena could ultimately be explained in terms of the logic of the market? Development economics was in trouble, and its "reason for being" had to be reasserted.

Critically examining the grounds on which it was being discredited, Sen argued that the failure of development economics was not so much in identifying the factors leading to economic growth, as in the inability to characterize development as distinct from growth. Development refers to improvements in areas such as life expectancy, literacy, and health that determine the quality of life—this is the notion of human development—and the growth of income is only a means to those ends. The limitation of development economics was that its exclusive focus on the question of growth had turned the means into an end in itself, keeping the real ends out of sight. It could claim the legitimacy of its existence as a relevant discipline if it only rid itself of this preoccupation with growth and adopted the broader vision of development based on human development indexes.

But isn't the growth of per capita income necessary for development? Sen, while agreeing that it is, points out that it is quite possible that growth may fail to produce the desired impact on the quality of life. On the other hand, it is possible for a country with a lower per capita income to achieve the same level of development as those enjoying a higher income level. Citing examples of several developing countries, he points out that China and Sri Lanka have achieved in 1980 the same life expectancy as Brazil and Mexico, despite the fact that the GNP per capita in the latter two are seven times higher. The achievement of China and Sri Lanka in this area was the result of direct public policies rather than the growth of income, and this highlighted, according to him, that "[not] merely is it case that economic growth is a means rather than an end, it is also the case that for some important ends it is not a very efficient means either". (1983: 496)

Thus by questioning the reduction of development into growth, and by highlighting the role of direct public action in this context, Sen redefines development and gives it a new lease of life. A new space is opened within the discourse in which development, instead of being defined merely in terms of plans and strategies for accumulation and growth, can now be posited as the project of designing and implementing public policies with the aim of improving the broader indexes of development.

Sen presents two crucial concepts, "entitlement" and "capability"—which he further develops in his subsequent works—that provide the foundation for the new space of development he defines. He defines entitlement as a relation connecting one set of ownership to another through certain rules of legitimacy. It "refers to the set of alternative commodity bundles that a person can command in a society using the totality of rights and opportunities he or she faces" (1983: 497). In a private ownership market economy, entitlement relations can be of various types such as, among others (*a*) exchange-based entitlements, (*b*) production-based entitlements, and (*c*) own labor entitlements, and (*d*) entitlements based on social security which supplements the exchange-based entitlement. But in all these cases, the relation captures a person's access to commodities that is considered legitimate within the existing legal and social arrangements.

The concept of entitlement provides the clue to why a high level of per capita income of a country may not translate into a high level of development. Economic growth means an increase in the availability of commodities, but such an increase may be associated with an absence of entitlements for some sections of the population and therefore may fail to realize developmental goals for those sections. In other words, poverty and deprivation may very well be the result of entitlement failure rather than non-availability of commodities.

While entitlement refers to the commodity bundle a person can command, capability refers to what that person can do: Can he adequately nourish himself? Live long? Read and write? Avoid preventable morbidity? These capabilities are the features of well-being that constitutes the content of development. Although capability depends on the bundle of commodities, the relationship between the commodity space and the space of capability is a complex one: the same set of capabilities may correspond to different sets commodities. The mapping from commodities to capabilities may differ both across and within countries depending on the differences in race, gender, age and other characteristics. Thus capability as a concept is broader and more complex than basic needs. The latter defines a set of needs and then identifies a bundle of commodities—food, housing, drinking water, etc.—that satisfy those needs, and thus the focus remains on commodities. In contrast, the former begins by recognizing the many-one correspondence between capabilities and commodities, and therefore is able to address the differences in the commodity requirement of different groups for achieving the same set of capabilities.

These twin ideas, entitlements and capabilities, constitute the analytical foundation of the poverty-oriented approach: development now means the expansion of the set of capabilities and entitlements of target groups. These goals can be better achieved by direct public action—such as ensuring food security through public distribution, public action in the sphere of health and education—rather than the growth of income. And the task of the development practitioners is to design "efficient" policies that will produce well-being of the poor at the minimum cost in terms of resources.

Thus in Sen's analysis, development as the space of governmentality is further crystallized and consolidated; it is a space where target groups are to be identified and addressed in terms of the technologies of governance. The point that needs to be stressed here is that the poor posited by the discourse as the target of policy is an empirical category identifiable in terms of empirically observable characteristics. She/He is one without access to an arbitrarily and exogenously given consumption basket as in the basic needs approach; or, one who does not have the capabilities necessary for functioning in society, as in the capability approach. Thus the developmental target is first set and then the poor is identified and marked as the member of a "population group" in terms of his/her empirically observable deficiencies. This poor as a target of policy is very different from the one who inhabited the space of underdevelopment in the earlier conceptualisation of the dual economy in terms of the traditional–modern division. There the traditional economy was depicted in terms of an inner logic of its own, a logic that constituted its inner essence, and the inhabitants of that economy were described in terms of that essence. But governmentality dispenses with the necessity of theoretically defining the poor; it constitutes him as an empirical category on which the techniques of governance can be applied.

Unsettling the "Economy"

Let us now see the implications of this new vision of development for the hegemony process we have already described in the preceding chapters. The space of development mapped in terms of entitlement, capability, and public action evidently unsettles the "economy" that was produced through articulatory practice in what we have called the first moment of the hegemony process. The discursive closure defining that moment was based on the choice of accumulation and growth as the nodal points. These nodal points organized the economy as a sutured space by fixing the economic categories with provisionally stable meanings. The recognition of the existence of absolute poverty outside the space of accumulation and growth allows other meanings to permeate through the sutures and unsettle the earlier representation. Developmental governance reconstitutes the economic space by positing need, entitlement, and capability as the new set of nodal points, and thus rearticulates the elements by investing them with new meanings. The developmental state was earlier seen as an institution with the sole aim of using its political authority to create conditions most conducive to growth. In other words, the state was reduced to a vehicle of primitive accumulation. The new nodal points discursively reconstitute the state and represent it as an active agent engaged in designing and implementing welfare promoting redistributive policies. The developmental role of the state is now defined in terms of providing entitlements to fulfill needs and expand capabilities of the population groups. The market was a channel through which resources—means of labor, wage-goods and labor power—could flow from the stagnant pre-capitalist sector to the domain of accumulation driven capitalist production. And consumption, i.e., the wage-bill, was instrumental in the production of surplus for accumulation, because it was the basis of the employment of surplus producing labor. In the new representation, the market is an arrangement that allows one set of entitlements to be converted into another through exchange, and consumption is for direct satisfaction of needs and creation of capability, an end in itself. Thus governmentality produces its own representation of the economy, a representation that is very different from the accumulation-centric one.

What is important to recognize however is that while the space of need and capability is predicated on a critique of the growth-centric view of development, it is not posited in radical opposition to the space defined by growth; need as a nodal point is not pitted against accumulation. The poverty-oriented approach claims that growth has failed to eradicate poverty but it never holds growth responsible for poverty. It clearly abstains from trying to explore whether the process of accumulation itself has anything to do with the existence of poverty. Poverty is an empirically observable phenomenon that coexists with growth, an initial condition that the latter seems to have failed to transform. The failure of growth in this regard only betrays its inability to perform the task that was assigned to it, and one can rightly be skeptical about its efficacy in dealing with the problem of poverty. But the existence of poverty is independent of growth: it is not a phenomenon produced by the growth process but a space that the chariot of growth has bypassed. And although confronting poverty calls for its reconceptualization and redesigning of policies for its alleviation, the newly constituted space of poverty is in no way antithetical to accumulation and growth. On the contrary, they are complementary in that successful and efficient management of poverty can secure the legitimacy of capital in the space of accumulation.

The narrative of primitive accumulation that we have built up in the preceding chapters however offers an entirely different perspective. We have conceptualized dispossession and poverty as an outcome of the arising of capital, of the expropriation and marginalization that are inevitably associated with it. Cast in terms of the concept of entitlement, it is a story of destruction and loss of entitlements caused by capital's arising. The estrangement of petty producers from the means of labor caused the destruction of their property-based and own labor-based entitlements. The other legal and semi-legal entitlements they had enjoyed within the pre-capitalist social arrangement were systematically withdrawn under the new bourgeois property laws. The dispossessed were left with only their labor power—the only commodity that they could sell in the market. But their exclusion from the space of capital led to the failure of that one exchange-based entitlement, condemning them to a wasteland of poverty and deprivation. Poverty thus is an outcome of the process of accumulation and growth itself; they are two sides of the same coin.

Seen from this perspective, the recognition of the existence of poverty clears a ground for a political critique of capital and its arising.

The coexistence of growth and absolute poverty poses political questions whose resolution is essential for addressing the problem of development. We have already demonstrated in Chapter 3 how the discourse depoliticized the accumulation-centric development by presenting it as a matter of techno-bureaucratic planning exercise based on politically neutral, rational calculations. Primitive accumulation was exorcised of its inherent contradictions and depicted as development in a dual economy driven by the impersonal law of the market. The persistence of absolute poverty brings these contradictions to the fore and thus opens up the possibility of politicizing development by interrogating the discourse.

But the discourse once again distances development from the world of politics by ridding the question of poverty of its political dimensions. It posits the realm of poverty as distinct and separate from the realm of accumulation, and claims that improving the conditions of the population groups inhabiting the former realm is only a matter of designing appropriate public policies. The designing of these policies is again a matter of rational and scientific calculations—a task for experts and professionals. Earlier, these development professionals prepared plans and designed policies for accumulation, now they will also formulate strategies for efficient public action for the eradication of poverty. It involves collection of information about the poor through enumeration, classification, and quantification, and then the use of that information to devise programs that will generate welfare for them—satisfy their basic needs and expand their capabilities—at the lowest resource cost. What could be a ground for a political critique of capital is thus turned into a domain of rational calculations. Thus the discourse subverts the possibility of locating poverty in a politically contested terrain by displacing the entire question onto the "politically neutral" terrain of governmentality.

In the beginning, there was some ambivalence within the discourse towards the poverty-oriented approach, as reflected in the debates within the World Bank on the McNamara model. Given the Bank's commitment to the ideology of the market, free-enterprise and non-interference of the state, the shift of emphasis onto the anti-poverty programs was seriously questioned on the ground that it would undermine growth and thereby weaken the long term basis of economic prosperity. Although the McNamara strategy came to be adopted, there was a strong tendency within the Bank to assert the primacy of growth. As Robert Ayres puts it:

[The] antipoverty emphasis of McNamara since 1973 posed some serious challenges to the prevalent Bank ideology. The result was a somewhat ambiguous pastiche of concepts and approaches. Thus, while there was heightened emphasis on questions of poverty and income distribution, this did not mean that the prevalent growth concerns could be forgotten. .... The result after 1873, then, was a rather tenuous gluing together of some markedly divergent approaches. Poverty-oriented emphases sometimes seemed to have been pasted on the prevalent ideology, without, however, altering its fundamental slant. (1983: 75)

However, the poverty-related goals were slowly assimilated within the broad program of the Bank and by the end of the 1970s, the "ambiguous pastiche" crystallized into a coherent agenda. Reconciliation was struck between growth and poverty alleviation, and they were posited as the twin goals of development. The *World Development Report* (1980) of the Bank explicitly recognized that growth might cause dispossession and poverty:

[L]ooking at changes over time within particular countries, the connection between growth and poverty reduction over periods of a decade or two appears inexact. There is a general agreement that growth, in the very long term, eliminates most absolute poverty; but also that some people may (at least temporarily) be impoverished by development—as when a tenant farmer is displaced by his landlord's tractor or a shoemaker by mass-produced shoes. (pp. 35–36)

And it goes on to emphasize the absence of any trade off between growth and the poverty-focused approach:

[T]he connection between economic growth and poverty reduction goes both ways. Few would dispute that health, education, and well-being of the mass of people in industrialized countries are a cause, as well as a result, of national prosperity. Similarly people who are unskilled and sick make little contribution to a country's economic growth. Development strategies that bypass large number of people may not be the most effective way for developing countries to raise their long-run growth rates. (p. 36)

Thus the discourse first produced its own critique of "growth essentialism" and then restructured the space of development on the basis of this auto-critique to posit the eradication of absolute poverty and accumulation as its dual objectives, with profound implications for the post-colonial developmental states. We now turn our attention to how this change of perspective was reflected in the trajectory of India's planned economic transformation.

The Changing Perspective of Development and the Indian Planning

Although its thrust lay in the expansion of large-scale modern industries through accumulation, planning in India from the very beginning had an explicit welfarist face. As we have already seen, Nehru was convinced that the pains and rigours inevitably associated with the arising of modern industries could be assuaged and mitigated with appropriate intervention by the state. This claim, that the state could ensure that the entire population shared the benefits of industrialization, constituted the ideological foundation of planning and the ground for its legitimacy. However, as the project of planned industrialization began to materialize, a contradiction emerged between the outcome of planning and the state's welfarist commitments.

After the first two plans were over, there was a growing feeling of unease among some of the architects of the Indian plans about whether planning was producing results consistent with the objectives laid down by the post-colonial developmental state. Were the fruits of industrial growth trickling down to the poor? Were people finding their basic needs satisfied? These questions unsettled the confidence with which the planners and policy makers had until then formulated plans and designed policies. "It was evident", wrote Sukhomoy Chakraborty in reviewing the Indian planning experience, "by the early sixties that something was seriously wrong" (1987: 30). A committee was formed with P. C. Mahalanobis—the chief architect of the Second Five-Year Plan that epitomized the Nehruvian vision of economic progress—as the chair to enquire into the impact of planning on the level of living. The finding of the committee could not assert that the level had improved. There was ground to believe that planning in India with its emphasis on modern industrialization had bypassed the poor.

The persistence of poverty despite impressive industrial growth had profound political implications. The nationalist movement succeeded in mobilizing the masses to demand an end to the colonial rule. When the newly born independent nation state presented itself as a developmental state and initiated the process of industrialization, it enjoyed popular consent as evident in the unchallenged supremacy of the Congress Party in the post-colonial political scene. But the failure of growth to improve the conditions of the poor was certainly a threat to the support base of the ruling party. The legitimacy of modern India with its impressive heavy industries could be secured only by going directly to the masses with programs that would provide a bridge between them and the developmental state.

The committee under the chairmanship of P. C. Mahalanobis was followed by the setting up of a working group comprising eminent economists to make recommendations on the "minimum level of living". In its report, the committee defined the "poverty line" in terms of a basic minimum of Rs. 20 per month for the rural areas and Rs. 25 for the urban areas, calculated at 1960/61 prices. It also distinguished between public consumption and private consumption: the former included health, education, and housing that were to be financed directly by the state, and latter was to be met by an individual's personal income. The concern about the persistence of poverty thus made its way into the planning exercise during the period of the Third Plan.

It is interesting to note that although the question was raised and deliberated, and some of the relevant technical and empirical work was done, it was not until the early 1970s that the goals of planning were revised in India. It had to wait till the new idea crystallized within the discourse at its international sites and forums. It was only after the idea of direct assault on poverty was authorized by the discourse, and new practices defined that the developmental state could change the nature and modalities of its interventions.

The shift was finally visible in the formulation of the Fifth Plan which explicitly emphasized the need to adopt a strategy of growth with redistribution. The macroeconomic model behind the plan underscored the impossibility of reducing poverty solely through growth. As Chakraborty puts it:

> The main message of the model was quite clear, however, despite all its limitations. It showed that if the growth rate of around 5–6% per annum was about the maximum one could have, *it was impossible to bring about a significant reduction in poverty, howsoever defined, without attacking the problem directly.* ... Further, the market determined commodity vector was far from what was necessary if basic needs were to be met. ... As a result, when the Sixth Plan was formulated in 1980, a number of poverty eradication measures were introduced. (1987: 36)

Thus poverty alleviation as a separate and distinct target of development planning, as distinct from growth, was proposed and accepted during the Fifth Plan. Although they were introduced in a more coordinated and organized manner in the 1980s, several direct anti-poverty programs were launched in the late 1970s, including the Small Farmers Development Agency (SFDA), Marginal Farmers and Agricultural Laborers' Development Agency (MFAL), Cash Scheme for Rural Employment (CSRE) and Food for Work Program (FWP). These programs however were not well coordinated or efficiently executed; quite often they had overlapping areas of operation and aimed at the same target group. An integrated approach to poverty was adopted with a more comprehensive and rigorously formulated programs in the Sixth Plan—the major ones being the Integrated Rural Development Program (IRDP), the National Rural Employment Program (NREP) and the Rural Landless Employment Guarantee Scheme (RLEGP). The last two were merged in 1989 to form the *Jawahar Rojgar Yojana* (Jawahar Income Scheme). These programs aimed at improving the condition of small and marginal farmers on the one hand, and creating employment opportunities for the landless agricultural laborers and artisans, on the other. The lack of assets and skill was recognized as the main cause of poverty; therefore the programs focussed on the creation of assets for the poor. These assets included sources of irrigation, implements for farming in the small and marginal farms, animals for dairy and animal husbandry as non-farm activities and tools and training for artisans in cottage industries and handicrafts. The objective was to empower the poor so that they could engage in income generating productive activities. In the area of health, family welfare, and nutrition programs for vulnerable groups such as pregnant women, nursing mothers and children were launched to provide health services directly to the rural poor. They also included schemes for controlling communicable and common diseases in the rural area through educating and training health specialists and health personnel. In short, massive efforts were made by the Indian state to reach the poor directly through planning without the mediation of growth.

Thus, Indian planning assumed a governmental role in order to ensure that it helped in the rise of the political conditions of existence of the post-colonial capital. For almost two-and-a-half decades after the independence it had been engaged in creating the conditions for primitive accumulation; now it was actively engaged in redistributing a part of the surplus generated in the capitalist sector to the poor through anti-poverty programs. And the space of planning was restructured to accommodate the non-capitalist goal of improving the condition of the victims of primitive accumulation.

Before the poverty-focussed approach was adopted, there was already a shift of emphasis in the Fourth Five Year plan onto the agricultural sector. Policies were designed and implemented to bring about radical changes in agricultural production. The new policies sought to increase agricultural productivity with the help of the new agricultural technology embodied in strategic inputs such as high yielding varieties of seed, fertilizers and pesticides, and modern mechanized implements. Not surprisingly, only the large farmers were in a position to take advantage of these new opportunities, and the Indian agriculture witnessed a "green revolution" in the northwestern provinces of Punjab, Haryana and western Uttar Pradesh. It was undoubtedly an attempt to inaugurate capitalist transformation in the Indian agriculture. Critical observers of the process of economic development in post-colonial India—especially the Marxists—interpreted this change as a reversal in the ideology of Indian planning, a change from its socialist orientation to an endorsement of capitalist development. But seen from the perspective of the arising of the post-colonial industrial capital, the thrust for an increase in agricultural production by providing incentives to the dynamic owners of large farms was perfectly consistent with the planned expansion of modern industries. An expanding industrial sector required an increased supply of food for its labor force, and at the same time had to have an external market in the agricultural sector for its own products. In other words, planned capitalist transformation in certain pockets within the agricultural sector was complementary to the planned development of modern industries. Seen thus, there wasn't much of a reversal in it as the Marxists claimed.

The real change within the realm of planning occurred after the Green Revolution, a change whose profound implications escaped the Indian Marxist. It was the change from the preoccupation with accumulation to the concern about the poor, and with it the emergence of the governmental face of the state. And it is crucial to grasp the importance of this change to arrive at an understanding of the dynamics of post-colonial Indian capitalism.

The goal of reaching the poor through direct public action remained an integral part of Indian planning throughout the 1980s, until the wind of globalization started blowing. In order to negotiate the rapidly changing global economic order, the Indian economy reorganized itself and governmentality took a new and more complex form, which I deal with in the following chapter.

Notes

1. Faubion (2001: 211).
2. *Measures of Economic Development of Underdeveloped Countries*, Department of Social and Economic Affairs, United Nations, 1951.
3. Patnaik (1995).

Chapter 5

Difference as Hegemony: Capital and the Need Economy

The Theme of Return

Talking about the dialectics of "old" and "new" in the introduction to *Mapping Ideology*, Slavoj Žižek has cautioned us against a possible confusion in identifying continuity and radical rupture in the understanding of social change. The problem arises "when an event" writes Žižek, "that announces a wholly new dimension or epoch is (mis) perceived as the continuation or return to the past"(1) The prevalent trend among critical theorists to characterize the current experience of capitalist globalization following the collapse of the actually existing socialisms as a return to the 19th century tradition of the nation state, according to Žižek, is an exemplary case of such misperception. These theorists, he claims, fail to see that far from a return to its earlier form, the emerging order is a radically new one, signalling a "withering away" of, rather than a return to the traditional concept of national sovereignty.

One may, in fact many would, find Žižek's withering–away–of–the nation–state thesis premature. However, one surely would agree with him on the point that the theme of "return" dominates the description of globalization by its proponents and detractors alike: both see the changes that are being wrought on the global economic scene as signalling a return to the Adam Smithian world of free market, unbridled capitalism, and the minimalist night watchman state. The neo-liberals who celebrate these changes argue that these will unleash productive forces and expand market opportunities on a global scale, and thereby bring prosperity to all members of the global economic community. The liberalization of the labor market for them is the necessary prerequisite for investment, accumulation and growth. The critics on the other hand see in the forces of globalization the imperialist face of capital, its naked 18th century form, trying to subjugate the third world to its absolute dominance. They describe it as a process wherein the welfare states of the Fordist regime are being dismantled, the collective bargaining power of the working class is being weakened, and the economic sovereignty of third world nations undermined. The dispersion of production on a global scale through subcontracting and outsourcing, and the consequent informalization of the labor processes, are, in the neo-liberal vision, serving as a substitute for the free international mobility of labor and hence are crucial for efficiency. But the critics interpret the informalization as a shift to primitive and more exploitative modes of labor. Despite their contrary, in fact opposing, views of globalization, both groups however share the same imaginary of a return to the past, to an earlier form of capitalism that, depending on the perspective adopted, is either vibrant and dynamic or primitive and retrogressive. For one, capitalism is returning to its vigorous and exciting youth; for the other, it is a return of the civilized capitalism to its brutal and coercive primordial form.

It is this preoccupation with the theme of return that I want to contest. I will argue that far from a return to the past, what we are witnessing is the emergence of a capitalism that is radically new in its form of governance and modalities of power. Driven by a similar urge, Michael Hardt and Antonio Negri have sought to characterize the emergent global system as what they call *Empire*, a capitalist order that is fundamentally different from the classical notion of imperialism based on the nation-state-centric sovereignty. Although I do not find their story of *Empire* very convincing—I do not wish to critically engage with it here—I do share their claim that the current juncture must be understood as the materialization of a new era of capital, an era that resists representation in terms of the traditional concepts of the political economy of capitalism.

My specific concern, as I have made clear in the preceding chapters, is the relationship between capital and the imaginaries of development: how the development discourse creates the conditions of capital's arising and reproduction. In this context, what is of particular importance to me is the widely held view that the phenomenon of globalization announces the "death of development". In Chapter 3, we saw how the British Development Act of 1929 marked a shift in the concept of development. The classical idea of development as a process that the economy experiences—a process to be described and analyzed—was supplanted with the new vision in which development meant changes to be brought about by purposeful action, by formulating plans and designing programs; it was now derived from the transitive rather than the intransitive verb. It is now claimed that capitalist globalization and the rise of the market economy has rendered the project of development obsolete and irrelevant. For now, the process of accumulation and growth will result from the internal logic of capital, from its innate urge for self-expansion. Development as purposeful and planned action by a rational agent located outside the realm of the market has no place in the global capitalist economy described by the neoliberals. Development planning is history.

If by development we mean planning for accumulation, then there is no denying it is an anachronism in the emergent new economic order. But it hardly means that development is dead. Far from it. The accumulation-centric vision—we have already characterized it as the first moment of the hegemony process—is fast fading away but it is yielding place to an entirely new imaginary of development, one that is rooted in governmentality rather than in the project of planned primitive accumulation. In the preceding chapter, I argued that there was already a mutation in the notion of development from the 1970s with the focus shifted from accumulation to promotion of welfare through direct intervention. It was the project of legitimizing capital's existence by resorting to a reversal of primitive accumulation for providing entitlements to the dispossessed. I will now claim that the development discourse in this era of capital is reorganizing itself entirely in relation to the world of the dispossessed produced by capitalist accumulation, and now it is governmentality in a form that is far more complex, with far greater material effectivity, than before. Its goal is to constitute an economic space outside and alongside capital, for its castaways, rather than to create entitlements for them through redistribution of income. Development is very much alive and kicking; only instead of identifying itself with capital, it now seeks to create the conditions of existence of the latter on the basis of an agenda of its own. What it is engaged in is the management of poverty—although couched in terms of the now fashionable "development management"—in a far more elaborate and complex way than in the 1970s and 80s.

The Challenge of the Slums

The Challenge of the Slums: Global Report on Human Settlement, 2003, published by the UN–Habitat, reports that there are 921 million urban slum-dwellers in the third world in 2001. They constitute 78.2 per cent of the urban population of the least developed countries and a third of the global urban population. The total slum-population is 20 million in the five great metropolises in South Asia (Karachi, Mumbai, Delhi, Kolkata, Dhaka). The figures are particularly stunning for Africa: In sub-Saharan Africa the proportion of urban residents in slums is highest at 71.9 per cent, according to the report; in both Ethiopia and Chad, 99.4 per cent of the urban population live in slums. However, although the concentration of slum-dwellers is highest in African cities, in numbers alone, Asia accounts for some 60 per cent of the world's urban slum residents.

On the basis of these figures, Mike Davis has drawn our attention to what he considers a puzzling phenomenon: urbanization decoupled from industrialization (Davis 2004). "Whereas", he observes, "the classic slum was a decaying inner city, the new slums are more typically located on the edge of the urban spatial explosion" (p. 14). This "urbanization of poverty", according to Davis, is largely the result of the structural adjustment program prescribed by the IMF and forced on the developing countries, especially in Africa and Latin America. The liberalization of imports, cut back on public investment and removal of food and fertilizer subsidies, have forced the poor out of the rural economy and to move to the city for survival; it is the push rather than the pull of expanding employment opportunities resulting from industrialization. The urban poor of the third world for Davis are a "surplus humanity".

While Davis and other sociologists of urbanization are bent on interpreting this phenomenon of urbanization delinked from industrialization and development as an outcome of the neo-liberal policies forced on the third world in the 1990s, the fact is that a large urban informal economy in which the poor have managed to survive entirely outside the "modern" industrial sector has always been there in these countries. It is the result of primitive accumulation that has accompanied the process of post-colonial development from the very beginning. The neo-liberal policies adopted during the 1990s have certainly exacerbated the process of exclusion, but the process has been operative during the entire post-colonial period. As far back as in the 1970s, ILO sponsored projects including the well-known Kenya Mission reported the existence of a large urban population in the big third world cities that belonged neither to the modern enclave economy nor to the traditional rural economy. But these empirical observations remained at the margin of the discussions on development for the two decades that followed, while the dominant discourse continued to project the imaginary of development based on the traditional–modern binary. The "new urban poverty" that the UN–Habitat report refers to this "indeterminate space" between the traditional and the modern sector, the space of the dispossessed, and there is hardly anything "new" about it. Only it was not visible until recently since the narrative of development kept it out of sight.

The foregrounding of this "surplus humanity"—the space of poverty that emphatically distances itself from the Marxian reserve army—constitutes the ground for the new face of development as the "management of poverty". In what follows, I will explore the genealogy of the "informal sector" to bring into visibility this emerging paradigm of development. I will argue that the dawn of the 21st century is witnessing the emergence and materialization of a capitalist order constituted by a synthesis of accumulation and developmental governmentality. And this I identify as the complex form of capital's hegemony resting on an implosion of what Foucault described as the productive and the restrictive forms of power.

The Discursive Constitution of the Informal Sector

Central to my theorization of the post-colonial *economic* developed in Chapter 2 was the space of the dispossessed, of those who are excluded from the space of capital, a wasteland created by capitalist development. This space has remained invisible in the narrative of capitalist development and my purpose is to reinscribe it within the story post-colonial capital's arising. But now I have to face the inescapable question: how do the inhabitants of this space survive? They must be eking an existence somehow by engaging in some economic activities, however petty and low-income, outside the capitalist space. I did not consider the existence of these activities in my theorization, but it was only a discursive strategy because what I wanted to highlight was the fact that the inhabitants of the wasteland are victims of primitive accumulation. But the space of the dispossessed is not an empty economic space, its inhabitants engage in a variety of economic activities for their survival, activities that constitute a sub-economy. But the point to be stressed is that this sub-economy is the result of exclusion.

The development discourse in the phase of its accumulation-centric approach never recognized the existence of this sub-economy; for the development planner there was only unemployment, people waiting to be absorbed in the modern capitalist sector. I have already located in the identification of absolute poverty in the 1970s as the target of direct intervention a shift in the discourse; but even in this new phase, the emphasis was on state-centric redistribution to the poor; the activities in the sub-economy, although their existence was reported in the early 1970s by development researchers, did not find a place in the representation of underdevelopment.

But things have changed in the last few years. At the beginning of the new millennium, development agencies are suddenly waking up to the fact that a sub-economy exists. The discourse is bringing this hitherto invisible space into visibility by describing it, naming it and allowing it a place within the framework of development policy. It is given the name "the informal sector", a sector comprising activities whose location is in the limbo space between the traditional and the modern sector. The informal sector is now common currency in the development circle; the space of the dispossessed has finally come under the gaze of development.

It is here that I locate a second shift within the discourse, a shift that marks a fundamental change in the governmental technology in the era of globalization. The management of poverty in terms of welfarist governmentality is, I argue, taking on a new form that is in consonance with the new global order. In order to comprehend the implications of this change, we need to briefly trace the history of the informal sector and its emergence as a target of developmental governance.

The concept of the "informal sector" has figured prominently on the ILO's developmental agenda since the 1970s. The ILO conducted a series of studies in the 1970s and 1980s on the informal sector in third world cities. I concentrate here on an *ILO Employment Paper* by Paul Bangasser published in 2000 that explores in detail the genesis and evolution of the concept within the ILO.[1] "To learn from history", writes Bangasser:

> we must know it. Over the past three decades, the ILO has been both the midwife and the principal international institutional home for the concept of the informal sector. *As we enter the next millennium, with a new Director General and a refocused mandate on "decent work" and an increased emphasis on to the marginalised and the excluded,* it seems timely to pause and look back. Over these past thirty odd years, how has this institution wrestled with the informal sector, both as a concept and as a painful reality for our constituents? Where did this concept come from? How has the ILO dealt with it over the years, with what successes ... and what failures? (Bangasser 2000: 4, my emphasis)

Here Bangasser, speaking on behalf of the ILO, explicitly states that in the new millennium, there is a shift in the ILO's focus away from the center and onto "the marginal and the excluded", and this new focus demands that the developmental experience of the preceding half-century be rethought, put in a new perspective in order to produce a space in which development can be reconceptualized for the era of globalization. This new vision will have to locate the "the marginal and the excluded" within the conceptual framework for the analysis of an underdeveloped economy and the dynamics of its development.

In delineating the contours of this new vision, Bangasser takes cognizance of the fact that the Lewis strategy has failed miserably to deliver the results it had promised; the "modern sector" has grown at an impressive rate but its capacity to absorb surplus labor has turned out to be far less than was claimed in the Lewis scenario. With people migrating from the traditional to the modern sector in search of employment, the outcome has been a huge army of the unemployed residing at the margin of the modern, urban economy. These people have so far remained invisible to the development planner; models of development planning and the calculus on which they have been based have ignored their existence with the implicit assumption that once the development process gaines momentum, the surplus labor force will eventually be absorbed in the modern sector. In other words, these people have so far been seen by the development bureaucracy—on both national and international level—not as castaways of development but as people waiting to be active participants of the process of modernization and growth. The discourse of accumulation-centric development has treated the space of the marginalized as a transient one that will ultimately wither away.

After 50 years, it has now dawned on the global architects of development that far from a transitory phenomenon in a dual economy, unemployment and underemployment are now a permanent and integral part of the process of development itself. As Bangasser puts it,

> [T]he "temporary problem" didn't go away; it got worse. An increasingly large and visible "modern jobs gap" could not be ignored. Demographic trends plus seemingly unstoppable urban migration meant that ever-increasing numbers of people were entering the urban labour market, which was the modern sector par excellence. The levels of capital investment needed to generate "modern sector" jobs to absorb them were simply not in the cards, even under the most optimistic assumptions about both domestic saving and foreign investment. By the middle to late 1960s, unemployment was clearly not responding to the planned development efforts as it was supposed to. And this was in spite of significant efforts, and successes, in areas like capital formation, infrastructure investments, human resources development, etc. (Bangasser 2000: 7)

Against this background, he traces the history of how the ILO has wrestled with the concept of the informal sector and argues that this idea, long ignored by other developmental organizations, is now indispensable for devising development strategies that the new millennium calls for. But before we get into the story of the informal sector's "coming into being" within the international development bureaucracy, and its materialization in terms of development practices, let us consider a shift that had already occurred in the concept of dualism within the academic discourse of development economics.

Calling the Boys Back Home

The problem arising from the inability of the modern sector to absorb surplus labor was not entirely unrecognized in the academic discourse. We saw in the preceding chapter that from the middle of the 1970s development was increasingly taking on the form of governmentality, with the international organizations and developmental states identifying absolute poverty as the target of interventions. About the same time a shift could be observed also in the conceptualization of the dual economy in the academic discourse. In an article published in the *American Economic Review* in 1970 that later turned out to be a very influential one, John Harris and Michel Todaro offered a description of the underdeveloped economy that was very different from the dual economy of Lewis. In addressing the question of rural–urban migration in Africa, they discovered a "curious economic phenomenon": "despite the existence of positive marginal product in agriculture and significant levels of urban unemployment, rural–urban migration not only continues to exist, but indeed, appears to be accelerating" (p. 126). To provide an analytical explanation of this phenomenon, they considered a rural–urban divide in which the "modern urban sector" offers a politically determined wage that is substantially higher than what an individual would earn in the agricultural sector. The wage differential lures rural workers to migrate to the urban center, but as the number of jobs in the modern sector is limited, many of them fail to secure one. They, however, prefer to remain in the urban area rather than return to the rural sector because each one of them has an expectation of landing a modern sector job some day. Although they live as unemployed in the city, they have an expected income that is equal to the higher urban wage times the probability of getting a modern sector job (which is less than unity). As long as this expected income is higher than the certain income in the rural sector, the rural–urban migration continues. The crux of the story in non-technical language is: if the modern sector provides limited number of high wage jobs, it results in a kind of "voluntary unemployment" in the urban area with people hanging around there with the hope of getting an entry into the modern sector even when they could find productive employment in the rural economy, albeit at a lower wage. Thus labor power remains unutilized, causing a loss, in the sense of non-realization of potential output, to the economy as a whole.

It is not the model as such but Harris–Todaro's portrayal of the underdeveloped economy that is important for our purpose. In comparison with the earlier vision of the dual economy, there clearly is a reversal in the representational strategy they adopt. The first thing to note is that they take a snapshot of the growth profile and thereby abstract from the dynamics of the dual economy. One of the two sectors that inhabit this timeless, static economy is labelled "modern", which by implication makes the other sector, i.e., agriculture, "non-modern" or "traditional". Their characterization of the two sectors however departs from the modern–traditional binary that serves as the basis of dualism in Lewis. It is not an inherent dynamism or drive for accumulation that makes the modern sector "modern" in their description; the only characteristic that distinguishes it from the other sector is the fact that it pays a higher wage. On the other hand, the existence of surplus labor is not the defining characteristic of the (non-modern) agriculture; it is a sector where productive employment is available, although at a lower wage.[2] The modern–non-modern divide in Harris–Todaro's economy thus rests exclusively on the fact that in the former the wage is "politically determined" implying that the workers there are in a privileged position to bargain with the employer compared to those working in agriculture.

This is a fundamental departure from the earlier description of dualism and underdevelopment. The dualism in Lewis consists in the twin assumptions that the modern sector is driven by its inherent logic of accumulation and growth, while in contrast the existence of surplus labor reflects an inefficiency that is internal to the traditional sector, condemning it to a state of stagnation. In the new scenario the non-modern sector, i.e., agriculture, is not "inefficient" in any sense: everybody is productively employed there with a positive contribution to the output and therefore migration to the city inevitably causes a fall in production. In other words, there is no surplus labor in the non-modern sector to be transferred to the modern sector.

I would interpret Harris–Todaro's description of the economy not merely as a "different one" but as a reversal in the representation of underdevelopment. The earlier representation described the modern capitalist sector as dynamic and vigorous as opposed to the stagnant and backward traditional sector and thus arranged the two in a hierarchy. The dynamics of development was rooted in this hierarchy, in the ability of the "modern" to draw labor and non-labor resources from the "traditional", and expansion of the former meant the ineluctable withering away of the latter. The "modern" was permanent because of its strength and fullness while weakness and lack made the "traditional" transient. The new representation denies the modern sector any inherent superiority in terms of developmental energy, and at the same time it endows the non-modern sector with the capacity to accommodate employment seekers in productive employment. While the existence of the former is responsible for unutilised idle labor power, the latter is inimical to such wastage. Thus, there is a reversal in the respective roles assigned to the two sectors in the context of unemployment.

In this new portrayal of underdevelopment, the "modern/urban" is an alien entity that unsettles the economic landscape by luring people away from their "traditional/rural" economic habitat and then denying them entry into its own space. It is not just a temporary demand–supply mismatch in the labor market at a particular stage of transition that will ultimately disappear with sufficient expansion of the modern sector. Harris–Todaro in fact emphatically makes the point that a larger modern sector in this scenario will further aggravate the problem because by increasing the expected urban income, it will induce more people to migrate and swell the ranks of the urban unemployment. Contrary to the earlier perception of development, the solution here lies not in an expansion of the "modern" but in policies that would induce people to return to the "non-modern".

Harris–Todaro's analysis of urban unemployment provided analytical support to World Bank's emphasis, during the McNamara phase in the 1970s, on rural development in Africa. But their story was soon extricated from the specificity of its context of the African labor-scarce economies and adopted by development economists as a general framework for studying rural–urban migration in less-developed countries. A voluminous literature emerged that sought to identify the factors affecting migration and to devise possible policies for its regulation. In this entire literature, migration in a dual economy is seen as a burden—something that encumbers the development process by producing congestion and squalor in the urban space. The flow of labor from the non-modern to the modern space constituted the very process of developmental transition described in the 1950s and 1960s, but the same flow is now a dead-weight on development.

What this representation completely suppresses is that migration is the result of dispossession. The migrants are the victims of primitive accumulation and there is no "traditional" space they can be induced, lured or even forced to return to. The genie uncorked by development simply cannot be sent back into the bottle; it can only be tamed, disciplined and, quarantined. To do that, new objects of governmentality must be constituted, new techniques of governance devised, new development practices animated. I propose to see the emergence of the "informal sector" and its rise to prominence in the development discourse in this light.

From the Unemployed to the Working Poor

In the Harris–Todaro narrative and the literature it spawned, we can see that the existence of a space between the "modern" and the "non-modern", the space of the excluded, was coming into visibility in the field of development economics since the 1970s. But it was not until the late 1990s that this "limbo space" came under direct surveillance of the development discourse with international organizations shifting their attention to the informal sector. Harris–Todaro described the inhabitants of this space as "unemployed" but it was "discovered" in the early 1970s that they survived by engaging in a variety of petty economic activities that fell neither in the so-called traditional sector nor in the modern sector. In 1972 the ILO's comprehensive employment mission to Kenya, a part of its World Employment Program (WEP), serendipitously stumbled on these activities and coined the term "informal sector" to represent the site where they took place. An active and vibrant informal economy, the report of the mission claimed, existed in Nairobi which was overshadowed by the glittering skyscrapers of the modern economy and kept out of the visibility of the observer from outside. And far from the then prevalent view that informal activity meant only petty services provided by street vendors, cab drivers or porters in the railway station, this economy consisted of a wide range of manufacturing activities in which material goods were produced, such as furniture making, masonry, and carpentry. The Kenya mission's report identified this sector in terms of the following characteristics:

(a) Ease of entry;
(b) Reliance on indigenous resources;
(c) Family ownership of enterprises;
(d) Small scale of operation;
(e) Labor-intensive and adapted technology;

(f) Skill acquired outside the formal school system; and
(g) Unregulated and competitive markets.

What is important for us is the fact that the mission's characterization of the informal sector is entirely descriptive and empirical; the sector is described in terms of observations about what it does, how and under what conditions. It is not posited as a theoretical category defined in terms of any inner logic of its own; its "informal-ness" is not the manifestation of an inner essence. Let us recall that the definition of the traditional sector in the dual economy was grounded in the question why it did what it did, in behavioral and institutional characteristics that were internal to it. In contrast, the Kenya report, while inaugurating a new approach to the question of urban poverty by shifting the focus from the unemployed to the *working poor*, presented the informal sector as an empirical category, and however exciting to a development practitioner, it was hardly a concept that economists could be comfortable with.

They were not. Development economists were unwilling to accept a concept that did not have an adequate theoretical foundation. What is the rationale behind viewing a collection of economic activities as constituting a "sector" distinct from the rest of the economy? If these activities are all taking place within a market economy, why should they be treated as a separate sector? Asked the economist. None of the characteristics mentioned in the report could possibly serve as the basis of a sectoral divide for him. Because within the market economy, entry into one market may be less difficult than into another, the production technology may differ across activities in terms of factor intensity or one may rely more on local resources than others; but these are only differences within the market economy. The activities can certainly be arranged in a continuum in terms of these variables (i.e., the degree of labor or local resource intensity, of ease of entry), but however different, they all exist in the homogenous and continuous space of the market and are driven by the one and the same logic of rational market calculations. What then is the basis of calling a collection of activities an informal sector and thereby allowing a discontinuity in the economy?

No convincing answer to this question could be found within the axiomatic structure of the mainstream economics. So the academic discourse of development economics was reluctant to endorse the informal sector as a conceptual category, and even recent textbooks on development economics, however rigorously they may treat other concepts and categories pertaining to a developing economy, still only mention the informal sector as an empirical category, as "invisible" economic activities the urban poor engage in for subsistence, activities that take place outside the purview of the legal norms regarding minimum wage, labor standards and of fiscal obligations.

Economists may have found the concept nebulous, but sociologists and anthropologists were the most enthusiastic participants in the discussions on the informal sector. In fact, the development agencies relied more on experts belonging to these disciplines, rather than on economists, to arrive at a functional category that could serve as the basis for policy practices.[3] Numerous ethnographical city studies probing various aspects of urban poverty were undertaken in the two decades following the Kenya report, and the materials produced by these studies led to the "identification of the 'working poor' as the target group requiring specific attention."[4] Most of these studies were inspired and actively supported by the ILO and thus within the ILO discourse, the idea of the informal sector took shape as an operational category to be deployed as a target of developmental practice. However dubious its theoretical standing, "the use of the concept of 'informal sector' in policy and planning [was] in itself a real phenomenon." (Peattie 1987: 851)

But this should not surprise us. Because we have already seen that in so far as governmentality is concerned, its object, i.e., *the population group*, is descriptive and empirical; it need not be defined in terms of an inner essence. When in the early 1970s absolute poverty was set as the target of developmental interventions, the "poor" was posited as an empirical category, identifiable in terms of an exogenously and arbitrarily defined minimum level of consumption. The task of developmental states and international agencies was to promote the well being of the empirically observable "poor", without having to endow him with the status of a theoretical category. Similarly, the informal sector was presented as a category described in terms of its empirical characteristics only to be turned into an object of welfarist governance.

The informal sector as a target of governmentality thus emerged as a distinct site of economic activities through the statements that were made about it within the development agencies, especially the ILO, at a particular juncture in the history of the project of development—statements that could not have been made earlier because the extra-discursive conditions under which these statements could emerge were not there. An important aspect of the constitution of an object of governance is its representation in terms of statistical information, because the statements made about the object derive their authority from, among other things, the manner and style in which they are made. So the informal sector that had till then escaped enumeration was now subjected to statistical enquiry, i.e., quantification of its various dimensions, collection and processing of data and their interpretation. The ILO was already engaged in preparing reports on how to collect statistical data on employment in the informal sector, but the issue came to sharp focus when the need to develop an accounting framework for that purpose was emphasized in the 15th International Conference of Labor Statisticians (ICLS) held in Geneva in 1993. It adopted a resolution that stated: "it is desirable that countries develop appropriate methodologies and data collection programmes on the urban informal sector and the rural non-agriculture activities" (Bangasser 2000: 22). And finally the international System of National Accounts (SNA)—the core schema used for calculating national products that are internationally comparable— recognized the existence and importance of the informal sector by explicitly incorporating it into its own conceptual framework. The earlier SNA was revised in 1993 to accommodate the formal– informal distinction. "Thus, within a few weeks of its adoption, the ICLS resolution of statistics on employment in the informal sector was formally included into this SNA (1993) and then formally adopted and recommended to the international community by the United Nations Economic and Social Council (UMESC). It is hard to imagine a more authoritative or universal endorsement!" (*ibid.*: 23, my emphasis). The dark space between the traditional and the modern, a space so far invisible to the development planner, was thus signified, represented, and brought within the gaze of the discourse. The shadowy figures inhabiting that space were now visible; they could be marked, enumerated, and then represented in terms of numbers, figures and statistical tables.

The final and the most important aspect of the discursive constitution of the informal sector as an object of developmental intervention is its valorization, its representation in terms of a set of positive characteristics. The Kenya report described it as a subsistence sector severely constrained by resource and technology, but it also discovered that it had remarkable dynamism, innovativeness, and vibrancy. The development bureaucracy welcomed the new sector within its conceptual framework, but its positive portrayal by the report was largely ignored. Throughout the 1970s and 1980s, the prevalent image of the informal sector within the development agencies was one of a last resort for those who failed to find a place within the formal/modern sector, of the space of the "poorest of the poor" who needed helped. This view, Bangasser calls it the "miserablist approach", was certainly consonant with the then prevailing idea of governmentality that sought to ameliorate poverty by redistributing income to satisfy basic needs. But "this 'miserabilist' view", in the words of Bangasser,

> drew us away from seeing the strengths of the informal sector. And it made it impossible to see the informal sector as what it had originally been presented, a viable alternative approach to the organisation of economic activities. In effect, we were still locked into the modern–tradition and urban–rural modes of dualistic thinking, we had just changed the terminology slightly to include formal–informal. (Bangasser 2000: 32)

But this negative vision changed in the late 1990s as it increasingly dawned on the development practitioners that the informal sector was going to be with us in any foreseeable future. The new millennium called for a reconceptualization of the informal sector, more in keeping with the optimism expressed in the Kenya report, as a site that contains the potential for an alternative growth path. Instead of describing it in terms of deficiency and lack, the international organizations, as a counter to the "miserabilist" image, began to paint the sector as one with inherent creativity and ingeniousness. Purposive development planning could now address this sector with a positive approach and promote it by bolstering its activities with credit, technology and training. A recent study of the ILO reflects the optimism:

> [T]he informal sector now stands out 'as a potential provider of employment and incomes to millions of people who would

otherwise lack the means of survival' or 'as a breeding ground for entrepreneurship on a mass scale'. It is now increasingly realized that the informal sector can significantly improve itself, practically in each aspect of its functioning, if only the past policy biases, under which it is denied access to the advantages (e.g., availability of credit, foreign exchange and tax concessions) offered to the formal sector, are removed. (Oberai and Chadha 2001: 4)

In sum, the discourse constituted the informal sector as an economic entity to implant it within the framework of development. This process of constitution involves three moments. It is first posited as a purely empirical category with little claim to theoretical foundation. Then it is brought within the internationally accepted accounting framework so that it can now be an object of statistical enquiry, enumerable and classifiable. And finally it is valorized and portrayed in a positive light so that new developmental interventions can be designed. Today, one only has to surf the Internet to find an enormous body of studies, discussions, and reports, produced by governments, development agencies, research institutes, NGOs, and even trade unions, on the ubiquitous and proliferating "informal sector" in the cities of developing countries.[5] It exists, one is told, even in European cities where the unemployed from the East European transitional economies are trying to eke out a living in the fringe of the economy. These reports and studies constantly reproduce the informal sector, recreate, and renew its identity by collecting, processing, and then disseminating information about it. It is in this sense that the discourse has brought the informal sector into existence.

According to the studies conducted on the informal sector, informal employment in the developing economies currently constitutes a major part of the economically active population: it is 57 per cent in Latin America; 50 per cent in urban Indonesia; and 65 per cent in Dhaka. In Asia, the informal sector accounts for 33 per cent to 40 per cent of the urban employment; in Central America, 60 per cent to 75 per cent; and in Africa, 60 per cent. An ILO study on the urban labor market in Zimbabwe revealed that while 10,000 new jobs per year were created in the formal sector, the urban workforce was increasing per year by 300,000. And it is estimated that 90 per cent of the new urban jobs in Africa over the next decade will be in the informal sector. (Davis 2004: 25).

The informal sector thus occupies a central place in the new representation of underdevelopment and the new narrative of development.

Coming Full Circle

With the focus shifted onto the informal sector, the new face of
development at the dawn of the new millennium displaces the
"traditional–modern" to make way for the "informal–formal". What
are the implications of this shift for us? How are we going to interpret this new representation? For the practitioners of development
the shift may be the reflection of very pragmatic governmental
concerns, but for us it is of significant theoretical importance. We
are concerned with the dynamics of the development discourse, and
here we discern an important moment of departure in which development is finally extricated from the narrative of transition. The
idea of traditional–modern dualism, as we have already argued,
is essentially historicist—the traditional precedes the modern, it is
"pre-modern"—and carries within itself the notion of a systemic
transition. The informal–formal dualism on the other hand has no
historicist connotation: unlike the traditional, the informal exists
in the same time and space with the formal; it is not a remnant of
the past that the modern has failed to transform. With the informal
taking the place of the traditional, the discourse thus jettisons the
entire historicist baggage it was made to carry for half a century
since its inauguration; it no longer has to talk in terms of the idiom
of transition.

Seen in the context of capitalist underdevelopment, the informal–
formal dualism is endogenous to the capitalist development process.
It is fundamentally different from the earlier notion in which dualism was constituted by an exogenous, historically given initial condition. The informal sector is the product of capitalist development,
of its primitive accumulation; the modern sector in the course of its
own arising creates the space of the dispossessed, the space in which
the informal activities take place. In this representation underdevelopment is the product of development rather than its initial
condition.

With the informal–formal supplanting the traditional–modern,
the development project, after struggling for half a century with

the task of managing the accumulation process, comes full circle. The journey began with an initially given state of underdevelopment waiting to be transformed—to be developed—by the process of capital accumulation and technological progress. A modern sector, driven by the logic of profit and accumulation, was instituted within this scenario; a sector that will expand and ultimately subsume the entire outside within its own domain, and dualism will dissolve into the one-ness of the developed, modern economy. The modern sector expanded but dualism refused to go away. The discourse sought to cope with this persistence of underdevelopment in terms of myriad of strategies and techniques of governmentality. Finally, it recognizes that the dualism that continues to inhabit the economic space is internal to capitalist development; the informal sector is the internal "other" of the modern capital.

Let us recall that we have already theorized the post-colonial economic precisely in terms of this endogenous dualism: the space of the dispossessed produced by the arising of capital is where a sub-economy is created by welfarist governmentality, and the mutuality and contradiction between these two spaces is what constitutes the dynamics of post-colonial capitalism. Let us also recall that central to our theorization is the problematic of hegemony, the process through which capital's rule is legitimized. How then does the shift from exogenous to endogenous dualism we have just located within the development discourse relate to our theorization? The recognition of internal dualism in the representation of the economy, I will argue, constitutes what I have already identified as the third moment of the hegemony process: hegemony in its complex form in which dominance expresses itself through difference rather than monism. But before we get into the question of hegemony, I must further probe the concept of the informal sector. The ILO and other development agencies may be content with an empirical category amenable to governmental interventions, but our purpose is different: we want to bring to the fore the contradictions that are inherent in the post-colonial economic formation and see how the discourse hides them by projecting a depoliticized face of development. In other words, we want to politicize development. In order to do so, we must add some theoretical flesh to the concept of the informal sector.

The Need Economy

Although policy makers finally settled for a descriptive category, a few stray attempts were made to provide a theoretical definition of the informal sector during the years of its germination within the ILO, but they were lost on the practitioners of development management who were eager to arrive at an operational category. A number of researchers suggested an approach somewhat similar to the structuralist theory of articulation of modes of production.[6] In their characterization, the informal sector is a system of petty commodity production in the urban economy that exists in an articulated relation with the formal capitalist sector. In contrast to the latter where production is organized on the basis of a strict separation between capital and labor, it is a system in which self-employed labor or family labor produce commodities for the market. It is almost like a peasant system inserted into an urban capitalist economy (McGee 1973). While the structuralists describe how a rural peasant economy is articulated with capitalist production, in this approach the "peasant" is engaged in manufacturing activities right at the heart of the city. The analysis

> entails the identification of different modes of production in the Marxist sense, and concerns itself with the articulation of these modes of production ... in which various modes adapt to each other, each becoming dependent on the other and losing its identity and independence to some degree. (Bienefeld 1975 quoted in Moser [1978])

Although an interesting way of looking at the formal–informal dichotomy, it is, I argue, premised on the historicist concept of the mode of production in which different modes are connected in a hierarchy in terms of past and present. In this hierarchy, petty commodity production is a system that belongs to the process of transition from pre-capital to capital, which ultimately dissolves in the capitalist mode of production. If the informal sector is seen as a system of petty commodity production existing on the fringe of the capitalist sector, then it is the same as saying that it is a remnant of the past, an initial condition that capital has failed to transform. But I have spared no pains to make it clear that my purpose is to exorcise the story of the post-colonial economic formation of historicism, to extricate it from the narrative of transition. And in keeping with that I have already interpreted the formal–informal divide as a dualism endogenous to capitalism, as a discontinuity that does not carry the mark of historicism. The informal sector is not pre-capital; it is non-capital, and therefore a historicist concept of petty commodity production cannot provide its theoretical foundation. It must be conceptualized as an economic space constituting an outside of capital and at the same time as a space without any historicist mooring.

I conceptualize it as a need economy. I see it as an ensemble of economic activities undertaken for the purpose of meeting needs, as distinct from activities driven by an impersonal force of systemic accumulation. It is a system of petty commodity production but— and it is an important "but"—not the one that precedes capital in the historicist narrative of transition. It is an effect of capital, its inescapable outcome—a non-capitalist economic space that is integral to the post-colonial capitalist formation. Let me explain.[7]

I presented a somewhat tentative concept of the need-economy in Chapter 2 in terms of the circuit of commodity, $C \sim M \sim C$, as distinct from the circuit of accumulation $M \sim C \sim C' \sim M'$. The commodity circuit here begins with C, implying a unity of producers and means of production. It is petty commodity production in its historicist form and the coexistence of the two circuits refers to a particular moment of the transition process. Now I have to further complicate matters and redefine the commodity circuit in order to posit the need economy as not a pre-capitalist but a non-capitalist space. The most important aspect of the informal sector is that its producers are estranged from the means of production as a result of primitive accumulation. They are proletariats in the sense of being alienated from the means of labor. But at the same time they are unable to sell their only possession, their labor power, and be a producer of surplus within the capitalist sector, and in that sense they do not belong to the "working class". What is important for us is that in order to engage in production activities, they have to acquire the means of production from the market through the mediation of money. And therefore the circuit $C \sim M \sim C$, beginning with commodity, cannot represent these activities; we have to further complicate the circuit in order to characterize informal commodity production. As production presupposes a stock of money for the purchase of means of labor, we have the following new circuit linking commodity and money:

$$M \sim C \sim C' \sim M' \sim (M'-M, M)$$

where (M'–M) *is spent on consumption.* Here the petty producer begins with a stock of money, M, (obtained through the informal market for petty credit or personal loan). With this money he buys the means of labor, C, and works on it (with his own labor or family labor) to produce C', which he sells for money. The sales proceeds is M' which is greater than the initial stock of money, M. Out of M', the initial stock is replenished and the rest (the difference between M' and M) is used to purchase commodities for consumption that is equivalent to the difference between the money value of C' and C. The replenished stock of money (M) allows the producer to initiate the entire process once again at the beginning of the next period. Stated in plain language, the producer purchases materials with his initial stock of money; he then adds value to them, sells the produced commodity, and uses the proceeds to replenish the initial stock and to purchase commodities for consumption (which is equal to the value added in the activity).

Unlike the circuit C ~ M ~ C, which begins with commodity, the circuit of informal sector production begins with money, and here lies the crucial difference between the historicist idea of petty production and production in the informal economy. The fact that the latter cannot begin without money reflects the absence of any unity of labor and the means of labor outside the circuit of money. Money allows the producer access the market for inputs and she/he is united with the means of production only through the mediation of money. In contrast, the unity of the petty commodity producer of the story of transition with his conditions of production is rooted in the pre-capitalist rules of property. Only after producing the commodity on the basis of this unity he enters into the realm of money. In the process of transition, the petty producer is estranged from his conditions of production and turned into wage-laborer, while his means of labor are transformed into capital. But our producer in the informal economy is caught up in a limbo: he is not a petty producer in the historicist sense, but not a "worker" of the capitalist system either. When T. G. McGee exclaims after discovering the "peasant" in the city's informal economy, he does not see that his peasant is actually a member of the proletariat let down by capital.[8]

Thus, the informal producer is not a petty commodity producer of the narrative of transition because his production activity in its entirety is embedded in the circulation of money. But if we characterize the informal sector in terms of this embeddedness, we face another question: how do we now distinguish the circuit of the informal production from the circuit of capital? Because the circuit of capitalist production is represented by $M \sim C \sim C' \sim M'$, and at first sight the two appear identical. But we must recognize that despite the fact they appear identical, the two circuits are different in a fundamental sense. First, commodities purchased by the informal producer, C, consist only of the means of labor, and it is transformed into C' with the producer's own labor (or family labor) and then sold for money. In contrast, in the case of capitalist production, the purchased commodities consist of both the means of labor and labor power, and C is transformed into C' in the capitalist labor process. In the former case, the producer in the interior of production has complete control over the labor process; while in the latter, the means of labor confront the worker as capital, as an alien power. The two circuits are thus different in terms of the nature of the labor process.

But there is a more fundamental difference between the two circuits, which is crucial for our conceptualization of the informal sector as a need economy. In the case of capitalist production, the circuit begins with an initial stock of money (M), which is spent to obtain labor power and materials (C). The value of C is augmented in the interior of the production process by transforming it into C', which is then sold for a larger amount of money (M'). What is important for us is that the entire amount by which the initial stock increases, i.e., the difference between the two quantities (M'–M), is used for accumulation: the next round of the circuit begins with M' as the initial stock. In other words, capitalist production is a mode of doing business in which the production activity is undertaken for the sole purpose of expanding the volume of the circuit by using the surplus to augment the initial stock. It is an activity driven by a relentless urge for accumulation and expansion. Thus we represent capital's circuit as:

$$M \sim C \sim C' \sim M' \sim C' \sim C'' \sim M'' \sim$$

Now let us contrast it with the circuit of the informal economy we have already described. Here the additional money obtained at the end of the circuit is used for: (*a*) replenishing the initial stock, and (*b*) purchasing commodities for the consumption of the producer. So, in the second round the circuit is exactly the same as in the first:

$$M \sim C \sim C' \sim M' \sim M \sim C \sim C' \sim M' \sim$$

Here the purpose of production is consumption for the satisfaction of need, although production and consumption are both mediated by the circuit of money. Production is undertaken with the goal of obtaining money to purchase a consumption basket, and the money obtained must also be enough to replace the initial stock so that the activity can be self-reproducing.

I call the realm of capitalist production the accumulation-economy and that of informal production the need economy. In the first, production is for accumulation, and in the second, it is for meeting need. They are two distinct economies, two systems, each with an internal logic of its own. While one is driven by the logic of accumulation, production in the other is organized to support a certain level of consumption. Although they both reside in the realm of exchange and money, their simultaneous presence marks a discontinuity in the space of the market. These two economic spaces together constitute the post-colonial economic, inscribing in it an inescapable dualism.

The conceptualisation of the informal sector as a need-economy requires further elaboration. Empirical studies have reported an immense heterogeneity within the informal economy: these activities take place within a wide variety of informal arrangements and a network of oral contracts and relations of reciprocity. The forms of labor on which they are based are also varied and many: pure self-employment, family labor, communal labor, or even wage-labor and their various combinations. The concept of the need economy encompasses the entire ensemble of these activities because despite the heterogeneity of their forms, they have one common characteristic: they all enable the producer to have access through the market to a consumption basket that will satisfy his need. As all heterogeneity and differences dissolve in the common pursuit of need satisfaction, the informal space allows itself to be represented as a need economy. In identifying the informal sector as an operational category, the National Sample Survey of India comes close to this idea—although being unaware of its theoretical implications—when it characterizes the sector as "consisting of units engaged in the production of goods or services with the primary objective of generating employment and incomes to the persons concerned."[9]

But isn't, then, the need economy the same as the subsistence economy? Where production allows the producer to have the subsistence level of consumption, without leaving any surplus? And the accumulation-economy the surplus economy, which produces a surplus over and above the subsistence requirements of the producer? In response to this question, what needs to be stressed here is that although they appear similar, *the need economy is not what is commonly understood as a subsistence-economy, an economy with no surplus. While the accumulation-economy must have a surplus, need satisfaction as a goal of production does not rule out the existence of surplus in the need economy.* Because when we say that production in the need economy is for consumption, we do not only mean present consumption but future consumption as well. The self-employed producer may use a part of his present income to augment the initial stock so that it may support a higher level of consumption in the future period. Empirical studies also suggest that a not-too-insignificant fraction of the informal income is actually ploughed back within the informal sector (Hart 1973). We can explicitly consider this by modifying the circuit of the need economy as

$$M \sim C \sim C' \sim M' \sim \{M' - (M + m), M + m\}$$

where "m" is the addition to the stock.

I used the circuit in its non-expanding form (i.e., when "m" is equal to zero) to represent the need economy only to highlight the difference between the systemic logics of the two economies. Production in the accumulation-economy is organized for the purpose of generating a surplus for accumulation. In the process it does satisfy consumption needs—wage-goods are produced within the accumulation-economy—but the satisfaction of need in this case derives from the logic of accumulation: the internal rationality of the system posits accumulation as prior to consumption. In contrast, the need economy posits consumption as its objective: production is organized for consumption, for acquiring consumption goods through the mediation of the market. Its representation in terms of the simple reproduction—when the circuit reproduces itself without any expansion—serves to underscore this fundamental difference. Now if we allow the need economy to expand—with a part of its production used to augment the stock—consumption still prevails over accumulation, here need still remains prior and accumulation derives from the logic of need. Although the need economy circuit now looks similar to the circuit of the accumulation-economy, the fundamental difference between the two remains constant: one satisfies need in order to accumulate, while the other accumulates in order to satisfy need.

Let me now further complicate the concept of the need economy. *I have in the preceding section used the term non-capital to describe the informal economy, but the need-accumulation division, strictly speaking, does not exactly coincide with the division between capital and non-capital on the basis of wage-labor.* The concept of the need economy covers the entire ensemble of non-capitalist production, but it also includes some activities that would otherwise be seen as "capitalist production". These are production activities organized by small entrepreneurs in the informal sector who hire wage-workers—termed as "micro-enterprise" in the current development rhetoric. According to empirical studies, such enterprises constitute a substantial part of the informal sector (Gerry 1974, Hart 1973). These are enterprises where production is organized for consumption, and where in most cases the employer himself is a worker who uses hired labor as a supplement. And because of the low level of technology and productivity, both the employer and his workers have a low level of income and consumption. Seen from the mode of production perspective, such an activity will be identified as belonging to the domain of capitalist production. If one adopts the notion of "class process" presented by Stephen Resnick and Richard Wolff (1987)—class as the process of production, appropriation, and distribution of surplus labor—to arrive at a classification, this activity will fall into the category of what one will then call the "capitalist class process". But when we divide the economic space between need and accumulation, the location of these small enterprises is the need economy since they are engaged in need-based production. If self-employment is interpreted as a generic term that includes all kinds of producers outside the capitalist space, then the petty employer and his workers together can be seen as constituting a self-employed productive agent who is engaged in production to realize his consumption goal. Neither the mode of production nor the class process allows this conceptualization of the numerous small capitalist producers who are an important constituent of the informal sector. In our conceptualization, therefore, the term "capital" refers exclusively to the accumulation-economy, and all other production activities driven by need, irrespective of whether they use wage labor or not, are constituents of the need economy.

In sum, the need economy is the space of all consumption driven production activities irrespective of their modes of labor, relations of production and organizational forms. These activities are entirely embedded in the circuit of money and exchange. They can generate a surplus for ploughing back and therefore are capable of self-expansion. In contradistinction, the accumulation-economy refers to the space of production activities that are driven by the logic of accumulation and are based on capitalist production relations with strict separation between capital and labor.

Difference as Hegemony: Capital's Self-Representation in a Globalized World

With the "informal" supplanting the "traditional" the new millennium disengages the project of development from the narrative of systemic transition and rids it of the historicist burden it has struggled with for half a century. But, at the same time by focusing on the informal sector, the discourse now explicitly recognizes a discontinuity within the space of the market: that there is a dualism internal to the capitalist economic formation of the third world. I interpret this new representation as a hegemonic articulation, as a moment of the hegemony process that turns the otherwise decentered economic space into a provisional discursive totality, and produces the "economy" as a contingent entity. This "economy" is very different from the one in which the accumulation-centric and need-centric developments were defined. In what I identified as the first moment of hegemony, the discourse represented the economy by treating *accumulation* as the nodal point and fixing the floating meanings of other economic entities (production, labor, market, the state) entirely in relation to the logic of accumulation. Whatever did not conform to that logic was kept out of the sutured totality as the "other" of accumulation, as an economic space that could be squeezed and bled to feed the accumulation-economy, and ultimately be allowed to wither away. In other words, it was hegemony in its simple form in which capital ruled with its own agenda, subjecting pre-capital to the violence of primitive accumulation. I discerned the second moment of hegemony in the reconceptulaization of development that followed in the 1970s and 1980s, when the economy was reorganized around the new nodal point "need," as distinct from "accumulation", unsettling the earlier fixity of the instances of the economy and allowing them new meanings. This inaugurated the era of governmentality in the domain of developmental practice.

The current representation in terms of the formal–informal discontinuity—as distinct from such discontinuities as the traditional–modern, subsistence–surplus or capital–non-capital—rearticulates the economy around two distinct nodal points: accumulation and need. These two nodal points define two distinct economic spaces. The formal sector is the site of the accumulation-economy, where capital is engaged in the production of surplus for its self-expansion. When economic entities are seen in relation to this space, their meanings are provisionally fixed by the closure imposed by accumulation as the nodal point. The informal sector, on the other hand, is the site of need economy, where the purpose of production is employment, income and consumption. It is an economic space produced by need as the nodal point, and the same economic entities acquire different meanings when posited within this space. For example, labor in the first space is the means to produce surplus for investment and accumulation, and the state is an institution for creating the most favourable conditions for the accumulation process. But when seen in relation to the second space, labor is the means to acquire entitlements to consumption through the production of marketable commodities, and the state's role is to create conditions to ensure these entitlements. Thus each entity carries plural and contending meanings when placed in the context of the "economy" constituted by the two spaces mapped by accumulation and need.

The two nodal points and their corresponding spaces are finally articulated at a different level by invoking the market as the master nodal point. The floating character of need and accumulation are arrested by the fact that they both reside in the commodity space defined by the market. They are two distinct economies, yet they both flow from the logic of commodity production. The market provides the ultimate discursive closure, turning them into moments; and these moments in turn serve as nodal points, defining their respective subspaces for accumulation and need-based production.

Thus what in the accumulation-centric representation was kept out of the discursive closure as the *traditional/pre-capitalist* as the "other" of accumulation, a space to be exploited in the interest of accumulation, is now incorporated within the discourse as the informal economy and is allowed to coexist with the formal economy within the network of commodity relations and the circuits of money. In the earlier case, capital and pre-capital were arranged in an explicit hierarchy—one dynamic and progressive and the other stagnant and retrograde—that served to legitimize primitive accumulation. The new articulation of the economy sees the market as defining the entire economic space, but recognizes a discontinuity within that space; the formal and the informal—the accumulation-economy and the need economy—are posited as two distinct systems within the market economy. They however are not placed in a hierarchy similar to capital and pre-capital. In fact, as we have already seen, the informal sector is described in a positive light with dynamism and innovativeness attributed to it, qualities that promote it to a level where it can be treated at par with the formal sector. In other words, the antithetical "other" of capital is now turned into a negotiable "other" and is allowed a place alongside the accumulation economy.

I discern in this formal–informal dualism a complex form of hegemony. In the Gramscian interpretation, hegemony is of complex form when the thesis incorporates a part of the antithesis to produce a surrogate synthesis. In our framework, hegemony is a discursive articulation that produces a regime of identities and meanings. It takes on a complex form when the provisional totality produced by the discursive closure accommodates discontinuity in the sense of the simultaneous presence of distinct spaces. In the new vision of development, the market is a complex space from which the two spaces of accumulation and need are seen as flowing. Development here fosters and foregrounds the need economy for legitimizing the accumulation economy, i.e. for ensuring the politico-ideological conditions of its reproduction. Capital can successfully reproduce itself only when the outside of the capitalist space, the space of the dispossessed, is politically managed in terms of developmental interventions.

Let me here recall the distinction between capital and capitalism that was made in Chapter 2. Capitalism refers to the realm of the market that contains both capital (the accumulation-economy) and the need economy. Thus capitalism is necessarily heterogeneous, and capital exists in capitalism not as the universal but as a particular. In the case of simple hegemony where development was identified with accumulation, capital ruled with its own agenda and was antithetical to difference, but hegemonic representation in its complex form promotes and valorizes the "other", instead of suppressing and silencing it, and revises the developmental agenda to incorporate the conditions of existence of the need economy. The post-colonial capitalism is a world of difference and heterogeneity in which capital appears to live in harmonious relation with other forms of production.

We have already seen that in the 1970s there was a shift of emphasis within the developmental thought from accumulation to the basic needs, from economic growth to the question of absolute poverty, from the productive participants in the process of accumulation to those left out of that process. But this new vision of development largely remained within the confines of state-centric redistribution of income and entitlements. Although developmental practices in this case aimed at ensuring a flow of resources from the space of capital to its outside—I characterized it as a reversal of primitive accumulation—these resources were to be used not so much for constituting production activities for the surplus population as for creating capabilities through direct consumption (e.g. health, education, and food security). In other words, it was a form of governmentality that sought to promote the well-being of the population groups within the framework of the traditional welfare state.

With the informal economy brought within focus by the development discourse, governmentality takes on a new form in which productive resources, rather than income or entitlements to consumption, are transferred from the space of capital in order to constitute need-based production activities for the dispossessed. Development now means the provision of credit, inputs, and technology for the informal sector, for those outside the domain of capital. It is a reversal of primitive accumulation but the purpose here is to constitute an economic space outside the domain of capital by either bolstering the existing economic activities or bringing into existence new ones.

But it is a dual process of creation and destruction, of conservation and dissolution. The circuit of capital, of the accumulation-economy, continually expands and inevitably encroaches upon the need economy and usurps its space within capital's own domain. This is the on-going process of primitive accumulation. Global cities are built in the third world—with impressive flyovers, magnificent office buildings, and swanky shopping malls—to attract global capital, displacing a huge number of people and subverting an entire ensemble of need-based production activities that were the sources of their livelihood. Hawkers and vendors on pavements, small workshops on illegally occupied government land are evicted to give the city a facelift so that corporate capital can flow in. Self-employed fishermen lose their access to the sea in the face of the aggressive expansions of the transnational corporations.[10] The informal producer is driven out of the market by the predatory pricing and marketing policies of the formal capitalist sector:

> ... [T]here are also situations in which the sector is fighting a battle simply to hold on to what it has already established. In certain branches its ability to retain established markets is threatened by the formal sector, e.g., food processing in India. There is evidence to suggest that the formal sector has in a few cases expanded its market share (sometimes by lowering the product quality and/or prices) in order to make its output affordable to low income groups, and in the process destroyed the market held hitherto by the informal sector (e.g., processed food, ready-made clothing, footwear, etc.). (Sethuraman 1997: 25)

In Latin America, supermarkets now control 60 per cent of food retailing, and evidence suggests that this concentration has caused the closing down of thousands of undercapitalized small enterprises. More than 60,000 small food retailers have gone out of business in Argentina between 1984 and 1993; in Chile, between 1991 and 1995, more than 5,000 small retailers have been pushed out of the market.[11] Thus the informal economy is constantly under the threat of subversion; its conditions of existence are always vulnerable; its reproduction plagued with uncertainty.

Yet at the same time, in a simultaneous process, the dispossessed are rehabilitated through the "pastoral functions" of the international organizations and the developmental state. Developmental interventions re-institute them within the need economy by re-creating their conditions of existence with resources transferred from the domain of capital; micro-credits are made available, self-employment promoted, common property rights restored, appropriate local institutions built to reconstitute the need-space. When David Harvey draws our attention to the fact that underlying the current phenomenon of globalization is a process of primitive accumulation—he calls it "accumulation by dispossession"—to argue that what we are witnessing now is imperialism as we knew it, he does not see that what he is highlighting is only one side of the story, that in a parallel and simultaneous move, governmentality is actively engaged in forming a need-economy by reversing the process of dispossession.[12] It is not Harvey alone. There is a general tendency among the critics and detractors of globalization to describe the current experience solely in terms of the predatory and malevolent expansion of global capital. The proponents of the new order, on the other hand, hold the opposite view and paint it as one that is opening up new economic opportunities for the poor and the underprivileged, and seek to demonstrate how assistance in terms of credit, technology, and information are allowing them to exploit these opportunities. But it is the simultaneous presence of these two processes, their mutuality and contradictions, what constitutes the dynamics of post-colonial capitalism in the era of globalization; forces of globalization are simultaneously enabling and constraining, empowering, and debilitating; to focus on only one is to endorse a story that is one-sided, partial, and misleading.

Although the discourse has liberated the informal economy from the "miserabilist approach" and described it in a positive light, and has presented the formal and the informal as derived from the same universal, i.e., the market, the two economies are locked in an asymmetric relation. I interpret the relation as one of dominance and subordination. Dominance was explicit in the case of simple hegemony when capital ruled with its own agenda. But the relation of dominance continues to be operative in the complex case, only hidden behind the apparently harmonious coexistence of the two circuits. However positively it may be painted, the need economy, I argue, remains subordinate to the accumulation-economy, because it is the legitimization of capital's existence that necessitates the reverse flow of resources and the constitution of need-based production activities. And seen from this perspective, the need economy is the combined effect of primitive accumulation and the imperative that capital's existence be legitimized: it owes its existence to welfarist governmentality. Capital strives to expand its circuit of accumulation, and governmentality responds to it in terms of welfarist intervention. While capital acts on its own, the inhabitants of the need economy—although valorized and endowed with an apparent autonomy in the representation of the economy—exist only as *population groups*, as constituted objects on which the techniques of governance can be applied. Thus the two spaces are locked in a hierarchy: one is subordinate to the other.

The asymmetry is also reflected in the rules governing the two economies. Need-based production, although allowed to take place in its own space, must conform to the logic of the market, of commodity production: it must be viable in terms of market calculations, i.e., revenue must cover costs, and the money with which the circuit starts must be replenished along with a residual for consumption. Now the rules of the market pertain to the system of capitalist production, but in this case they also govern the need-based production. But while the need economy has to subject itself to the logic of commodity production, the accumulation-economy cannot be subjected to the criterion of need: production for accumulation cannot be questioned from the perspective of consumption and need.

These fundamental asymmetries constitute a relation of dominance between the two economies. But the formal–informal dualism hides this asymmetry by describing them as two autonomous and parallel spaces without any contradiction, and thereby places them on a non-political terrain. And it is in this sense that I interpret this dualism as a complex hegemonic construct. Hegemony is a representational strategy, a discursive articulation that either sanctions dominance or denies its existence by positing a harmonious totality. In the simple case, the dominance of capital was explicitly posited and justified by appealing to the notion of accumulation as progress. But, in the complex case, hidden in the apparently harmonious formal–informal dualism is a relation of dominance that subordinates the need economy to the power of capital. And it is the task of the critical theorist to deconstruct the hegemonic representation and bring to visibility the underlying relation of power and dominance, and reinscribe the relation on a politically contested terrain.

The Return of z-goods

There was one important aspect of the discussions on the informal sector within the development organizations that I have not mentioned so far. Although, in the two decades following the Kenya mission's report, the urban economy occupied the central place in the discussions, the concept was finally extended to encompass the rural economy as well. In 1993, Gustav Ranis and Frances Stewart (R–S hereafter) drew the attention of the architects of development policy to the fact that there were economic activities in the rural sector of developing countries that did not fall within the category of agricultural production; they dubbed these "rural non-agricultural activities (RNA)". Development practitioners soon embraced the idea and it became an important object of studies and discussions within the development circle in the 1990s, spawning a sizable literature.

R–S invoke Hymer and Resnick's z-goods (which I have already mentioned in Chapter 3) to identify RNA. Hymer and Resnick locate the production of z-goods in the pre-colonial, self-sufficient peasant economy. These activities include food processing, production of handicrafts and services within the household or the village, catering mainly to local needs. The emergence of the colonial regime, they argue, caused the withering away of z-goods. In the colonial period, as the peasant economy was linked with the international economy, there was a shift toward the production of cash crops and primary products for exports, providing alternative use of labor; on the other hand, cheaper and better quality consumption goods became available through imports. These changes destroyed the conditions of z-goods production from both demand and supply sides, and they disappeared. R–S contest Hymer and Resnick's claim and insist that a lot of these activities actually survived the colonial onslaught and they proceed to explore what happened to them in the period of post-colonial industrial development. They consider two contrasting post-colonial scenarios: the unfavourable archetype and the favourable archetype. In the unfavourable case, the emergence and growth of the modern large-scale industrial sector in the post-colonial economy—they name it the U sector—leads to the destruction of z-goods. The developmental state's policies favor the U sector in terms of credit, infrastructure, and foreign exchange, and z-goods are ultimately displaced by the consumer goods produced by this sector. In Chapter 3 this is precisely how we described the Indian experience in the first phase of planning: the modern Indian industries playing the same role that the steel and textile mills of Manchester and Lancashire had played in the colonial period. India fits in well with the unfavorable archetype.

The favorable case described by R–S is one where z-goods, instead of withering away, actually flourish. They divide the sector into two parts and argue that while one is petty rural production, characteristically primitive, stagnant, and vulnerable, and therefore unable to survive changes that development entails, the other is dynamic and vibrant, and capable of adapting to, and taking advantage of such changes. Contrasting the two cases of Taiwan and Philippines, they demonstrate that in the former, under favorable government policies, the z-goods sector actually flourished as a complement to modern industries, but the latter largely conformed to the unfavorable archetype.

It is not the model or the policies it suggests that we are interested in here; we would rather like to locate R–S's intervention in relation to the dynamics of the representation, and grasp its implications for the production of identity and meaning in the indeterminate and contingent space of the "economy". It is interesting to note here that after almost twenty-five years they restore a concept that was subjected to the discourse's erasure and deploy it as a new instrument of developmental governance. What is important is that not merely are z-goods reinscribed in the economic space, R–S extricate them from the negative approach of Hymer and Resnick and imbue them with developmental energy, much in the same way as the urban informal sector is freed from the "miserablist approach" and valorized as vibrant and innovative. In the earlier vision of the dual economy, the binary of modern industry and traditional agriculture ruled out any third sphere of economic activity: there could be no non-agricultural material production outside the modern sector. The Kenya mission's observation that there were manufacturing activities within the informal economy marked a significant departure from this conceptualization in that it brought within visibility an economically active sphere outside the strict modern/traditional dichotomy. The "discovery" of z-goods in the rural economy is a complementary move in the discursive field, and they together inscribe an "in-between space" in the imaginary of development and populate it with economic actors who are dynamic and innovative, albeit severely debilitated by unfavourable conditions. In other words, it is a space that carries unrealized development potential. Thus, the "economy" is restructured in the new representation, its space reorganized, to accommodate plural and heterogeneous identities.

What I have described as the need economy thus consists of both the urban informal sector and what R–S call RNA. One may characterize the goods produced in this need-economy, both in urban and rural areas, as z-goods—as non-agricultural goods produced outside the modern sector—but, as I have already argued at length, the need-based production is entirely embedded in the circuit of money and there is no unity of labor and the means of labor in this sphere of production, and it is true for RNA as well. Hymer–Resnick's z-goods was a historicist concept—a concept related to the story of transition. As a constituent of the need-economy, RNA has no historicist connotation and therefore are not z-goods in the strict Hymer–Resnick sense, just as the urban informal manufacturing activities are not petty commodity production. They are all z-goods in their displaced form, reconstituted, recreated by capital, and they all belong to capital's extended commodity space.

Capitalism as a World of Difference

Thus the dominant imaginary of capitalist development stretches the market beyond the accumulation-economy to map a space for "capitalism" and then populates it with need-based production activities, and this space is necessarily heterogeneous. It accommodates a variety of forms and organizations of production with one common feature: they all reside in the commodity space and within the circuit of money. The women's self-help group breeding aquarium fish in their micro fishery in West Bengal, India; the man running a cheap fast food stall on the pavement of Sao Paolo; the housewife in Bangladesh, with a micro-credit from the Grameen Bank, making bamboo stools at home for sale; the small fishermen's cooperative in Sri Lanka; the artisan in Haiti making metal sculptures at home from recycled oil drums and scrap metals for sale—they all inhabit the space of the market and therefore are encompassed by capitalism. And within this capitalism, the accumulation-economy of capital exists as a particular, distancing itself from the need economy, yet subjecting the latter to its dominance.

In its self-representation, capital thus describes capitalism as un-centered, multiple, diffused and fluid, defining it as a space that is flexible enough to accommodate any activity, whatever its form of organization and mode of labor, as long as it is amenable to the rules of the market. And this has profound implications for the politics of representation. We can here recall J. K. Gibson–Graham's encounter with capitalism we dealt with in chapter 1. She claims that the description on which the "hegemony of capitalism" is predicated is monist and therefore antithetical to difference: it allows the term "capitalism" to subsume the entire economy with its varied and plural activities, and thereby either keeps heterogeneity and difference completely out of visibility or marginalizes the "non-capitalist" sites to an extent where they are overshadowed by capitalism's overwhelming presence. In a counter-hegemonic move, she seeks to contest this prevalent discursive practice by foregrounding those non-capitalist sites. In other words, her deconstruction of the dominant image of the economy aims at simultaneously emaciating capitalism and liberating the non-capitalist activities from the grasp of what she calls the capitalocentric vision of the economy.

Gibson–Graham's conceptualization of hegemony, clearly, refers to its simple form: when capital seeks to organize the world after its own image, and for her the decentering of the economy serves to undermine the hegemonic order. But when hegemony takes the complex form by expressing itself through diversity and the dominant representation highlights heterogeneity rather than monism, it subverts this counter-hegemonic politics of difference. As the stable binary of capital and non-capital now dissolves into a hybrid "capitalist space", the strategy of decentering capitalism coincides with, or even reinforces, the dominant order. Michael Hardt and Antonio Negri rightly call our attention to this danger:

> When we begin to consider the ideologies of corporate capital and the world market, it certainly appears that the post-modernist and post-colonialist theorists who advocate a politics of difference,

fluidity and hybridity in order to challenge the binaries and essentialism of modern sovereignty have been outflanked by the strategies of power. Power has evacuated the bastion they are attacking
and has circled around to their rear to join them in the assault in
the name of difference. These theorists thus find themselves pushing against an open door. (Hardt and Negri 2000: 138)

Although my characterization of hegemony is very different from
what Hardt and Negri call Empire, I share their critique of the politics of difference celebrated by authors such as Gibson–Graham.
The diversity and plurality that constitute "capitalist development"
in the dominant imaginary, as I have already argued, are produced
through a process of valorization and promotion of the non-capitalist
forms of production in the need economy, a strategy, ironically, the
advocates of the politics of difference are bent on adopting in their
battle against capitalism. It is important to recognize that when
need-based production is painted in a positive light, the discourse at
the same time confines it to a space outside the world that is capital's own. It is in this sense that the constitution of the need economy through developmental interventions signals an implosion of
the two regimes of power described by Foucault: the restrictive and
the productive. The interpreters of Foucault have the tendency to
present the two as distinct and separate regimes; Foucault's texts
also give the reader the impression that he was in favor of such a separation. While power in *Madness and Civilization* works in terms
of restriction, exclusion, and silencing, welfarist governmentality
and bio power produces subjectivity and activates the human multiplicity, and Foucault's diachronic analysis focuses on the passage
from one to other. But in the now prevalent development imaginary,
while governmentality, through a reversal of primitive accumulation,
activates the need-space by promoting newly formed subjectivities—
the self-employed, the z-goods producer, the subsistence producer in
a small cooperative—the need economy remains the space of confinement for the dispossessed and castaways of capitalist development. It is a space that prevents them from banging on the doors
of the glittering world of capital.

Let us listen to the case of Lola Tasuna of Manila—reported by *Economic Perspective*, an electronic journal of the US Department of State—whom a microcredit from Opportunity International has enabled to become a "successful micro-entrepreneur".

> *[Her] tenement in Manila faces a sidewalk sewage ditch. She and the five people she lives with are squatters. Like their neighbours, they live in shelters constructed from scrap materials......*
>
> *Her business is making kerosene lamps, a necessity in a neighbourhood where blackouts are frequent. With a loan from Opportunity International, she buys clean jars at 5 cents a jar, paints the lids, adds wicks, and attaches metal handles. She sells them for 10 to 25 cents, depending on the size.*
>
> *Life is easier for Lola than it was before she could buy clean jars. Then she had to scratch through the garbage dump every morning to find jars. She washed them in a bucket of cold water, scraping off the labels and the filth with her fingernails.*
>
> *Lola's pride in her handiwork and in her ability to earn her livelihood shines out, despite her grim surroundings. She does not feel poor, act poor, or talk poor. In a land with no safety net of social services, Lola knows she is a survivor.*[13]

The narrative in a way epitomizes the twin mechanisms of power. A meagre transfer of resources from the accumulation-economy "empowers" Lola to become a self-employed producer of a marketable product, and her "success" in business is celebrated in the official commentary on development. Yet, she remains quarantined in a need-space outside the world of capital. In other words, the subjectivity of a self-fending "micro-entrepreneur" is produced and valorized, but at the same time its location is permanently fixed in the exterior of capital's own space.

In the following section, I seek to demonstrate how the current developmental interventions are aimed at constructing a need economy, and how through this process the complex hegemonic formation of post-colonial capital—the third moment of the hegemony process—is materializing. The emphasis placed on the issue of microcredit by the World Bank and other international organizations provides the clue to this new formation, for it is through the provision of micro-credit that the informal sector and rural non-farm employment are created, promoted, and renewed.

Financing the Need Economy: Governmentality and the Global Management of Poverty

A new global order is being inaugurated in which capital—both financial and real—commodities and images will circulate freely in an integrated global economy. Capital in this new order will expand on a global scale, and the process of accumulation and growth will be governed by the global rules of property and contract. And at the same time, the need to define a global regime of development is simultaneously being emphasized. Although the Washington Consensus focuses on the first, the agenda of the World Bank explicitly recognizes the second:

> We know that nations are dependent on one another. We know that nations are no longer the sole masters of their destinies. We need global rules and global behaviour. We need a new international development architecture to parallel the new global financial architecture." (2000: 17)[14]

A new architecture of development must complement the new global capitalist order, and this new paradigm of development focuses on the management of poverty from a global perspective. More precisely, the creation and renewal of the need economy is now a global process driven by a global discourse. When speaking on the role of the U.S. Agency for International Development (USAID) in promoting micro-enterprises in developing countries, the former US Secretary of State, Colin Powell, asserted that

> I am proud that America's key role in promoting microenterprises. US objectives are threefold: to improve access to financial services for the world's poor; to support access business services that specifically address constraints felt by poorer entrepreneurs; and to improve the business climate through regulatory, legal, and policy reforms. *Our efforts are global, from Mali in Africa and Jordan in the Near East to Azerbaijan in Europe and Peru in Latin America. Our success will be universal, with the concerted efforts of the international community.* (My emphasis)[15]

Thus, poverty eradication is a project that encompasses the entire developing world, from Africa to Latin America, bringing it within a global web of governmentality, of which the international organizations, the NGOs and even the national governments are functionaries. The USAID—whose average annual funding for micro-enterprises is $155 million—is but one of the numerous international organizations engaged in providing micro-credit to the poor of the third world. The question of micro-credit is increasingly coming to the center of the developmental agenda of global organizations such as the World Bank and the UNDP. For us, it is of great significance because the issue of micro-credit encompasses both the urban informal sector and rural non-farm employment—the two constituents of the need economy—and thus provides us with the clue to the process of creation, nurturing, and improvement of need-based production activities.

The question of micro-credit has arisen out of the concern of the international organizations in recent years about what they call "pro-poor growth". Almost a decade ago, the UNDP in the Human Development Report (1997) questioned the presumed one-way causation between growth and poverty, i.e., that growth reduces poverty:

> Increases in GDP seem to be connected to reduction in poverty .... This is usually taken to mean that growth is good for poverty reduction, but it explains only about half of it. Correlation is not causation ..... Might it be that poverty reduction causes growth? There are certainly reasons for it to do so. (p. 74)

The concern there was how the poor could possibly contribute to growth; the current architects of development are now voicing the same concern with a lot more force. In 2005, the UNDP sounds convinced of the potential of pro-poor growth:

> The progressive [pro-poor] growth can be thought of as a dynamic process in which poor people produce their way out of poverty, while increasing their contribution to national wealth.
>
> The progressive [pro-poor] growth approach focuses attention on the structural inequalities that deny poor people and marginalized groups an opportunity to contribute to and participate in growth on more equitable terms. It puts redistribution alongside growth, at the center of the policy agenda for reducing extreme poverty.[16]

The kind of pro-poor growth advocated here is one that involves *redistribution of productive assets* to the poor rather than mere *redistribution of income and consumption* through public policy. The distinction is important because it distances the current strategy from the "basic need approach" adopted in the 1970s that primarily sought to provide the poor with necessities such as housing and health. What is being aimed at now is redistribution of assets so that the poor can be engaged in productive economic activities that are sustainable over time. In other words, there must be "empowerment"—a buzzword in the current lingo of the development practitioners—not only in terms of basic necessities but also in terms of economic resources that will enable the poor to be a self-sustaining productive agent. And it is here that development moves beyond the second moment of the hegemony process we have described, and the third moment of hegemony in its complex form—where the outside of capital takes the form of a sub-economy for the rehabilitation of the dispossessed—begins to materialize. This shift of focus is also apparent in the UN–Habitat's 2003 report on slums that I have already mentioned:

....that policies should more *vigorously address the issue of the livelihoods of slum dwellers and the urban poor in general, thus going beyond traditional approaches that have tended to concentrate on improvement of housing, infrastructure and physical environmental conditions*. This means enabling urban informal activities to flourish, linking low-income housing development to income generation, and ensuring easy access to jobs through pro-poor transport and low-income settlement location policies.[17] (My emphasis)

We, from our perspective, will interpret the core content of this pro-poor growth strategy as the creation of the need economy. It is a strategy that seeks to reunite the pauperized with the means of labor to constitute an economic space outside the economy that is driven by the logic of accumulation. While talking of growth, the strategy refers to the one-ness of the economy—there is an economy that grows—but underlying this growth is the process of creation and reproduction of a dualism. Whatever the poor contributes to growth is in terms of the income he generates in the need-based activity as distinct from the income generated within the accumulation-economy of capital.

Both the World Bank and the UNDP now identify micro-credit as an efficient instrument for the development strategy premised on pro-poor growth.[18] In the words of James Wolfensohn, the former president of the Bank:

Micro-finance—providing loans and savings services to the world's poorest people—fits squarely into the Bank's overall strategy. ...[T]he Bank's mission is to reduce poverty and improve living standards by promoting sustainable growth and investment in people through loans, technical assistance, and policy guidance. Microfinance contributes directly to this objective[19]

And the intended beneficiary of micro-credit, the "poor", is one who belongs to the informal economy that exists outside both agriculture and the modern industrial sector. We have already seen how the informal sector has been freed from the "miserablist" approach and is being described as a vibrant economic space for the working poor. Numerous studies in the recent years have tried to throw light on the size, composition, and characteristics of this sector, and its role as an important source of employment to the poor. According to one ILO study conducted in 2002, the informal economy accounts for 78 per cent of non-agricultural employment, 61 per cent of urban employment, and 93 per cent of the new job creation for the entire African continent.[20] In Kenya, 40 per cent of the urban employment is in the informal sector, in Zambia 43 per cent, and 1.56 million people work in the informal economy, compared to 1.26 million in the formal economy, in Zimbabwe. Another study reports the share of the informal sector in urban employment in Latin American economies in 1999: 48.7 per cent in Argentina, 53.4 per cent in Columbia, and 50.8 per cent in Peru.[21] The overall picture is more or less similar for the Asian economies. Put together, these studies strongly suggest the immense significance of the informal sector in providing livelihood to the poor.

The same studies also emphasize that lack of access to credit is a debilitating factor for the informal sector. Due to his inability to access formal credit, the informal producer has to rely primarily on credit from informal sources. One important feature of these economies is the existence of a wide variety of traditional informal arrangements for small finance. As the World Bank notes:

> A major constraint to the participation and contribution of poor and vulnerable households in economic growth is access to financial credit.... It has been estimated that more than 500 million people worldwide need access to financial services. However, formal financial intermediaries such as commercial banks often do not serve poor households for reasons that include the lack of traditional collateral, high costs of small transactions, and geographic isolation. Poor households' access to financial services is generally limited to informal transfers or loans, either individually or through savings clubs, rotating savings and credit associations, and mutual insurance societies.[22]

The informal arrangements for credit are various forms of ROSCA (Rotating Saving and Credit Association) such as *tontine* in Niger, *tanda* in Mexico, *pasanaku* in Bolivia or *arisan* in Indonesia, to name a few.[23] They raise money from within a clearly defined group to provide small short-term credit to its members—who are producers in the informal economy—on a rotational basis. Members of the group are bound together by traditional kinship or community relations, and it allows disbursement and recovery of loans at very low transaction costs, providing these arrangements an edge over the impersonal, collateral-based formal financial system.

In the same way as the informal sector is being valorized by the development discourse, the "efficiency" of these informal arrangements to cater to the credit–need of the poor is increasingly being highlighted by the international organizations, but at the same time, the inadequacy of funds as the major constraint on these arrangements is also emphasized. And therefore, as the World Bank argues,

> [a]mong the continuing challenges faced by developing societies and the international community is to find ways to build the capacity of the micro finance sector to complement the existing informal and private institutions, promote access to those markets for the poor, and help ensure that they are sustainable.[24]

It is here that the micro-credit schemes designed by the international development organizations plan to intervene. The purpose of these schemes is to "complement the existing private institutions" so as to ease the credit constraint faced by the poor in the informal sector. Numerous micro-credit schemes have been designed with the purpose of providing funds both for bolstering the existing arrangements and for forming new credit associations for the poor. For the Bank, micro-credit is

....understood to incorporate programs which extend small loans to very poor people for *self-employment projects that generate income, allowing them to care for themselves and their families.* It has proven an effective and popular measure in the ongoing struggle against poverty, enabling those without access to lending institutions to borrow at bank rates, and start small business.[25] (My emphasis)

Micro-credits, provided by international organizations, NGOs and national governments, have already reached a significant part of the very poor in the developing countries. According to one World Bank estimate, "the number of poor people with access to micro-credit schemes rose from 7.6 million in 1997 to 26.8 million in 2001 (growth by 350 per cent)—21 million of them women. The overall number for all people involved in micro-credit programs is even higher—as of December 31, 2001, 2,186 micro-credit institutions reported reaching 54,904,102 clients. Assuming five persons per family, the 26.8 million poorest clients reached by the end of 2001 affected some 134 million family members."[26] The Bank itself provided loans of $88 million through national governments in 1996; in 1997 it financed the largest micro-finance project of $105 million in Bangladesh while the overall portfolio was $128 million. And in 1998, James Wolfensohn, the then president of the Bank, stated: "In the next few years, as we develop new lending instruments with greater flexibility and as our staff gains more experience in microfinance, these amounts should increase."[27]

It is evident from the reports on micro-credit projects that the kind of economic activities micro-credit promotes fall within what we have described as the need economy: it aims at providing funds to the poor for, as the World Bank puts it in the preceding quote, "self-employment projects that generate income, allowing them to care for themselves and their families". The case of the Grameen Bank of Bangladesh—the icon of micro-credit institutions—and

SEWA (Self-Employed Women's Association) in India are but two examples that adequately illustrate the point. The Grameen Bank has experienced a phenomenal growth since its inception in 1976 and is believed to have made significant dent in rural poverty in Bangladesh. The total amount of loan disbursed by the Bank is to the tune of $380 million.[28] It offers small loans to the rural poor on a group-lending basis where peer pressure ensures repayment. The borrower uses the loan to engage in various non-farm self-employment activities: simple processing such as lime making; manufacturing such as pottery, weaving, and garment sewing; services such as storage, marketing and transport.[29] These income-generating activities allow the borrower to repay the loan with interest in order to get fresh loan. Adopting a similar approach, SEWA in India has extended micro-credit, amounting to Rs. 100 million in 1995, to women both in the rural non-farm sector and the urban informal sector.[30] The credit has enabled the women to engage in need-based production activities and SEWA has promoted cooperatives within which such activities are undertaken. The cooperatives involve women in diverse manufacturing and service production such as weaving, garment stitching, block printing, tobacco processing and dairy, to name a few.[31] Thus, these organizations through an initial transfer of funds from the formal economy promote existing need-based production activities and create new ones, constituting a self-sustaining need economy.

The need economy thus constituted through micro-credit, however, is required to conform to the rules of the market. The activities financed by these schemes must be "economically viable" in the sense of being able to generate income sufficient for the repayment of the loan with interest so that a larger fund can be put back into circulation to expand the volume of need-based production. The case of SEWA is a particularly interesting example of need-based production activities acquiring the capability of self-reproduction. In the beginning, the organization concentrated on attracting deposits from self-employed women and helped them to get loans from nationalized banks on the basis of those deposits. However, soon the SEWA bank started advancing loans to the depositors from its own funds and finally withdrew entirely from the credit arrangements with the nationalized banks.[32] While the official commentary on development will celebrate it as a case where the poor is empowered to be a self-reproducing productive agent without any external assistance, from our perspective it captures the very essence of the hegemony process we have described: an initial transfer of surplus from the accumulation-economy brings into existence a need economy that, eventually, is able to reproduce the conditions of its own existence outside the domain of capital ("ship of fools, sail away from me").

The need economy, in other words, must survive the test of the market. As the World Development Report (2002), entitled *Building Institutions for Markets*, asserts, development and the liberation from the poverty-trap requires the building of institutions that support what it calls "inclusive and integrated markets"—markets that stretches beyond local and informal arrangements and encompass a greater number of economic agents. And for the development of such inclusive markets, already existing local and informal institutions have to be imaginatively modified and integrated with other formal and global institutions. In other words, the space of the market must be stretched to incorporate the *informal*; it is the universal space in which the *formal* and the *informal* will both reside. This is the construct of complex hegemony in the current post-colonial context—in which the market is the universal space that unites the *formal* and the *informal*, but a discontinuity within the space is explicitly recognized—discontinuity in the sense that two distinct economies driven by the logics of accumulation and need exist within the compass of the market. The development discourse, and the practices it is currently defining, is aimed at constituting this paradigm of complex hegemony of capital.

In its early phase, the development discourse saw the poor as located in the space that was traditional and underdeveloped. The dominant imaginary described development as a process in which this space shrinks in the face of the expansion of the modern sector and the poor is transferred to the new space of the "modern" and the "developed". But in the new imaginary, the location of the poor is fixed in his/her own space, one that is distinct from the "formal" and the "modern", and governmentality seeks to "reconstitute and improve" the former space with the help of a transfer from the latter. This is the new international architecture of development.

The important point here is that although the management of poverty is a part of a global project, its architecture has to rely on the knowledge about the *local*. There is now a discernable shift in the focus of the development discourse from the "*global*" to the "*local*". This foregrounding of the "*local*" at a time when the "*global*" is being universally celebrated may appear somewhat paradoxical, but it is precisely through this kind of discursive stance that knowledge about the "*local*" is "produced", and this knowledge is used in the global management of the need-economy. Not only the informal credit arrangements, many other local institutions are being painted in positive light and their role in development asserted. For example, the World Bank is highlighting the concept of social capital—connectedness that is local—as a key to economic development; traditional systems of insurance are being "discovered" as efficient institutional arrangements. In all these cases, the "*local*" does not dissolve into, nor is suppressed by, the *global*; it appears to stand on its own but is ultimately made an integral part of a global regime of knowledge–power defined in terms of the knowledge-institution nexus. This is an important feature of the new global architecture of development: the "*global*" recognizes, searches for and discovers the "*local*", and then a dwarfed, censored form of it is turned into an instrument to be deployed for the effective management of poverty.

In sum, there are two aspects of the emergent structure of global governance. The neo-liberal face of the international organizations, reflected in the Washington Consensus, seeks to ensure the conditions of existence of a global capitalist order based on the international mobility of footloose capital and dispersion of production across national boundaries. The accumulation-economy of globalized capital engages in primitive accumulation and thus causes dispossession, exclusion, and marginalization. But at the same time, this capitalist order must be legitimized and its broader politico-ideological conditions of existence must be created. And this is where the developmental face of those organizations and the NGOs becomes visible, with governmentality addressing the issue of creating, protecting and monitoring an informal sector to rehabilitate the victims of the capitalist onslaught in a need economy. These two distinct goals—one destructive and one supportive—constitute the structure and modalities of global governance in the current era of capital.

Informalization within the Accumulation-Economy

So far, we have described the informal need economy as existing outside the accumulation-economy of capital. We now have to contrast it to a phenomenon that is increasingly being highlighted in the commentary on globalization: informalization of production activities within the circuit of capital—a phenomenon that results from the internal logic of the accumulation economy itself. Studies in the informal sector have emphasized the observation that a part of the sector is deeply implicated in the modern formal economy through various linkages of subcontracting and outsourcing (Sethuraman 1997, Tabak 2000). There is a tendency among development theorists and practitioners to see the informal sector entirely in terms of this embedded-ness and to focus exclusively on these linkages for designing policies. But what is to be emphasized here is that need-based production that resides within and is organically related to the accumulation circuit is very different from the need-economy that exists outside the circuit.[33] It is the latter that has been our concern in this book, and it should be emphatically contrasted with the former.

Informalization within the accumulation economy and its relationship with the circuit of capital however is of a complex nature and can take different forms. To conceptualize these, let us first recall the circuit of accumulation we have already described: $M \sim C \sim C' \sim M'$, where $(M'- M)$ goes into accumulation. The capitalist purchases commodities (labor-power and materials), C, and produces C' within the capitalist labor process. Now the laborer sells his labor power as a commodity for wages to purchase the necessary consumption basket that will fulfill his need. Seen from the laborer's side, there is a circuit that runs from commodity to money to commodity, $C \sim M \sim C$. Thus the flip side of the capitalist's accumulation circuit is a circuit that refers to need. But the need-circuit here is completely dominated by the logic of accumulation because the laborer is allowed to perform the labor necessary for his consumption only if he produces surplus labor for accumulation. In other words, capitalist production under the factory system—where wage-labor produces surplus for capitalist accumulation—allows itself to be described as an articulation of the two circuits with one dominating the other.

But capitalist production—the circuit of accumulation—need not restrict itself to the factory system; it can take on a variety of forms based on different articulations of the two circuits. Each of these forms corresponds to a particular way in which the accumulation-economy implicates the need-economy in a relation of dominance and subordination. We can think of three possible cases:

Case 1: The Putting-out System

The capitalist provides the laborer with materials and the means of labor, but the laborer, instead of working within the factory in a capitalist labor process, works in the household, and delivers the product to the capitalist for a payment. The capitalist then sells the product for an amount larger than what he has spent. It should be noted here that, unlike in the case of factory-based capitalist production, the capitalist in this case purchases only the means of labor and not labor power. Household is the site where the producer works on the materials, in most cases with family labor, and transforms the means of labor into commodities, which he delivers to the capitalist. She/He receives a payment that she/he spends on consumption.

Case 2: The Self-employed Sub-contractor

Unlike case 1 in which the capitalist provided the materials, the informal producer in this case produces for the capitalist but she/he has to borrow or raise on his/her own the money required to begin the circuit. He/She purchases the materials and other means of labor, and then works within the household to produce the commodity, and sells it to the capitalist for an amount that allows him to replenish the initial stock and fulfil his consumption needs.

Case 3: The Sub-contractor as the Informal Employer of Wage-labor

In this case, the informal production is organized by a small entrepreneur who employs a few wage-laborers—often he himself is an owner worker—but is driven by a consumption goal. Here the small entrepreneur begins the circuit with a stock of money, which he obtains by borrowing or from personal savings, buys materials and labor power, produces the commodity, and then sells it to the capitalist in the formal sector for a larger amount of money.

After replenishing and augmenting the initial stock, he spends the remaining part of the revenue for consumption. The capitalist in the accumulation-economy sells the commodity for an amount of money that is larger than what he has paid the small entrepreneur, and which becomes the initial stock of his circuit in the next round.

In all these three cases, informalization of production leads to the creation of a need-economy within the circuit of capital. The incentive for the capitalist to go for this kind of arrangement arises primarily from cost considerations: informalization of production means lower cost of both labor and supervision. Although the surplus produced by the informal producer accrues to the capitalist, the latter does not directly control the labor process as in the factory system, and the payment is made on a piece-rate basis to ensure efficiency. The three cases, however, are different when seen in terms of their respective labor processes. Both in case 1 and case 2, the labor process is under the control of the direct producer, but in the latter case he procures the means of labor while in the former, they are advanced by the capitalist. Thus, while in case 2 the producer can be described as self-employed, in the putting-out system of case 1, she/he has property right neither over the materials nor the product, and therefore, is not self-employed in the sense of case 2. The producer under the putting out system is not a wage-worker of a capitalist factory, and she/he is not a purely self-employed producer either: she/he is best described as a hybrid of these two modes of labor. In case 3, the small entrepreneur employs wage-laborers and therefore controls the labor process, but as she/he in most cases herself/himself participates in production—and as in most cases, the employer and the employees are related through kinship and community ties or personal acquaintances—the nature of the control is not an impersonal one as in the capitalist factory system.

We should also take note of the fact that the surplus of informal production is extracted by capital—especially in case 2 and 3—at the point of exchange rather than in the interior of production as in the case of factory-based production. In other words, the informalization of production involves a mode of generation and appropriation of surplus by capital that is fundamentally different from the direct extraction of surplus from wage-labor. While the need economy is the site of production, the surplus it generates flows to the accumulation-economy through contractual arrangements and is used for the expansion of the circuit of accumulation.

Finally, it is to be recognized that the informalization of capitalist production is fast becoming a global phenomenon. With the death of distance and compression of time and space brought about by the development in communication technology, the circuit of accumulation is increasingly extending itself beyond the national boundaries. Attracted by the availability of cheaper labor power, global capitalist enterprises are shifting their relatively labor-intensive processes of production to distant third world countries in the form of subcontracting and outsourcing: Nike gets its sports shoes produced in Indonesia; AT&T's standard telephones are assembled in Thailand; Paris-designed shirts are cut and stitched in Bangladesh. And in most cases, local subcontractors, who are networked to the parent firm, organize these production activities either in a putting-out system or in small factories operated with wage-labor. This decentralization in the sphere of production, however, is accompanied by a simultaneous shift towards a more centralized system of managerial control over the network by the parent firms from the global cities of North America and Europe. The surplus generated at the sites of production in the third world is extracted by the parent firm at the point of exchange with the subcontractor.[34] Thus through this dispersion of production on a global level, a part of the informal need economy of the third world finds itself implicated in the circuit of the global accumulation-economy.

The important point here is that we must sharply contrast the need economy that results from developmental governmentality— the one we have described in this book—with informalization within capitalist production described above. Case studies in the context of Central American economies help illustrate the difference between these two spheres of informal production.[35]One such study reveals how a Honduran—US baseball manufacturing company engages women belonging to a rural community in Northern Honduras to make baseballs. The women carry out only one part of the manufacturing process—sewing the balls—under subcontracting arrangement. The balls are then finished in another plant to be exported to the United States. This subcontracting arrangement has been a response on the part of the company to trade union pressure from the organized labor. The women engaged in this activity are typically housewives who do house work along with other chores with the help of children, and are paid at piece rate. This serves as an illustration of the globalization-driven informalization in which the labor force in the interior of capital's circuit is atomized and the site of production is shifted to the household as a strategy to counter the demand of the organized labor for higher wages.

The case of the women retrenched from the state sector in Managua, Nicaragua, offers a very different scenario. As a part of the structural adjustment programs implemented in Nicaragua in the final years of the Sandinista regime, the state sector was downsized and a large number of employees, mainly women, lost their jobs. They became self-employed "entrepreneurs" in the informal sector, primarily, retail sales.

While the Honduran case is one of informalization within the circuit of capital, in the Managuan case, it is the "exclusion" from the formal economy, rather than dispersion and fragmentation of capitalist production on a global level, which results in the formation of informal need-based activities. The point that is to be emphatically made here is that informalization of production within the circuit of capital is different in a fundamental way from the need economy that constitutes the outside of that circuit, and it is the latter that has been my concern in this book. While the latter is a sub-economy resulting from primitive accumulation, the former phenomenon is a result of the dispersion within the circuit of capital. As we have already pointed out at the beginning of this section, the circuit of capitalist production is an articulation of accumulation and need (workers producing surplus value for the capitalist in order to be able to perform the necessary labor for themselves) in which need is subjugated to accumulation. Informalization within capitalist production means that the site where labor is performed is distanced from capital, and then is rearticulated with it through a different network of surveillance and control. Put differently, it is a process whereby the moment of need is apparently separated from accumulation, but is subjected to the latter in a more complex way through the network of exchange. In contrast, the parallel need economy, the result of exclusion, resides in a space entirely outside the circuit of capital, although, as we have argued, inside capitalism.

There is a strong tendency in the current literature on informalization to interpret the phenomenon primarily as one that occurs in the interior of capital, as a process driven by the logic of capitalist production, of surplus value, profit and accumulation.[36] The informal producer in this view is ultimately a source of surplus value, and informalization is a particular mode of surplus extraction. In sharp

contrast to this view, the narrative in this book is about informalization that results from exclusion from the sphere of capitalist
production, about the world of informal producers who are not
seen by capital as a potential source of surplus value, about the victims of primitive accumulation who do not find a place within the
accumulation-economy because of the involution of the space of
capital.

The Indian Economy goes Global

I now make an attempt to understand, in the light of what I have described as complex hegemony, the structural changes that the Indian
economy has been undergoing since the 1990s in the course of its
integration into the emerging global capitalist order, and discern in
these changes the contours of the new regime of capital and its
mode of governance.

Things are still in a flux; the old order in which the Indian economy functioned for the half-century of its post-colonial existence is
slowly but irreversibly yielding place to a new one. The contours of
the new order are coming into visibility but it is yet to take a clear
shape and to consolidate itself as a coherent regime. The changes
that are being wrought on the economic landscape are multi-faceted
and complex, and therefore if one wants to discern in these changes
the materialization of a coherent order, the vision of that new order
will inevitably differ depending on the particular perspective from
which the changes are approached. As I have already said, I will
interpret the changing structure of the Indian economy from the
perspective I have proposed and developed so far, a perspective that
focuses on the relation between capital and its outside, on how the
outside space is negotiated with the purpose of creating the politico-
ideological conditions of capital's reproduction. I will claim that
the emerging order conforms to a regime of accumulation that is
grounded in the incorporation of the formal–informal separation
within the framework of planning and in the deployment of governmental technologies to reproduce the dualism.

Although the talk of reforms was up in the air from the late 1980s,
the new regime was inaugurated in 1991 when the union government
announced the reform package and initiated the process of its implementation. Aggressive changes were made in the areas of industry,
finance, international trade, capital flows, and the exchange rate.

The process continued throughout the 1990s with further changes in these spheres. Taken together, these changes meant a restructuring of the economy in a way that would enable it to integrate with the emerging global capitalist order.

The new industrial policy explicitly sought to extricate the Indian industry from the grasp of bureaucratic control that had characterized the earlier regime. There were three important features of this policy shift. The first of these was in the sphere of industrial licensing. Previously, the private industrial sector was under the purview of a strict system of licensing: no new industry could be set up, and no investment could be made to expand capacity in the existing ones without prior approval of the government. The new policy totally abolished the licensing system, irrespective of the level of investment, except for the few sectors that were considered important from the standpoint of strategic concerns, especially about the environment or social objectives. The scope of de-licensing was further extended in the following years to include the majority of these exceptions, leaving only five sectors under the purview of the licensing system in the end of the 1990s.

Second, the existing Monopoly and Restrictive Trade Practices (MRTP) Act was considerably amended in favor of the large firms. Earlier, the Act required all firms with assets exceeding Rs. 100 million to seek separate approval for their investments and expansion in addition to the usual industrial license. Arguing that such requirements discouraged growth and diversification of large enterprises, the new policy dispensed with the threshold limit and allowed these enterprises total freedom in their investment decisions.

Third—this was perhaps the most aggressive aspect of the new industrial policy—the centrality of the public sector in the economy was denied by allowing private capital to enter the areas hitherto reserved for the state. The post-colonial strategy for industrialization accorded a central role to the public sector by having the key sectors of the economy, such as capital goods, public utilities, and telecommunication under the exclusive monopoly of state capital. The new policy not only opened the majority of these sectors to private investments, in addition it proposed privatization of the existing state enterprises through disinvestments in the form of selling shares to private individuals and institutions. The space in which the state capital had operated was thus considerably shrunk to allow private capital to ascend to a central and decisive position in the economy.

Regarding the overall approach to industrialization, the general thrust of the reform package was to move away from the inward looking strategy of import substitution pursued in the first three decades of planning towards a more outward looking model based on export promotion. And in consonance with this shift, radical changes were introduced in the external sector regarding foreign trade and investments. The previous regime had severely restricted the entry of foreign capital and import of goods to provide protection to domestic industries. In a significant change of policies, quantitative restrictions on imports were converted into tariffs, and the average rate of tariff was cut down drastically to allow unrestricted flow of imports. What is more important, the government withdrew the regulatory framework within which foreign capital had to operate and adopted an open door policy towards Foreign Direct Investment (FDI). It emphatically committed itself to creating conditions that would lure as much FDI as possible into the Indian economy.

Apart from substantial reduction in tariff and non-tariff restrictions on trade, the external sector witnessed another significant shift in policy: the earlier system of exchange rate based on strict government regulation was replaced by a radically, new and liberalized regime. The earlier system allowed a substantial overvaluation of the rupee, and this high value had been maintained through total control by the government on the sale and purchase of foreign exchange. The new regime left the determination of the value of the rupee to the market forces by introducing at first partial and then full convertibility in the current account, and partial convertibility in the capital account.

Perhaps the most striking feature of the new order was the integration of the Indian financial sector into the global financial system. The process of capitalist globalization has increased the mobility of financial capital on the global level to an unprecedented degree. With its open door policy towards foreign capital and liberalization of the exchange rate regime, the Indian economy succeeded in inserting itself into the global circuit of finance and in attracting a staggering amount of foreign institutional investments (FII).

The stated objective of the reforms was to minimize the state's involvement in the economy and thus to have a "leaner and fitter" state sector. In keeping with this objective, the government decided to cut back on the budget deficit and eventually eliminate it. Various subsidies, an integral part of the earlier regime, were withdrawn or reduced considerably. It was strongly argued that the subsidy given to the unprofitable public sector units was a burden on the state exchequer and therefore these units must either close down or be sold to the private sector.

Put together, these reforms significantly altered the structure of the Indian economy in favor of a system driven by the market forces and private entrepreneurship. Although the neo-liberal advocates of reforms complain about the insufficient implementation of the proposed reform package, there is no denying that the Indian economy in the preceding decade-and-a-half has experienced a rupture with the past. The post-colonial regime of economic development through planned accumulation, with the state as its most important agent, has been virtually abandoned to embrace a system in which accumulation is driven entirely by the market forces and the logic of capitalist calculation.

Jobless Growth

It cannot be denied that the reforms have had an effect on the growth of the economy. The 1990s experienced an impressive average of growth rate, and after a temporary decline in the subsequent years, it again shot up to its earlier level. The evidence on the whole strongly suggest that, despite fluctuations owing to factors such as a poor monsoon or a recession on the world level, the growth performance of the Indian economy has been and will continue to be satisfactory. Reforms therefore cannot be opposed on the ground of growth.

The growth rate figures however belie a phenomenon that the Indian economy has been experiencing in this period of boom: the growing level of unemployment. The evidence also points to the fact that while the economy is growing steadily in terms of the GDP, its impact in terms of employment generation has been negligible. It is not India alone, the entire developing world—and to a certain extent the developed countries as well—is witnessing this growth–employment paradox.

Even in the early years of globalization, the UNDP, in its Human Development Report of 1993, took note of this fact: "many parts of the world are witnessing a new phenomenon—jobless growth. Even when output increases, increase in employment lags way behind."(p. 36) It ascribed the lack of employment generation to the capital intensity of investment and the pattern of income distribution.

[The] prevalent technology reflects the existing pattern of income distribution—20 per cent of the world's population has 83 per cent of the world's income and, hence, five times the purchasing power of the poorer 80 per cent of the humankind. Clearly technology will cater to the preferences of the richer members of the international society. (1993: 37)

An interesting observation on the multinational corporations was made in this context:

The pattern is similar for multinational corporations with subsidiaries in developing countries: they have made substantial investment without creating large number of jobs. In 1990, there were at least 35,000 transnational corporations with more than 1,50,000 foreign affiliates. Of the 22 million people they employ outside their home country, about seven million are directly employed in developing countries—less than one percent of their economically active population. (*ibid.*: 35)

The jobless growth thus found a place within the discourse and gained currency within the international development organizations more than a decade ago. We have seen earlier in this chapter that this concern about the phenomenon of exclusion of a significant part of the population from the growth process finally culminated into a rethinking of the informal sector.

Coming back to the Indian case, there is little doubt that the impressive growth rate has failed to generate employment. As the *Global Employment Trends of the ILO* reports:

In spite of steady and robust growth since 1995, productive employment generation has not been forthcoming. Between 1993–94 and 1999–2000, India's GDP grew at a rate 6.6 per cent annually, but the employment growth rate was only 1 per cent. In the previous decade—1983 to 1993—India's GDP growth averaged 5.4 per cent, yet the employment growth rate was 2.1 per cent—

twice the employment growth rate of the "booming" 1993–94 to 1999–2000 period. The employment intensity of production—measured by the employment elasticity of GDP growth—declined from 0.36 in 1993–94 to 0.13 in 1999–2000. (2003: 51)

The fall in the employment intensity of production was due to two main reasons. First, as the areas reserved for the public sector were opened to private capital, competition forced the public sector industries to reduce cost by downsizing the labor force through Voluntary Retirement Schemes. Faced with competition from abroad, the organized private sector also sought to retain competitiveness by rationalizing the structure of existing production processes, which meant shedding of excess labor. And second, in response to the threat of quality competition in an open economy, the private industries switched to more capital-intensive technologies in their new investment projects. These twin factors caused the employment elasticity to fall sharply from 0.36 to 0.13.

While the euphoria over growth still continued, the grim employment situation also started coming into focus from the late 1990s, providing a ground for a forceful political critique of reforms. To assert the legitimacy of the new order, the question of mass unemployment had to be addressed. The following statement made by K.C. Pant, the deputy chairperson of the Planning Commission, betrays the crisis of legitimacy:

> In recent years, however, two trends have become apparent, which dictate a reappraisal of our approach to development and employment generation. First, the demographic trends indicate that the rate of growth of population in the working age group is accelerating due to high birth rates.... Second, the pace of creation of work opportunities has not kept pace with the growing requirements during the 1990s, despite an acceleration in the growth rate of the economy. Taken together, these trends imply that if nothing is done, the country will face the spectre of rising unemployment with all its attendant economic, social and political consequences.[37]

A target of ten million new jobs was set for the Tenth Five Year Plan, scheduled to begin in 2002, and a task force was formed in 1999 under the chairmanship of Montek S. Ahluwalia, a member of the Planning Commission, to suggest appropriate policies for the realization of the target. In its report submitted in 2001, the task force strongly argued that instead of trying to change the employment intensities of production, it would be better for the government to promote growth, and growth alone would solve the problem on the employment front by creating sufficient number of jobs. The government, however, was sceptical about the recommendation's exclusive focus on growth, and another special task force was formed in 2001 with S.P. Gupta as the chairman to review the entire matter.

The report prepared by this group, submitted in 2002, has a very different story to tell about the employment scenario. It observes that there has been a deceleration in both population and labor force growth between 1983 to 1993–1994 and 1993–94 to 1999–2000, and that the economy has experienced a significant acceleration in GDP growth during this period; but despite these favorable changes, the employment growth rate has suffered a significant decline. The report identifies the decline in the labor-intensity in production—in almost all sectors and also in the aggregate—as the reason behind this paradox. Probing further into the employment-output connection and the sectoral composition of employment, the report presents striking information about the relative contribution to employment of the organized and what it called the "unorganized sector"—which is our informal sector—in the economy. The total contribution of the organized sector to employment in the year 1999–2000 was only 8 per cent—of which the private segment's contribution was a meagre 2.5 per cent. The remaining 92 per cent of the employment came from small businesses and self-employment in the unorganized sector. As production in the latter is significantly more labor intensive, its employment elasticity of output is also significantly higher than in the former.

On the basis of these observations, the Gupta task force argues that the solution to the unemployment problem lies in the unorganized sector. It claims that seen in the light of the current trends, even if the organized segment of the economy grows at a rate of 20 per cent per annum and the organized private segment at 30 per cent, their contribution to employment will increase hardly by 1.5 to 2 per cent of the total over the Tenth Plan. Therefore, it recommends that:

[on] the basis of this ground reality ... exclusively for generating the desirable high level of employment, *we have to target the*

unorganized sector, including small and medium enterprises, which also cover a large part of the service sector of the economy. (my emphasis)[38]

Such targeting involves careful designing of policies aimed at creating conditions favorable to the unorganized sector. The report identifies credit, technology and training as the key areas for policy interventions. The flow of credit, availability of technology, and the nature of education are visibly biased in favor of the organized sector under the existing arrangements. In order to realize the employment goal, the report strongly suggests, these biases must be reversed to eliminate the constraints within which the unorganized sector operates.

Contrasting it with the report of the first task force, one can see that the recommendations of the second task are derived from the very different representation of the economy it adopts. The former views the economy as a continuous space and reduces the employment question to the question of growth of the single homogenous "economy". While the latter explicitly recognizes a discontinuity within the economy and highlights the instrumental role of the discontinuity in realizing the employment goal—a goal that it posits as separate and distinct from growth per se. In terms of our story, the strategy is one of constituting and fostering the need economy to provide income-entitlements, as the accumulation-economy is incapable of accommodating the surplus labor force. The fact is that the unorganized sector has always been there, providing subsistence to an overwhelming majority of the working population, but the discourse of planning in India never recognized its existence—it was a dark space between the traditional agriculture and the modern industry. The discourse now illuminates this space, "discovers" the unorganized sector and turns it into an object of planned governmentality. The accumulation-economy, driven by the logic of capitalist calculation and the forces of the market, will grow on its own, but at the same time the need economy has to be created, fostered and managed by purposeful planned intervention for providing livelihood to the excluded. Resources have to be shifted to the need-space, and for that purpose, if required, the accumulation-economy has to be restricted, disciplined, and tamed. This vision of developmental governance is increasingly coming to prevail over the exclusively growth-centric approach and is currently shaping the nature of governmental practices in the Indian economy.

Globalization and reforms in India have had its ramifications in the sphere of electoral politics. The Congress Party that initiated the process was voted out of power. After a short phase of unstable coalition governments, the National Democratic Alliance (NDA)—a coalition led by the Bharatiya Janata Party (BJP)—took office in 1999. During its five years in power, it vigorously pursued the unabashed neo-liberal agenda of liberalization of the economy and its integration into the global commodity and financial markets, ignoring its devastating impact on the employment front. The result was an ignominious defeat of the NDA in the general election of 2004, in which the Congress came back to power, this time as the leader of the United Progressive Alliance (UPA)—a coalition of several regional parties, notably with the support of the Indian parliamentary Left led by the Communist Party of India (Marxist). The election campaigns of both the Congress and the Leftists centered on a critique of the NDA's reforms in neo-liberal style and its consequences in terms of inequality, unemployment, and loss of livelihood. Immediately after taking office, the UPA announced its Common Minimum Program (CMP) with the purpose of adding "a human face" to the reform process.[39] The CMP on the one hand emphasizes on industrial growth and the inflow of foreign capital:

The UPA will take all necessary steps to revive industrial growth and put it on a robust footing through a range of policies, including deregulation, where necessary incentive to boost private investment will be introduced. FDI will continue to be encouraged and actively sought, particularly in the area of infrastructure, high technology and exports…The country needs and can absorb at least two to three times the present level of FDI inflows. (p. 6)

On the other, it expresses its commitment to create entitlements through direct public action:

The UPA government will immediately enact a National Employment Guarantee Act. This will provide a legal guarantee for at least 100 days of employment… on asset-creating public works programs every year at minimum wages for at least one ablebodied person in every rural, urban poor and lower-middle class household. (p. 1)

And more importantly, recognizing the role of the informal sector in realizing the employment goal, the government will:

[e]stablish a National Commission to examine the problems facing enterprises in the unorganized, informal sector. The Commission will be asked to make appropriate recommendations to provide technical, marketing and credit support to these enterprises. A National Fund will be created for this purpose. (p. 1)

It also emphasizes on the revamping of the functioning of the Khadi and Village Industries Commission, and on expanding credit facilities for small-scale industry and self-employment. Thus the government sets the twin goals: it will create conditions for the expansion of the accumulation economy, and at the same time, through its governmental role, will promote the need economy for creating employment and entitlements. Together, they constitute the new regime of post-colonial capital.

As I said at the beginning of this section, things are still in a flux: the forces of globalization and the political imperatives of legitimizing the existence of globalized Indian capital are apparently pushing and pulling the economy in different directions. Yet, in this complex dynamic, one can discover a new order that is slowly materializing, an order in which capital's reproduction is ensured in the de-politicized terrain of governmentality, by an elaborate mechanism of welfarist policy interventions that seek to create a need economy in which the victims of the accumulation economy can survive. And with it, the project of planned development in post-colonial India is coming full circle. It all began with the vision of the planned arising of capital that would bring about the transition of the economy and society from a state of poverty and backwardness—a historically given initial condition—to a state of prosperity and progress. After struggling for half-a-century with this elusive project, the project of post-colonial development is finally coming to terms with the fact that there is a dualism endogenous to post-colonial capital, and the role of the developmental state is to create the conditions within which the two-tier world of capital can be reproduced.

Notes

1. Bangasser (2000).
2. Harris–Todaro assume away surplus labor in the Lewis' sense in agriculture on the ground that they are dealing with African economies that in fact are plagued by a shortage of labor in agriculture.
3. The literature on the informal sector is vast. A few important and frequently cited works are: Hart (1973), Weeks (1975), Sethuraman (1977), McGee (1973), Gerry (1974), Moser (1978) and Tokman (1978). For a critical overview of different approaches to the informal sector, see Peattie (1987).
4. Moser (1978: 1051).
5. On this, see Bhattacharyya (2002).
6. See McGee (1973) Gerry (1974) and Bienefeld (1975) and Bryant (1976). See also Moser (1978) for a survey of the literature.
7. Chakraborty and Cullenburg (2003) use the term "need-based economy" to describe an economy of subsistence producers as distinct from a surplus economy with class. My conceptualization of the need-economy is fundamentally different from theirs in that it does not rule out the existence of surplus within the realm of need-based production. More important, I posit the need-economy in opposition not to the class-economy but to an economy driven by the logic of systemic accumulation. In fact, Chakraborty and Cullenburg's treatment of need-based production, as distinct from class-based production, is highly problematic because there is nothing that prevents class-based production from being driven by need.
8. See McGee (1973).
9. The NSS Report no. 456, 1999–2000, I: 1.
10. In the UN Earth Summit held in Johannesburg in August 2002, hundreds of angry African farmers and fishermen demonstrated for more access to natural resources. "We are from fishing villages on the (South African) west and south coast and we want access for subsistence fishermen", organizer, Manfred van Rooyen, said as fishermen waved posters saying "There are more sharks on land than in the sea".
11. Haggleblade, Steven et al. 2004 (164).
12. Harvey (2003).
13. *Economic Perspective* (2004: 34).
14. World Bank Partnerships for Development (2000). Creative Communications Group for the World Bank: Washington.
15. *Economic Perspective*, op.cit.
16. *Human Development Report*, 2005: 65.
17. Warah (2003).
18. See "Micro-finance and Other Credit Mechanism", The World Bank Group, 2001, and the *Human Development Report*, 1997: 109.
19. The World Bank: Making a Difference with Micro-finance" Countdown 2005, Vol. 1, Issue 4, May–June 1998.
20. Xaba, Jantjie et al.(2002).

21. Vishwanath and Narayan (2001).
22. The World Bank Group (2001).
23. World Development Report (1989: 114).
24. The World Bank Group (2001).
25. The World Bank Group (2004: 4).
26. *Ibid.*: 4.
27. "The World Bank: Making a Difference with Micro-finance" op. cit.
28. "Grameen Bank—Banking on the Poor", *http://www.gdrc.com.au*
29. "Grameen Bank- Bangladesh: Breaking a Vicious Circle by Providing Credit", *http://www.gdrc.org*.
30. "The SEWA Bank: A Women's Self-help Organization for Poverty Alleviation In India", *http://gdrc.org*.
31. "The SEWA Tree: A Women's Support Network", *http://www.gdrc.org*.
32. "The SEWA Bank: A Women's Self-help Organization for Poverty Alleviation In India", *http://gdrc.org*.
33. Little, Mazumdar and Page (1987) in a World Bank Study on the small-scale industries in India, observes that for most of the products, the small and large industries are potentially competitive.
34. Chossudovsky (1997) presents some figures related to the distribution of earnings in the garment export sector of Bangladesh: "the factory price of one dozen shirts is US$36 to $40 (fob).... The shirts are retailed at approximately US$22 a piece or US$266 a dozen in the United States. Female and child labor in Bangladeshi garment factories is paid approximately US$20 a month.... Less than two percent of the total value of the commodity accrues to the direct producers (the garment workers) in the form of wages. Another one percent accrues as industrial profit to the 'competitive' independent Third World producer." (p. 88).
35. See Perez Sainz, J.P. (1998).
36. See Tabak (2000).
37. See the foreword to the report of the S.P. Gupta Commission on employment, 2002.
38. The figures and the quote is from the Gupta Commission Report, p. 4.
39. Common Minimum Program of the UPA, Government of India, New Delhi, 2004.

Chapter 6

Conclusion: Towards a New Political Imaginary for the Post-colonial World

It has been one long story of post-colonial capitalist development, built up step by step in the preceding chapters. A story of primitive accumulation of capital, dispossession and exclusion; of ship of fools and developmental governmentality; of the hegemony process and the formation of a complex hegemonic order; of an emerging global capitalist regime in which the reign of capital rests on an implosion of the productive and the restrictive form of power. The central points made by our exploration of the post-colonial capitalist formation are the following:

(a) The phenomenon of exclusion and marginalization is an integral aspect of post-colonial capital and it resists being addressed in terms of the concept of exploitation as extraction and appropriation of surplus. An understanding of the post-colonial capitalist formation must explore how capital negotiates the space of the dispossessed to create the conditions of its own reproduction.

(b) Contrary to the claim of the traditional Marxist political economy of underdevelopment, hegemony of capital is not antithetical to difference. The presence of an outside of capital does not signal its weakness, the lack of its transformative power. On the contrary, the continued existence of the non-capitalist need economy, encompassed by the commodity space, is the sign of capital's strength: its ability to successfully carry out primitive accumulation on the one hand and to confine the outcasts and the dispossessed to the need economy created through welfarist governmentality. The post-colonial economy is necessarily heterogeneous, and the post-colonial capital does not represent itself as a monolith; its hegemony is expressed through difference rather than monism.

(c) Developmental governmentalty is made possible by a reversal of primitive accumulation whereby a part of the capitalist surplus is transferred from the domain of capital to the need economy. Development cannot be reduced to capital: the space of development is one that is distinct from the space of capital with the former securing the legitimation of the latter by creating and renewing the need economy.

(d) The understanding of post-colonial capitalism as a complex of capital and a need economy extracts the story of underdevelopment from the narrative of transition and reinscribes it within a non-historicist framework with the claim that poverty and underdevelopment is the outcome of the arising of capital rather than a residual of the pre-capitalist past.

Conceptualization of post-colonial capitalism in these terms brings into visibility a new political imaginary which foregrounds the politics of exclusion rather than the politics of transition that has so far dominated radical thinking about the third world. The latter, rooted in a historicist notion of transition, has sought to characterize underdevelopment as the result of the insufficiency of capital's transformative power in the third world context: its inability to transform pre-capital and revolutionize the economy; and the critique of capital has been centered on its inability to be the vehicle of the historicist journey from backwardness to progress. The anti-capitalist politics proposed by this view has posited as its goal a macro-level socialist transformation of the economy under the agency and leadership of the working class.

The politics of exclusion, in contrast, unyokes the anti-capitalist political project from the story of transition by envisioning post-colonial capitalism as a complex of capital and a need economy and focuses on the space of the marginal and the dispossessed. Its critique of capital is centered not on the inability of capital to transform pre-capital but on the wasteland of the dispossessed created by the very process of primitive accumulation. The goal of this politics is to politicize development. As we have seen, developmental governmentality posits itself as "politically neutral" practices, the purpose of which is to improve the conditions of the population groups with the help of rational calculations by experts and professionals. The politics of exclusion subjects the depoliticized face of governmentality to a political critique and seeks to posit the terrain of governmentality as a politically contested terrain.

Politicization of the governmental functions of the developmental state and the international organizations means pitting the need economy in radical opposition to the accumulation-economy of capital. The new anti-capitalist politics claims autonomy for the need economy and asserts its demand for resources (means of labor, credit, training, information). Governmentality creates and renews the need economy but at the same time confines it to an "informal" space outside the space of capital. In the complex hegemonic order of capital that I have described, the dominant discourse of development allows capital an autonomy in the sense that the accumulation-economy can expand on its own. The expansion of the accumulation-economy is the result of both capitalist accumulation—creation of new capital with surplus produced within the capitalist production system—and primitive accumulation. As primitive accumulation results in dispossession, development rehabilitates the dispossessed in the need economy. Thus, the need economy remains a passive space that is obliterated and recreated in the course of capital's autonomous process of expansion, although in the representation of the development process the two are posited as complementary and parallel. The precise goal of the politics of exclusion is to unsettle the dominant regime of representation to bring to light this asymmetry and then to endow the need economy with autonomy that will allow it to posit itself as the radical "other" of capital. In other words, the purpose of the new politics is to liberate need-based production from the informality and spatial fixity that the dominant discourse imposes on it so that it can encroach upon and unsettle the space of capital.

The politics of pitting need against accumulation operates in two directions. The need economy we have described resides in a space outside the domain of capital. We have also noted at the end of the preceding chapter that informalization of capitalist production associated with subcontracting and outsourcing on a global level results in need-based production activities within the circuit of accumulation. These activities generate economic surplus that flows to the accumulation fund of capital and is used for expanding the volume of the circuit. The politics of exclusion aims to resist the invasion of the accumulation-economy into the parallel need economy and to assert the latter's demand for resources to create the conditions for its expanded reproduction. At the same time, it strives to extricate the implicated part of the need economy from capital's circuit, to liberate these activities from the grasp of the systemic logic of capitalist accumulation, and unite them with the parallel part of the need economy to constitute a unified economic space where production is grounded in the logic of need.

The Politics of the Governed

Exploring the political dimensions of governmentality in the post-colonial context, Partha Chatterjee in his recent book has introduced us to what he calls the politics of the governed (Chatterjee 2004). He offers the concept of *"political society,"* which is constituted by population groups, as distinct from *"civil society"* inhabited by the citizenry. Political society is identified as the site where population groups engage in contestation, confrontation, and negotiations with governmental agencies of the state to ensure the reproduction of their conditions of existence. While citizens of civil society see themselves as representatives of the sovereignty of the state, inhabitants of political society are mere targets of governmental policy; they are the poor and the underprivileged—the urban dispossessed, slum dwellers, street venders, squatters of public land—whose very livelihood and habitation often involve violation of the law. According to Chatterjee, while civil society and the state with its constitution and law constitute the high ground of modernity in the post-colonial world, the site for actual political practice in these societies is the terrain of political society where governmental agencies have to deal with population groups and promote their well-being to secure legitimacy of the existing order. In this process, population groups, while asserting their demands, contest, confront, and negotiate with the agents of governmentalty to reproduce their precarious and ever vulnerable existence at the margin of the economy and society.

Although the concept of political society does not explore the link between governmentality and capital, it refers to what we have described as the management of the wasteland produced by post-colonial capital's primitive accumulation. The inhabitants of political society are the victims of the ongoing process of primitive accumulation whose rehabilitation in the informal sector is the precise goal of governmentality. But since in this conceptualization the distinction between civil society and political society is not posited in the light of the political economy of post-colonial capital, the political struggles of population groups remain multiple and diverse, their success and failure contextual and temporary. Of particular importance to Chatterjee is the observation that population groups in the course of these struggles cease to be mere targets of governmentality and acquire the characteristics of a community that binds its members in a kinship relation. This communal form is not grounded in any pre-given association based on ethnicity, race or religion; it is produced by the very political process in which the "governed" confronts, contests, and negotiates with the agents of governmentality. These communities and their forms of solidarity, however, remain plural, disparate, and local, each with its own specificity and uniqueness. Seen thus, the politics of the governed is unable to posit a unified "other" of post-colonial capital.

But once the space of the dispossessed is conceptualized in terms of need-based production, multiple population groups in political society and their plural struggles can be seen as grounded in the need-economy. Communities that emerge from these struggles, with their various forms of solidarity, can find a common identity in relation to their location in a unified "informal economy". The politics of the governed then rises above its temporary and contextual nature and is able to posit a radical critique of capital's accumulation-economy. Governmental technology necessarily presents the social as heterogeneous and the outside of capital is represented in the discourse of welfarist governmentality as fragmented, consisting of multiple population groups. And the precise task of the anti-capitalist politics of exclusion is to ground these fragments in the space of need to produce a unified and stable "other" of capital.

I have in the preceding chapters repeatedly made the point, and let me iterate, that the need economy belongs to the exterior of capital but to the interior of capitalism: the compass of capitalism extends beyond capital to accommodate need-based production. It is not a residual of the past that refuses to go away, it is a product of the arising of capital. Thus when it contests the accumulation-economy of capital, it does so from within capitalism. Its inhabitants are distinct from the "worker" who belongs to the interior of capital. Laclau and Mouffe in *Hegemony and Socialist Strategy* have drawn our attention to the fact that the nineteenth century witnessed struggles by artisans against the destruction of their artisanal identity in the face of the emerging capitalist order. According to Laclau and Mouffe, these were "without a doubt radically anti-capitalist struggles..... but they were not struggles of the proletariat—if by proletariat we understand the type of worker produced by the development of capitalism" (1985: 156). What is noteworthy here is that the struggles of the artisans against the capitalist order during the period of the arising of capital in Europe reflected the resistance put up by a system that was withering away against the one that was emerging. The two parties in this battle had their specific positions along the historical trajectory of progress. In sharp contrast to this, the anti-capitalist politics of the governed—although the dispossessed is not a worker—are struggles that are internal to capitalism without any historicist connotation.

But where is class in all this? The indomitable Marxist will ask. It is true that I have kept the concept of class as surplus labor out of focus. I have done it purposely because the narrative of post-colonial capital I have built is animated by the urge to explore a space that lies beyond class, a space that the concept of class as a relation based on the extraction and appropriation of surplus labor fails to address. It is the space of the excluded and the dispossessed who have nothing to lose, not even the chains of wage-slavery. I have read Marx's mid-nineteenth century discussion on primitive accumulation from my early twenty-first century vantage point to bring into visibility this dark space of "classlessness", which has been implicit and hidden in the Marxian discourse as a part of the discourse's forgetfulness. My purpose has been to make it explicit and visible, allow it to claim its place in the broader Marxian discursive field, and foreground it as an inescapable and defining aspect the post-colonial capitalist formation. My purpose has also been to posit the phenomenon of exclusion on a politically contested terrain—the terrain of the politics of exclusion. And this politics does not speak the language of class.

Unfortunately, Marxists of orthodox persuasion have failed to recognize the radical potential of this political space arising out of the process of primitive accumulation and the contradictions between need and accumulation. They either try to explain the need-based politics in terms of class contradictions, thereby reducing it to the space of class politics; or, when such reduction fails to be convincing, dismiss it as non-class politics devoid of any capacity to bring about radical transformation of the economy and society.

Class essentialism has thus refused to allow the politics of exclusion/ dispossession to have a space of its own in the overall project of social transformation.

My conceptualization of the post-colonial economic is largely motivated by the urge to break with this essentialist deployment of the concept of class. But "class", I hasten to add, still continues to offer a conceptual framework that is indispensable for imagining a post-colonial politics of transformation. Even after the devalorization of the Marxian class perspective following the collapse of the 'actually existing socialisms', radical politics in the post-colonial context still finds expression in the idiom of class; and the class analytic framework continues to define and energize subject positions that engage in the project of eliminating class-based exploitation.

The important point, however, is that class politics based on exploitation in terms of surplus labor and the politics of exclusion based on poverty and need map two separate and distinct spaces. Politics in these two spaces can be complementary or conflictual, depending on the specific context in which they are practised. The need economy, for example, is a space in which the distinction between capital and labor is, in most cases, blurred. The small entrepreneur in the informal sector maybe an employer of a few wage-workers, and seen from the perspective of class politics, it is an exploitative class process as surplus value is extracted from wage labor in the form of profit. However, productivity is so low owing to low level of technology and other resource constraints that wages and profits taken together allow for a very low level of income and consumption for both the producer and the appropriator of the surplus labor. Anti-capitalist class politics in this case will be bent on pitting the workers against the "capitalist employer" and is thus likely to subvert the very conditions of existence of the enterprise. Thus the politics that is effective in the interior of capital and its accumulation-economy can be totally counterproductive in the need economy. The need-based politics, on the other hand, will see the enterprise, with its employer (in most cases an owner–worker) and employees, engaged in production for consumption and seek to protect it from the predatory practice of big capital and the expansionary thrust of its accumulation-economy. Clearly, class politics here does not conform to the politics of exclusion.

The relation between these two realms of politics is thus a complex one and a radical political agenda for the post-colonial world must be grounded in an imaginative articulation of them. The concept of need itself, however, may be seen as a possible ground for such articulation. I have described in chapter 5 the capitalist accumulation-economy in terms of the circuit M ~ C ~ C' ~ M', where M is the initial stock of money spent by the capitalist to buy materials and labor power C, which is then transformed into C' within the capitalist production process. C' is sold for a larger amount of money, M', which is used to repeat the sequence in an expanded form. Now the sale and purchase of labor power can be seen as a complementary circuit of the form commodity ~ money ~ commodity, where the first commodity is the labor power which is sold for money (i.e., wages) which in turn is spent by the worker to buy the basket commodities she/he consumes. The worker sells her/his labor power in order to acquire money for the purchase of goods that are essential for the reproduction of his/her existence. Thus the worker's circuit can be interpreted as a need-circuit but one that is subjugated to the circuit of accumulation. The worker can realize her/his consumption goal only if she/he produces surplus value for the capitalist. Marx in *Grundrisse* repeatedly draws our attention to this subjugation of the world of need to the logic of accumulation, to the fact that the worker can perform the necessary labor for his/her own reproduction only if she/he performs surplus labor for the capitalist. Seen thus, the existence of the direct producers belonging to the three distinct parts of the economy—the need economy that exists outside the domain of capital, the informalized production activities that are implicated in the circuit of capital and the formal capitalist labor process—is grounded in production for the satisfaction of need, and they are all subjected to capital's dominance although the nature and form dominance is different in each case. The perspective of need can thus provide a common ground for both the "excluded" and the "included" in their battle against capital.

A radical political agenda for today's post-colonial world, deeply implicated in a global capitalist order, thus must be rooted in an articulation of these two terrains of politics: the terrain that foregrounds the need economy in radical opposition to the continual and ongoing process of primitive accumulation of global capital, and the one that focuses on class-based exploitation within capital's own space. It is only by articulating these two realms of politics—instead of reducing one into the other or placing them in a hierarchy—that we can carve out from their criss cross a complex space, a space politically far more fertile than the one defined by class alone; a space in which radically new counter-hegemonic imaginaries, and the contours of strategies and actions to turn those imaginaries into actualities, can be made visible.

Those who demonstrated against the WTO and G8 summits in Seattle, Genoa, Prague, and elsewhere were protesting against the tyranny of capitalist accumulation—against the loss of livelihood, loss of environment and disempowerment of millions of people in the third world resulting from predatory practices of the multinationals. Among those protesters were also the industrial workers of the developed countries, who had lost, or were anticipating the loss of their jobs as a result of outsourcing and off shoring. In other words, it was the need economy that fought in the streets of Seattle with the riot police, the Swiss Guards of the accumulation-economy. And it is on this rough and uneasy terrain that one can catch a glimpse of the politics of exclusion and resistance for the post-colonial world today.

Bibliography

Ahmed, Izaz. 1983. "Imperialism amd Progress" in Ronald Chilcote (ed.), *Theories of Development: Mode of Production or Dependency?*, California: Sage Publications, 33–72.
——. 2001. "Introduction" in Izaz Ahmed (ed.), *On the National and Colonial Question*. Delhi: Leftword, 33–72.
Althusser, L. and E. Balibar. 1970. *Reading Capital*. London: New Left Books.
Amin, Samir. 1976. *Unequal Development*. London: Monthly Review Press.
——. 1977. *Imperialism and Unequal Development*. Harvester: Hassocks.
Arndt, H.W. 1981. 'Economic Development: A Semantic History', *Economic Development and Cultural Change*, 29(3): 457–66.
Ashton, T.S. 1948. *The Industrial Revolution 1760–1830*. New York: Oxford University Press.
Ayres, Robert. 1983. *Banking on the Poor: The World Bank and World Poverty*. Cambridge: MIT Press.
Balibar, E. 1970. 'On Basic Concepts of Historical Materialism', in Althusser and E. Balibar (eds), *Reading Capital*. London: New Left Books.
Bangasser, Paul E. 2000. 'The ILO and the Informal Sector: An Institutional History', ILO Employment Paper 2000/9. *www.ilo.org*.
Bennholdt–Thomsen, V. 1981. 'Subsistence Reproduction and Extended Reproduction—A Contribution to the Discussion About Modes of Production' in K. Young et al. (eds), *Of Marriages and the Market*. London: Routledge and Kegan Paul.
Berger, S. and M. Piore. 1980. *Dualism and Discontinuity in Industrial Societies*. Cambridge: Cambridge University Press.
Bhagwati, J. 1994. *India in Transition: Freeing the Economy*. Delhi: Oxford Univesity Press.
Bhattacharyya, R. 2002. 'The Burden of Development'. Unpublished M.Phil dissertation, University of Calcutta.
Bienefield, M. 1975. 'The Informal Sector and Peripheral Capitalism: The Case of Tanzania', *Bulletin of the Institute of Development Studies*, 6(3): 53–73.
Boeke, J.H. 1953. *Economics and Economic Policy of Dual Societies*. New York: International Secretariat of Pacific Relations.
Bradby, B. 1978. 'The Destruction of Natural Economy', *Economy and Society*, 4(2).
Braverman, Harry. 1975. *Labor and Monopoly Capital: The Degradation of Work in the Twentieth Century*. New York: Monthly Review Press.

Brenner, R. 1977. 'The Origins of Capitalist Development: A Critique of Neo-Smithian Marxism', *New Left Review*, 104, July–August.

Bryant, J. 1976. 'The Petty Commodity Sector in Urban Ghana'. Working Paper (unpublished), British Sociological Association, Development Group.

Byres, Terence J. 1994. 'State, Class and Development Planning in India', in *The State and Development Planning in India*. Delhi: Oxford University Press.

Chakraborty, Sukhomoy. 1987. *Development Planning: The Indian Experience*. Delhi: Oxford University Press.

Chakraborty, A. and S. Cullenburg. 2003. *Transition and Development in India*. New York and London: Routledge.

Chatterjee, Partha. 1986. *Nationalist Thought and the Colonial World*. London: Zed Books.

———. 1988. 'On Gramsci's "Fundamental Mistake"', *Economic and Political Weekly*, 23(5): 24–27.

———. 1993. *The Nation and its Fragments*. Delhi: Oxford University Press.

———. 2004. *The Politics of the Governed: Reflections on Popular Politics in Most of the World*. Bombay: Permanent Black.

Chaudhury, A. 1988. 'From Hegemony to Counter Hegemony: A Journey in a Non-Imaginary Unreal Space', *Economic and Political Weekly*, 23(5): 19–23.

———. 1992. "From Hegel to Gramsci: Capital's Passive Revolution", *Society and Change*, VIII(3&4).

Chilcote, R. 1983. 'Dependency or Mode of Production? Theoretical Issues' in Chilcote, R. and Dale Johnson (eds), *Theories of Development*. California: Sage Publications.

Chilcote, R. and Dale Johnson (eds). 1983. *Theories of Development*. California: Sage Publications.

Chossudovsky, M. 1997. *The Globalization of Poverty*. Penang: Third World Network.

Cohen, G.A. 1978. *Karl Marx's Theory of History: A Defense*. Oxford: Oxford University Press.

Cohn, B.S. 1980. 'History and Anthropology: The State of Play', *Comparative Studies in Society and History*, April, 22(2).

Common Minimum Program of the UPA. 2004. Government of India, Delhi.

Cordoso, F.H. 1973. 'Associated Dependent Development: Theoretical and Practical Implications' in Alfred Stepan (ed.), *Authoritarian Brazil: Origins, Policies and Future*. New Haven: Yale University Press.

Cordoso, F.H. and Faletto Enzo. 1979. *Dependency and Development*. Berkeley: University of California Press.

Custers, Peter. 1997. *Capital Accumulation and Women's Labour in Asian Economies*. Delhi: Vistaar Publications.

Davis, Mike. 2004. 'Planet of Slums: Urban Involution and the Informal Proletariat', *New Left Review*, 26 (March–April): 5–34.

Dos Santos, T. 1970. 'The Structure of Dependence', *American Economic Review*, 60(May): 231–36.

Durkheim, E. 1947. *The Division of Labor in Society*. New York: The Free Press.

Durkheim, E. 1957. *Professional Ethics and Civic Morals*. London: Routledge and Kegan Paul.

Emmanuel, A. 1971. *Unequal Exchange: A Study in the Imperialism of Trade*. New York: Monthly Review Press.

Escobar, A. 1995. *Encountering Development*. Princeton, New Jersey: Princeton University Press.

Esteva, Gustavo. 1997. 'Development' in W. Sachs (ed.), *Dictionary Development*. New Delhi: Orient Longman.

Faubion, James. 2001. *Essential Works of Michel Foucault 1954–1984*, III (2111). The Penguin Press.

Femia, Joseph. 1980. *Gramsci's Political Thought*. London: Blackwell.

Ferguson, James. 1990. *The Anti-politics Machine: 'Development', Depoliticization and Bureaucratic Power in Lesotho*. Cambridge: Cambridge University Press.

Folbre, N. 1982. 'Exploitation Comes Home: A Critique of the Marxian Theory of Family Labor', *Cambridge Journal of Economics*, 6(4): 317–29.

Foster–Carter, A. 1978. 'The Modes of Production Controversy', *New Left Review*, 107(January–February): 47–77.

Foucault, Michel. 1972. *The Archaeology of Knowledge*. New York: Pantheon Books.

———. 1979. *Discipline and Punish*. New York: Vintage Books.

———. 1980. *Power/Knowledge*. New York: Pantheon Books.

———. 1988. *Madness and Civilization*. New York: Vintage Books.

———. 1990. *The History of Sexuality: An Introduction*. New York: Vintage Books.

Fraad, H., S. Resnik and R. Wolff. 1994. *Bringing It All Back Home: Class, Gender and Power in Modern Household*. London: Pluto Press.

Frank, A.G. 1967. *Capitalism and Underdevelopment in Latin America: Historical Studies of Chile and Brazil*. New York: Monthly Review Press.

———. 1969. *Latin America: Underdevelopment and Revolution*. New York: Monthly Review Press.

———. 1978. *Dependent Accumulation and Underdevelopment*. London: Macmillan.

Frankel, Francine, R. 2005. *India's Political Economy: 1947–2004*. New Delhi: Oxford University Press.

Gandhi, M.K. 1958. 'Hind Swaraj' in *The Collected Works of Mahatma Gandhi*, vol. 10. New Delhi: Publications Division.

Gerry, C. 1974. 'Petty Production and the Urban Economy: A Case Study of Dakar', ILO–WEP Working Paper (unpublished), Geneva.

Gibson–Graham, J.K. 1996. *The End of Capitalism*. Cambridge, USA: Basil Blackwell.

Gibson–Graham, J.K. and David Riccio. 2001. '"After" Development: Reimagining Economy and Class' in J.K. Gibson–Graham, S.A. Resnick and R.D. Wolff (eds), *Re/Presenting Class: Essays in Post-modern Marxism*. Durham: Duke University Press.

Global Employment Trends. 2003. Geneva: ILO.

Gorz, Andre. 1989. *Critique of Economic Reason*. London: Verso.

Gramsci, Antonio. 1971. *Selections from Prison Notebooks*. New York: International Publishers.

Guha, Ranajit. 1982. 'On Some Aspects of Historiography in Colonial India', in Ranajit Guha (ed.), *Subaltern Studies I*. New Delhi: Oxford University Press.

Gupta, A. 2001. *Post-colonial Development: Agriculture in the Making of Modern India*. Delhi: Oxford University Press.

Gupta, S.P. 2002. 'On Targeting Ten Million Employment Opportunities Per Year over the Tenth Plan Period', Planning Commission, Government of India, New Delhi.

Hardt, Michael and Negri Antonio. 2000. *Empire*. Cambridge, Mass: Harvard University Press.

Harris, J. and M. Todaro. 1970. 'Migration, Unemployment and Development: A Two-Sector Analysis', *American Economic Review*, 40(March): 126–42.

Hart, K. 1973. 'Informal Income Opportunities and Urban Employment in Ghana', *Journal of Modern African Studies*, 11(1): 61–89.

Harvey, David. 2003. *The Imperialism*. New York: Oxford University Press.

Hoogvelt, Ankie. 1982. *The Third World in Global Development*. London: Macmillan Press.

———. 1997. *Globalization and the Postcolonial World: The New Political Economy of Development*. London: Macmillan Press.

Hill, C.P. 1985. *British Economic and Social History 1700–1982*, 5e, Edward Arnold: London.

Hirst, Paul and Graham Thompson. 1996. *Globalization in Question*. Cambridge: Polity Press.

Hunt, Diana. 1989. *Economic Theories of Development: An Analysis of Competing Paradigms*. Hertfordshire: Harvester Wheatsheaf.

Hymer, S and S. Resnik. 1969. 'A Model of an Agrarian Economy with Nonagricultural Activities', *American Economic Review*, 50: 493–506.

Illich, Ivan. 1997. 'Need' in W. Sachs (ed.), *Development Dictionary*. New Delhi: Orient Longman.

Kalecki, M. 1971. 'Selected Essays on the Dynamics of the Capitalist Economy'. Cambridge: Cambridge University Press, Ch 13.

Kay, J. 1975. *Development and Underdevelopment: A Marxist Analysis*. London: ELBS & Macmillan.

Kuhn, Thomas. S. 1962. *The Structure of Scientific Revolutions*. University of Chicago Press.

Laclau, Ernesto, and Mouffe Chanthal. 1985. *Hegemony and Socialist Strategy*. London: Verso.

Latouche, Serge. 1993. *In the Wake of the Affluent Society: An Exploration into Postdevelopment*. London: Zed Books.

———. 1997. 'Standard of Living' in W. Sachs (ed.), *Development Dictionary*. New Delhi: Orient Longman.

Leibenstein, H. 1957. *Economic Backwardness and Economic Growth*. New York: John Wiley & Sons.

Lewis, A. 1954. 'Economic Development with Unlimited Supply of Labor', *Manchester School*, May, 1954.

Little, Ian M.D., D. Mazumdar and John Page. 1987. *Small Manufacturing Enterprises: A Comparative Analysis of India and Other Economies*, World Bank Research Publication. New York: Oxford University Press.

Luxemburg, Rosa. 1951. *The Accumulation of Capital*. London: Routledge & Kegan Paul.

Marx, Karl. 1954. *Capital*, Vol I, Part VIII. Moscow: Progress Publishers.

———. 1973. *Grundrisse*. Harmondsworth: Penguin Books.

———. 1975. 'On the Jewish Question', in Karl Marx and Friedrich Engels *Collected Works*, Vol. 3. Moscow: Progress Publishers.

Mazumdar, D. 1991. 'Import Substituting Industrialisation and Protection of the Small Scale: The Indian Experience in Textile Industry', *World Development* 19(9): 197–213.

McCloskey, D. 2000. 'Postmodern Market Feminism: A Conversation with Gayatri Chakravorty Spivak', *Rethinking Marxism*, 12(4).

McGee, T.G. 1973. 'Peasants in Cities: A Paradox, A Paradox, A Most Ingenious Paradox', *Human Organization*, 32: 138–62.

Meillassoux, C. 1972. 'From Reproduction to Production', *Economy and Society*, 1: 93–105.

———. 1981. *Maidens, Meal and Money: Capitalism and the Domestic Community*. Cambridge: Cambridge University Press.

———. 1983. 'The Economic Bases of Demographic Reproduction: From the Domestic Mode of Production to Wage-Earning', *Journal of Peasant Studies*, 1: 50–61.

Meier, Gerald. 1984. *Emerging from Poverty: The Economics that Really Matters*. New York: Oxford University Press.

Moser, Caroline O.N. 1978. 'Informal Sector or Petty Commodity Production: Dualism or Dependence in Urban Development', *World Development*, 6(9): 1041–62.

Nehru, Jawaharlal. 1981. *The Discovery of India*. New Delhi: Oxford University Press.

NSS (National Sample Survey) of India. 2000. 'Report No. 456: Non-agricultural Enterprises in the Informal Sector in India, 1999–2000—Key Results'.

Nun, Jose. 2000. 'The End of Work and the "Marginal Mass" Thesis', *Latin American Perspective*, 27(1).

Nurkse, R. 1952. *Problems of Capital Formation in Underdeveloped Countries*. New York: Oxford University Press.

Oberai, A.S. and G.K. Chadha. 2001. Introduction in 'Job Creation in the Informal Sector in India: Issues and Policy Options' (eds), A.S. Oberai and G.K. Chadha, ILO, New Delhi.

Patnaik, Prabhat. 1995. *Whatever Happened to Imperialism*. Chennai: Tulika.

Patnaik, Utsa (ed.) 1990. *The Mode of Production Debate In India*. Sameeksha Trust. Bombay: Oxford University Press.

Peattie, Lisa. 1987. 'An Idea in Good Currency and How It Grew: The Informal Sector', *World Development*, 15(7): 851–60.

Perelman, M. 1983. 'Classical Political Economy: Primitive Accumulation and the Social Division of Labor'. London: Frances Printer Ltd.

Perez Sainz, J.P. 'The New Face of Informality in Central America', *Journal of Latin American Studies*, 30(1), February 1998.

Piore, M. and C. Sabel. 1988. *The Second Industrial Divide: Possibilities for Prosperity*. New York: Basic Books.

Planning Commission of India. 1951. *The First Five Year Plan: Draft Outline*.

Quijano, A. 1983. 'Imperialism and Marginality in Latin America', *Latin American Perspective*, 10(2/3): 76–85.

Rahnema, Majid. 1997. 'Poverty', in W. Sachs (ed.), *Development Dictionary*. New Delhi: Orient Longman.

———. 1997. 'Introduction' in M. Rahnema and V. Bawtree (eds), *The Post-development Reader*. London: Zed Books.

Ranis, G. and F. Stewart. 1993. 'Rural Nonagricultural Activities in Development Theory and Application', *JDE*, 40: 75–101.

Ray, Debraj. 1998. *Development Economics*. New Jersey: Princeton University Press.

Resnick, A., Stephen and Richard D. Wolff. 1987. *Knowledge and Class*. Chicago and London: University of Chicago Press.

Rey, P.P. 1971. *Colonialisme, Neo-colonialisme et Transition au Capitalisme*. Maspero: Paris.

———. 1973. *Les Alliances des Classes*. Paris: Maspero.

Ricardo, David. 1911. *The Principles of Political Economy and Taxation*, London and Melbourne: Everyman's Library.

Rosenstein–Rodan, P. 1943. 'Problems of Industrialization in Eastern and South-Eastern Europe,' *Economic Journal 53*, reprinted in A.N. Agarwal and S.P. Singh (eds), *The Economics of Underdevelopment*. Bombay: Oxford University Press, 1958.

Roemer, John. 1988. *Free To Lose*. Cambridge, Mass.: Harvard University Press.

Rosen, George. 1985. *Western Economists and Eastern Societies: Agents of Change in South Asia 1950–1970*. New Delhi: Oxford University Press.

Sachs, Ignacy. 1991. 'Growth and Poverty: Some Lessons from Brazil' in J. Dreze and A. Sen (eds), *The Political Economy of Hunger*. Oxford: Clarendon Press, pp. 93–116.

Sachs, Wolfgang (ed.) 1992. *Development Dictionary: A Guide to Knowledge as Power*. London: Zed Books.

Said, Edward. 1978. *Orientalism*. London and Henley: Routledge and Kegan Paul.

Sanyal, K. 1988. 'Accumulation, Poverty and State in the Third World: The Capital–Pre-Capital Complex', *Economic and Political Weekly: Review of Political Economy* 23(5): 27–30.

———. 1991–92. 'Of Revolution, Classical and Passive', *Society and Change*, 8(3 & 4): 21–35.

———. 1993. 'Capital, Primitive Accumulation and the Third World: From Annihilation to Appropriation', *Rethinking Marxism*, 6(3): 117–29.

———. 1996. 'Post-Marxism and the Third World: A Critical Response to the Radical Democratic Agenda', *Rethinking Marxism*, 9(1): 126–33.

———. 2001. 'Beyond the Narrative of Transition: Postcolonial Capitalism, Development and the Problematic of Hegemony', *Margin*, 1(2).

Sasoon, Anne Showstack. 1983. s.v. 'Hegemony' in Tom Bottomore, Laurence Harris, V.G. Kiernan and Ralph Miliband (eds), *A Dictionary of Marxist Thought*. Cambridge, Mass.: Harvard University Press, 201–3.

Sen, Amartya. 1983 (1984). 'Development: Which Way Now?' *Economic Journal*, vol. 93, December. Reprinted in Amartya Sen, *Resources, Values and Development*. Oxford: Oxford University Press, 19, 485–504.

Sen, Asok. 1988. 'The Frontiers of Prison Notebooks', *Economic and Political Weekly*, 23(5): 31–36.

Sethuraman, S.V. 1975. 'Urbanization and Employment: A Case Study of Djakarta', *International Labor Review*, 112(2–3): 191–206.

———. 1997. 'Urban Poverty and the Informal Sector: A Critical Assessment of Current Strategies', *ILO Employment Paper*.

Slater, David. 1992. 'Theories of Development and the Politics of the Postmodern: Exploring a Border Zone', *Development and Change*, 23(3).

Schuurman, Frans J. 2001. 'The Nation State, Emancipatory Spaces and Development Studies in the Global Era' in Schuurman (ed.), *Globalization and Development Studies*. New Delhi: Vistaar Publications.

Smith, Adam. 1975. *The Wealth of Nations*. New York: Everyman's Library.

Shiva, Vandana. 1989. *Staying Alive: Women, Ecology and Development.* London: Zed Books.

Singer, H.W. 1952. "The Mechanism of Economic Development", *Indian Economic Review*, August.

Sunkel, Osvaldo. 1972. "Big Business and Dependencia", *Foreign Affairs.* vol. 50.

Tabak, F. 2000. 'Introduction: Informalization and the Long Run' in F. Tabak and M. Crichlow (eds), *Informalization: Process and Structure.* Baltimore and London: The Johns Hopkins University Press.

Taylor, J. 1979. *From Modernization to Mode of Production.* London: Macmillan.

Tokman, Victor. 1978. 'An Exploration in the Nature of Informal–Formal Relationship', *World Development*, 6(9/10): 1065–75.

UN–Habitat. 2003. 'The Challenge of the Slums: Global Report on Human Settlements', London: UN Publication.

UNDP. 1993. *Human Development Report.* New York: Oxford University Press.

———. 1997. *Human Development Report.* New York: Oxford University Press.

———. 2005. *Human Development Report.* New York: Oxford University Press.

Veltmeyer, Henry. 1983. 'Surplus Labor and Class Formation on the Latin American Periphery' in Chilcote et al. (eds), *Theories of Development: Mode of Production or Dependency?* New Delhi: Sage Publications.

Wallerstein, I. 1974. *The Modern World System.* New York: Academic Press.

———. 1979. *The Capitalist World Economy.* Cambridge: Cambridge University Press.

Warren, Bill. 1980. *Imperialism: Pioneer of Capitalism.* London: Verso.

Weeks, J. 1975. 'Policies for Expanding Employment in the Informal Sector of Developing Economies', *International Labor Review*, 91(1): 1–13.

Wolff, R.D., S. Resnick and H. Fraad. 2000. *Bringing it All Back Home: Class, Gender and Power in the Modern Household.* London, Boulder, Colorado: Pluto Press.

Wolpe, H. (ed.) 1980. *The Articulation of Modes of Production: Essays from Economy and Society.* London: Routledge and Kegan Paul.

World Bank. 1980. *World Development Report.* New York: Oxford University Press.

———. 1989. *World Development Report.* New York: Oxford University Press.

———. 1998. 'The World Bank: Making a Difference with Micro-finance', *Countdown 2005*, 1(4), May–June.

———. 2002. *World Development Report*. New York: Oxford University Press.

———. 2006. *World Development Report*. New York: Oxford University Press.

World Bank Partnerships for Development. 2000. Creative Communications Group for the World Bank: Washington.

Žižek, Slavoj. 1994. 'The Spectre of Ideology' in Žižek (ed.), *Mapping Ideology*. New York: Verso.

Sources from the web

Economic Perspective, Electronic Journal of the US Department of State, *http://usinfo.state.gov/journal/journals.htm*, February 2004, 9(1): 34.

"Grameen Bank-Banking on the Poor", *http://www.grdc.com.au*.

"Grameen Bank-Bangladesh: Breaking a Vicious Circle by Providing Credit", *http://www.gdrc.org*.

Haggleblade, Steven et al. 2004. 'The Rural Non Farm Economy: Pathway Out of Poverty or Pathway in?', *http://www.worldbank.org*.

"The Sewa Bank: A Women's Self-help Organization for Poverty Alleviation in India", *http://www.gdrc.org*.

"The Sewa Tree: A Women's Support Network", *http://www.gdrc.org*.

Vishwanath, Tara and Ambar Narayan. 2001. "Informal Economy: Safety Valve or Growth Opportunity", *http://www.worksandskills.ch/info@workandskills*.

Warah, Rasna. 2003. "The Challenge of Slums: Global Report on Human Settlements 2003", *http//www.globalpolicy.org*.

World Bank Group. 2001. "The Social Safety Net", *www.worldbank.org*.

———. 2001. 'Micro-finance and other Credit Mechanism", *www.worldbank.org*.

———. 2004. 'Recommendations for Micro-credit Disbursement Policies', *www.worldbank.org*.

Xaba, Jantjie, Pat Horn and Shirin Motala. 2002. 'The Informal Sector in Sub-Saharan Africa'. Working Paper of the Employment Sector, ILO, *www.ilo.org*.

About the Author

Kalyan Sanyal (1951–2012) was Professor of Economics at the University of Calcutta, India. Prior to this, he was Visiting Professor at the University of Notre Dame, US; Visiting Associate Professor at the Universities of Waterloo, Canada and Graduate Institute for International Economic Studies, Geneva, Switzerland; Visiting Fellow at the Institute for International Economic Studies, University of Stockholm, Sweden; and Raymond Ball Fellow and Rush Rees Fellow at the University of Rochester, US. His publications include papers in professional journals including *The American Economic Review*, *Economica*, *Rethinking Marxism*; and chapters and articles in edited volumes.

Index

For Product Safety Concerns and Information please contact our EU
representative GPSR@taylorandfrancis.com
Taylor & Francis Verlag GmbH, Kaufingerstraße 24, 80331 München, Germany